college of
arts +
sciences

The 33rd

Editors	Albert DiBartolomeo
	Scott Stein
	Kathleen Volk Miller
Publicity Director	Amy Weaver
Layout Editor	William Rees
Graphic Design	Sheena Lewoc
Editorial Co-ops	Jacob Harte
	Ian Micir
Student Interns	Jack Belli
	Lauren Boyle
	Lea Burns
	Allison Cahill
	Jennifer Fromal
	Elise LeMay
	Timothy Seidel McGovern
	Jordan Schilling
	Andrew Segedin
	Jessica Iaboada
	Eric Zrinsky

Sponsors

Drexel University
The College of Arts & Sciences at Drexel University
The Department of English & Philosophy at Drexel University

Dr. Constantine Papadakis, President, Drexel University
Dr. Donna M. Murasko, Dean, College of Arts and Sciences,
Drexel University
Dr. Abioseh Michael Porter, Department Head,
English and Philosophy, Drexel University

The 33rd
Drexel University
Department of English and Philosophy
3141 Chestnut Street
Philadelphia, PA 19104
www.drexelpublishing.org

Cover photo by IMS Graphics

Copies of this volume are available for $10 by writing to the above address.

ISBN 978-0-9820717-0-0

Thank you, thank you, thank you and thank you to: Dr. Donna Murasko; Dr. Abioseh Porter;
Dr. Constantine Papadakis; All the judges from both the Publishing Group Contest and
the Week of Writing Contest (Lloyd Ackert, Ken Bingham, Paula Marantz Cohen, Albert
DiBartolomeo, Diane Downs, Dan Driscoll, Bob Finegan, Leonard Finegold, Valerie Fox,
Ted Fristrom, Robert Gilmore, Sandy Hingston, Scott Gabriel Knowles, F.E. De Lancey,
Lynn Levin, Diamantino Machado, Emilie Passow, Daniela De Pau, Don Riggs, Gail Rosen,
Chris Satullo, Jonathan Seitz, Fred Siegel, Kathryn Steen, Susan E. Stein, Eva Maria Thury,
Scott Warnock); Department of English and Philosophy, esp. Mary Beth Beyer, Eileen
Brennen and Nicole Kline; Contest Participants; Week of Writing Panelists and Attendees.

Printed by T-Shore, Dexter, MI
Distributed by the Drexel Publishing Group
The fonts used within this publication are Archer and Avenir.

Credits

Welcome

When my daughter came home for winter break after her sophomore year in college, she announced that while she still hadn't chosen a major, she was quite sure of her minor; she wanted to study English. I was absolutely delighted. I had been the primary research advisor for 19 Ph.D students in microbiology and I feel very deeply that what often limited the success of my students was not their understanding of science or their ability to design experiments, but rather their inability to explain their work both orally and in writing. My daughter's decision to pursue a minor in English was, to me, not only a mature decision but one that would facilitate her success regardless of what field she ultimately chose.

I experienced this same excitement when several faculty members from the Department of English and Philosophy recently proposed the development of this anthology. Their goal is to showcase the writing of students and faculty from across the University and to use this collection as a learning tool in freshman writing courses. In addition to celebrating writing, the anthology provides interested students with the opportunity to gain experience in the process of editing and publishing such a volume. These dual ambitions reflect the commitment of the College of Arts and Sciences to enhance writing skills across the University.

I hope you enjoy these essays and articles. I hope you learn from the mistakes and successes of your peers and professors. More importantly, I hope you realize that you also can become a successful writer. Maybe your goals don't include being published in an anthology, but in your work as a student, as a professional, and even in the simple act of emailing, your writing is a reflection of who you are and thus, you should strive for it to be of the highest quality. I hope this anthology inspires you.

Sincerely,

Donna M. Murasko, Ph.D
Dean
College of Arts and Sciences

Preface

The Department of English and Philosophy has established a well-deserved reputation not only as a place where instructors of all ranks are passionate about teaching and learning—derived from classroom and other such experiences—but also as the one locale at Drexel where outstanding writing is seen as a daily, achievable goal. It should thus not be surprising that, with the extraordinary efforts of all of our student participants and our dedicated faculty, but especially Albert DiBartolomeo, Scott Stein, and Kathleen Volk Miller, some thoughts that were mere abstract ideas just a few months ago have now become a proud reality.

Using varying approaches that, even in these early stages, reveal the complexity, density of texture and meaning, and the richness of vision and artistry that often characterize good quality writing, the students—guided by their very able instructors—have carefully demonstrated in print some famous words of wisdom by Diane Stanley, author and illustrator: "Good writing is clear thinking." What I now hope the students, again with guidance from all of us, will continue to do from this point on is to apply the other half of Ms. Stanley's statement: "Reading is how you learn what good writing sounds like."

My personal congratulations—as well as those of the whole department—go to all who participated in this laudable and practically useful project. To those whose selections were published, I would like to conclude by offering some more words by the British writer, Thomas Carlyle: "In every phenomenon the beginning remains always the most notable moment." Bravo!

Abioseh Michael Porter, Ph.D
Department Head
Department of English and Philosophy

Table of Contents

Freshman Writing
Introduction

Publishing Group Essays
Introduction

Math & Science

Social Sciences & Humanities

Graduate

Week of Writing

Introduction

Poetry

Fiction

Non-Fiction

Humor

Opinion/Editorial

Faculty Writing
Introduction

Contributors

Freshman
Writing

Introduction

Each year, Drexel freshmen write thousands of projects and papers. Many of these are excellent, yet they are only read by the students' instructors and maybe a peer reviewer or two. The goal of the Freshman Writing Awards is to recognize student excellence and provide students with an opportunity to reach an audience beyond themselves. This contest is a highlight of the Freshman Writing Program. The awards are given at the English Awards ceremony in the spring term, and for years this contest has been supported by the Erika Guenther and Gertrude Daemmrich Memorial Prizes, the College of Arts and Sciences, and the Department of English and Philosophy.

The contest process is rigorous. From the 130 fall freshman writing courses, faculty members nominate the best examples of student writing. These papers are distributed to a panel of judges from the program. Last year, the judges narrowed down the 58 initial entries to a finalist list of 20. A smaller panel of faculty judges then re-read the final 20 and ranked them to make the final determination of the top three prize winners and seven honorable mentions.

The winning essays all received a reading beyond their own classrooms. Now, because of this anthology, they can reach an even wider audience. One of my favorite aspects of the contest is how many academic disciplines are represented by the winning students, reminding me of a Kurt Vonnegut line from *Slaughterhouse-Five:* "He did not think of himself as a writer for the simple reason that the world had never allowed him to think of himself in this way." This contest may be the first time some of these students are seriously recognized as writers; that is fitting, because, to me, that is exactly what they are.

Scott Warnock, Ph.D
Director
Freshman Writing Program

Rebecca Dorne

The Annual Circus

Like clockwork, every summer on the Fourth of July the performers gather their posters, their Bibles, and their chalk, and position themselves on the sidewalk around our house. They sing religious songs, blare chants, and make a general racket for a three-hour dog-and-pony show to entice the neighbors to come running out of their homes to join the fun. But the neighbors don't. They call the police instead, while trying to quiet the troupe with reason before they bring in the clowns for the final act in the main ring. The performers never listen, and they never provide a legitimate argument for their ballyhoo and beliefs, either. They are not violent, and they are not threatening, but they love the attention and share one common purpose—to protest my mother's profession.

My mother did not always specialize in abortions. She began working as a standard Obstetrician Gynecologist and had her own practice for fifteen years, but grew tired of the liabilities and unpredictable work hours that came along with delivering babies. For the last seven years, she has been working at a clinic specializing in high-risk pregnancy termination, mostly for rape victims and for pregnancies in which there are serious deformities. But the Ringmasters know all of this. They know everything about my mom including her birthday, when she graduated from medical school, what her father's occupation was, where she grew up, and, obviously, her home address. We suspect that the Internet provided all the information, except the address. A proud and silly amateur must have followed her home from work one day.

Despite the fact that they are irritating, any time the protestors come, a good show is always guaranteed. They hold up life-size pictures of my mother—taken from her website—with captions that read, "Murderer" and "Baby Killer." With chalk, they scribble biblical literature and character-bashing phrases directed towards my mother all over every sidewalk in the cul-de-sac. The neighbors like to get into altercations with them, scream at them, turn their sprinklers on them, and remind them how unwelcome they are in our neighborhood. Strange as it may seem, my mother accepts the attention even more than the protestors accept attention on themselves, once the police arrive. She refers to them as her "fans," blows them kisses from the window, and collects whatever pro-life posters and paraphernalia they leave behind. Her attitude towards the situation is that there is nothing we can do to stop them from coming, so we might as well demonstrate that we do not take them seriously.

I always wish that I could interact with them as the neighbors do, but I am forbidden from going outside when they come because my mother claims that they do not need anymore ammunition against our family to add to their circus act. The only time I had ever been outside to talk to them was when I was fifteen. A female protestor had brought her baby along with her in a stroller, as if to show how lucky that baby was to be alive and to not have been aborted. All I could think about was how unfair it was to that innocent, unbiased child for his mother to expose him to the stress and commotion of a hundred people screaming and shouting at once. I snuck outside to get a closer look because I was not sure if she actually had the audacity to bring a real baby, or if instead she had brought a doll. I found it strangely ironic that I empathized with a baby when the protestors were there, harassing my own mother and calling her a "baby killer." I had crossed an ethical quandary, similar to the one described by Nancy Gibbs in her essay, "If We Have It, Do We Use It?" The idea of teenage pregnancy horrified me not only because it had the potential to literally ruin two people's lives, but also because it limited the child to most of the things it could have had, if the pregnancy had been expected. Although Gibbs' essay questions the fairness of genetic engineering in human fetuses, her article poses an interesting argument, applicable to the abortion issue. When she states that "Parents would be making decisions over which their children had no control and whose long-term impact would be uncertain," (410) her reasoning implicates people who are not prepared to bring an infant into the world and, therefore, limit the potential success of that child. At fifteen, I knew that I would never have wanted to be brought into the world unless my parents were completely ready to raise me. My view has since been confirmed from many sources, including Henry P. David's study, "Unwanted Pregnancies," in which he compares the lives of children born from wanted and unwanted pregnancies. He concludes by noting the negative health effects on children who are unwanted (American Psychological Association).

As soon as I had stepped off the porch, I heard crying, and my suspicions were confirmed. They videotaped me standing outside of my home and asked me if I knew that my mother was a "baby killer." I laughed to myself, thanked them for informing me, and went back into the house. That was the only time I had ever been outside to talk to them. On a separate occasion, they dropped by, rang our doorbell, and warned my sister that they were coming to town sometime in the next three days and were planning on camping out on the sidewalk overnight. My sister called the police and stood in front of their large, white van so that they could not leave. To retaliate, they took photographs of my sister and used them in their brochures.

Since we cannot go outside to share our thoughts with them, we remain spectators, watching all of the commotion from a safe distance. We can never seem to figure out why the circus returns every year. The audience does not appreciate them; the reviews are clearly negative, yet they feel that the show must go on. By protesting at our home instead of just at my mother's clinic, their goal is to shock the neighbors and to have them become so disturbed by the attention and disorder that they will turn against my mom and her profession. But the neighbors are supportive of us and never tire of trying to reason with this cast of characters. Meanwhile, my sisters and I wearily look to other venues for a more engaging and thought-provoking entertainment.

Works Cited

David, Henry P. "Unwanted Pregnancies." American Psychological
    Association. Apr.

2004. 4 Dec. 2007 <http://gateway.tx.ovid.com/gw2/ovidweb.cgi>.

Gibbs, Nancy. "If We Have It Do We Use It?" Reading Life: A Writer's
    Reader. Eds. Inge Fink and Gabrielle Gautreaux. Boston:
    Wadsworth, 2005. 409-11.

Kelly Collett

Awkward Silence

Click click clickity click click click. Typing away. As usual. And then my mom comes in. Mouse click: hide all IM windows. Nothing inappropriate, it's just weird having someone read over my shoulder. She doesn't question the hidden messages. Peculiar. She sits. Silence. Except for clicking as I type in the web address for Journey's. "I really need to order new shoes." Still silence. I lurk the Journey's page for a bit, comparing various styles and making mental notes of the ones I like and the ones I don't. And then finally:

"I read your book. The black spiral one."

Oh. My. God. No she didn't. No. No no no no no. She couldn't have. Could she?

"Gee, Mom. Thanks for uh, you know, going through my things?"

Not my sketchbook. *Please* tell me she's kidding. She's not kidding is she? I draw in that! I journal! Oh man. All the things I don't want her to know. The things I can't tell her. Sweating. Unsteady breathing. She probably hates me.....

About a month ago, I was to be leaving for the great big world of college in about two days. Cookout? Sure. Why not? I love cheeseburgers. I love my friends. I love my family. Let's party!

So we ate. And then my family sat outside talking family things, and by family things I probably mean my dad and uncles sat around making jokes tinted with innuendo. Read: my family is ridiculous. I sat in the living room with my friends: Doug, Monica, Brian, my brother Eddy, and his friend, our neighbor, Sara.

I once heard someone on TV remark on the living room as being misnamed because no one actually lives in it; it's more like, that room that is not touched and kept clean always and no, don't let the kids in there with grape juice! What are you thinking?!

And it's really true. The living room has the nicest pictures, the more expensive vases with the more expensive silk flowers or those little pebbles, the piano Nana gave as a birthday gift that we never learned to play, and the comfiest sofas. No joke, these are probably the most comfiest of sofas. Yes, the most comfiest. Ever notice how it's so much easier to relax and be yourself when you're comfortable? Yeah. These sofas are made for creating inside jokes: the epic one-liners you will never forget, and the moments you wish you hadn't.

We sat there, talking science, talking politics. Read: trashing George Dubya. Sara didn't say much. She was the youngest in the room, four years younger than me. She's only a year younger than my brother, but he has been around me and my friends long enough to know our humor and at least have something witty up his sleeve. I felt bad. Sara didn't belong there. At least, that's what I thought.

We reached an awkward silence. Awkward because normally we don't stop. Awkward because we didn't know what to do. Five seconds passed. And then another five.

"You know, they say every time there's an awkward silence, a gay baby is born."

What? Where did *that* come from?

We all turn and look at Sara in disbelief. Our eyes are wide. It still hadn't fully set in what she said. And then Monica says, "Damn. Kelly, you know, I'd really hate to have been there for the awkward silence that made you." Insert: hysterical laughter.

I'm eleven. Sitting in the living room on the comfiest sofa. Just sitting. Well, curled up. Fetal position. Staring at the ceiling. It wasn't a good day. Sixth grade is a nightmare. Too many new people. Too many rules regarding lockers and what hallways we're allowed to traverse. Too many teachers telling me I didn't read, when I definitely did. I just couldn't remember. Who cares what color shirt he was wearing when he killed the buffalo?! Seriously!

Enter: Mom.

"What do you want for dinner?"

"I don't care."

"What's wrong?"

"Nothing."

She sits. She always sits.

She puts her arms around me. She always puts her arms around me.

"Bad day at school?"

"No."

"Well, what is it then?"

"Nothing!"

She gets up and walks back into the kitchen to start dinner. The pasta boils and the sauce simmers. She comes back in. She always comes back in.

"Okay. Now tell me. What happened?"

I roll over. "Mmmpph."

"See now that doesn't tell me anything."

I roll over again. "I don't wanna talk about it, okay?"

She goes back to cooking dinner.

Ten p.m. Looking at shoes. Freaking out. Did she seriously read it? Why would she tell me she did if she didn't?

"I just want you to know," her voice cracks and I turn to look at her. She's crying. "I just want you to know, you can talk to me about anything. You really can. I'll always be here for you no matter what you think."

I don't know what to say. I don't know what to do.

I'm crying.

I throw myself out of the chair and into her arms.

How could I forget?

I'm eleven years old again. Sitting on the big comfy sofa. Waiting for dinner to be done so I can eat. And she comes back in and sits down, "You know, I mean, I know you don't wanna talk about it, but you can tell me anything. If something's bothering you just tell me and I can try and help. It's what I'm here for."

And so I just tell her, "Okay well we're reading this stupid book for English and it's really hard to get into and I read it and we had a quiz on the chapter today and apparently I did really bad and my teacher was going through the papers after she graded them as asked me if I had even read the chapter in front of the whole class and now I feel really stupid and I don't want to fail at school and you know it just really sucks. It sucks. There."

How could I forget? Not even forget, just not care enough to remember?

What happened to me in seven years?

And there I am with friends, laughing hysterically at a joke that's all too true, and at one time taboo, sitting on the most comfiest sofas where I used to sit when I couldn't just go up to Mom and ask her to talk. And there I am, sketchbook packed away in a bag, waiting to head for Philly. There I am, getting ready to leave behind the most comfiest sofas, getting ready to say goodbye to my friends and family who have always been there. And Mom, who always knew.

Elisabeth Collins

My First Experience as "The Foreigner"

Without a doubt, my visit to the Philippines in the fourth grade ranks as one of the most exciting, frightening, rewarding, awkward, and *defining* experiences of my life. Needless to say, my emotions ran the gamut. However, the more negative sentiments I experienced throughout this trip, particularly those of being an outsider, bear striking resemblance to those of two characters from class readings, Max Vigne, of Andrea Barrett's short story, "Servants of the Map," as well as Caroline Hwang, author of "The Good Daughter," a short story in *Reading Life* by Inge Fink and Gabrielle Gautreaux. In all three instances, the individuals were alienated, even mocked for their inability to conform to the social or cultural standards of an unfamiliar cultural environment.

Since I was just an infant during my first stay in my mother's homeland, I considered my trip in the fourth grade my first true glimpse of the dazzling archipelago. I was excited beyond belief, but extremely nervous as well. Would I like my relatives, or more importantly, would they like *me*? Would I fit in with my cousins and their friends? Would I immerse myself in the culture quickly, or would everybody think me ignorant? Such questions plagued me relentlessly during the twenty-three hour flight, and immediately upon arrival I became overwhelmed by self-consciousness. Although I had inherited my mother's Filipina coloring—the dark hair, skin and eyes—my blatantly American, bright white Nike sneakers gave me away as I stood at the Manila Airport baggage claim. Also, despite being only nine years old, the height genes from my Caucasian father caused me to tower over all of the other children, and a few adults as well. I felt the penetrating gazes of hundreds of eyes, the piercing stares fiercely intensified by the ungodly heat. I felt exceedingly awkward, and we had not even left the airport yet! Knowing that entry into Filipino society could only amplify the culture shock, I assumed that the situation would worsen before improving.

My younger brother and I became overnight celebrities in my grandparents' neighborhood on account of our Game Boy Color hand-held games and our seemingly endless supply of Hershey's Chocolate. This enjoyable sense of distinction was fleeting, however, and was quickly replaced by intense insecurity. For the first few days of our visit, my cousins rarely spoke to me, but although I did not speak the dialect, I could tell from their stares and curious intonations that they spoke *about* me quite a bit. Furthermore, judging from the brief yet heated discourses between my aunts and my cousins, and from the obviously irritated manner in which my cousins spoke to me immediately afterward, I knew that they only initiated conversation or invited me to play because they were told to do so.

I also learned not to trust my cousins' Tagalog or Ilocano dialect translations after T.J., one of the youngest, feigned charity by telling me, "Hey, Lisa, if you want to impress Gramma, go up to her and say '*mabaho ang puet mo.*' That means, 'hello, how are you.' I never ascertained the true meaning of that sentence, but I noted the force with which my Grandmother slapped my cousin after I proudly showcased what he had taught me.

My thoughts and feelings during this time bear striking similarity to those of Max Vigne, the protagonist of Andrea Barrett's novella, "Servants of the Map." While surveying in the Himalayan Mountains, Max, "finding his companions uncongenial... read out of boredom and loneliness" (Barrett 25). Needless to say, my own companions were less than congenial; so I occupied myself by reading. Also, I missed my friends in the United States terribly, and was shocked at how shyly I behaved in the Philippines, whereas at home I had always been known as the outgoing, loud, rambunctious girl. Likewise, in Servants of the Map, Max writes his wife, Clara, "with my own family, with you, I can be myself, but here, with strangers, it is terrible, the old shyness seizes me" (Barrett 37). Clearly, both Max and I acted out of character in our unusual circumstances. In both experiences, being ostracized discouraged attempts to socialize, and, out of shyness or fear of incurring ridicule, the individuals behaved in a far more reserved or taciturn manner than usual.

In retrospect I realize that many of my feelings throughout my trip can also be likened to those of Korean American Caroline Hwang, author of the *Reading Life* short story, "The Good Daughter." Like me, she cannot speak the language of her parents' native country. She also notes that her parents viewed her as "all American," just as I was perceived in the Philippines (Hwang 140). No matter how hard I tried to assimilate myself, one month was simply not enough time for me either to learn to mask my Western habits or to display authentically Filipino ones. Moreover, Hwang addresses the difficulty one experiences when he must "straddle two cultures" (Hwang 140). From a child's perspective, the dissimilarity of

Filipino and American cultures was highly apparent to me in their different senses of humor. Much to my frustration, I found that my Western style of quick-witted humor and sarcasm were not considered even remotely amusing in the Philippines. Quite the contrary, many of the remarks I made in a purely well-intentioned effort to fit in were taken much more seriously than I had intended, and were thought caustic, even offensive at times. From the opposite viewpoint, I was not the least bit amused by the Southeast Asian sense of humor, dominated by stating the obvious.

My feelings as an outsider during my visit to the Philippines as a nine-year-old girl were almost identical to those of Max Vigne and Caroline Hwang, characters from class readings. The problems in all three cases arose from cultural disparities as opposed to racial, religious, or economic inconsistencies. Also, all three characters were mocked for their failure to successfully assimilate themselves into their new environments. These instances demonstrate that no matter where or in what time period one may be, being treated as an outsider is a common obstacle which, at some point, people all over the globe must face.

Works Cited

Barrett, Andrea. *Servants of the Map*. New York: Norton, 2003.

Hwang, Caroline. "The Good Daughter." Reading Life. Ed. Inge Fink and
    Gabrielle Gautreaux.

United States: Michael Rosenberg, 2005. 139-141.

Shanowya Jackson

The Museum

There aren't many people of color here at Drexel. Only 7 percent of the freshman population is black (2007 Freshman Class Stats). So let's do the math here. Out of 2,410 incoming students, only 169 are black. Besides my roommate and a couple of friends I have (which is under 20 for sure), everyone around me is white. At first I was happy to be away from the loud, ignorant people I was used to. There were no drive by shootings, no drug dealers, no whistling or abstract names. It was nice to be around people who were oblivious to the fact that the girl next to them might have a razor blade in her cheek, or the guy walking toward them might have a gun in his waist band. Soon, I started to feel displaced from my people. I needed my shot of "black love." This is when I decided to go to the African American Museum Philadelphia.

Built in 1976 as the first institution in Philadelphia for African Americans, this museum is exactly what I needed. I loved it, not only because I love my African heritage, but because the exhibits were amazing. One of the exhibits at the museum was about the "black church" (I was always taught that different races have different ways of worshipping, so it's a habit to distinguish the black church from other churches). Another one of the exhibits explained the origins of Cheyney University, a historically black university here in Philadelphia. There was also an abstract art section that included African masks and modern paintings of children and parades. These exhibits were nice, but there was one that truly made a lasting impression on me.

The exhibit that caught my eye was so subtle I almost missed it. It was crammed between the exhibit about the black church and the following exhibit about Cheyney University. This exhibit was about teen pregnancy and some of the stereotypes associated with the African American community. There were five pictures on the wall. The central picture was of a teenage girl who was still pregnant. The other four pictures were of teen mothers holding their babies, none of the babies over a year old.

What struck me the most was a little recorded voice playing through a small speaker at the beginning of the exhibit. I almost missed it because it was right next to the television blasting a sermon by a black preacher.

When I listened to this, I was so amazed because I'm usually not a good listener. One of the mothers from the pictures was talking. She was explaining how she was never promiscuous. She had only slept with one guy one time and gotten pregnant. Another young lady explained how she still went to school and raised her baby for an entire year. I had always thought that pregnancy meant dropping out of school and abandoning your future. (This is probably because my mother, my grandmother, and my great-grandmother all had children at 16 and none of them completed high school.)

As I was observing this exhibit, I noticed two families making their way toward me. The first family consisted of a mother and two daughters. There was no man with this family. Yet, the mother stopped in front of the speaker box and let her daughters listen to what the young ladies had to say. She then explained to them what the pictures meant. She didn't go into the details of sex. The mother simply explained that we shouldn't judge people based on their conditions or their circumstances. The daughters were listening attentively. When the daughters had questions, I could tell the mother was at ease because of the way she smiled. She used a lot of hand movements, and after every statement, she asked her daughters if they understood. It seemed like parenting came naturally to her.

This almost made me cry because she reminded me of my own mother. My mom was a single parent until I was about twelve years old. Since single parenthood is more acceptable today ("Problems in the Black Community," Fleming) my mom also raised me with relative ease when it came to social issues. Single parenthood originated when the male slaves were sold off, leaving the mothers to care for the young alone ("Problems in the Black Community"). So in the black community, single parenthood is nothing new, nothing taboo, or nothing to be ashamed about.

In the second family, there was a mother, a father, and two children. The mother saw the first exhibit first and tapped the dad to let him know that the exhibit was approaching. It was kind of like a warning or a signal, letting him know that the children couldn't see this part of the museum. As soon as the children got close enough to know what the pictures were expressing, the parents whisked them by, not even stopping to take in what the exhibit meant. The parents didn't even study the exhibit themselves. They simply rushed by until the mother and father shared eye contact. The family had reached the exhibit about Cheyney University. That's when the parents let the children look at pictures and read the text.

This second family disturbed me. Seventy percent of African American teenagers say that lack of communication between girls and their parents is often why teenage girls have babies ("General Facts and Stats"). It has also been proven that teenage girls who have strong emotional attachments to their parents are much less likely to become sexually active at a young age ("General Facts and Stats"). The second family had no communication, and one of their children was a little girl, about the age of seven or eight. If they didn't start exposing her to the ideas of alternative lives and families, such as single parenthoods, homosexual homes, and inter-racial households, what would she think about them when she got older? If they didn't start to explain to their children that the world was not perfect and that sometimes there are people who make mistakes and live abnormal lives, how would they deal with these situations when the time came?

My mom always told me that she would never let the street and television raise her child (Fleming). The second family was doing just that. Television has become the new parent. Rap videos, reality television, and magazines give most children the information they use to make everyday decisions. Since the parents of the second family didn't even want their children looking at pictures of young men with babies, most likely, those children are going to learn about teen pregnancy, sex, and parenthood from sources that are not reliable.

It's time that parents swallow their pride and start talking to their children about those difficult topics. It would be so much easier to feel uncomfortable talking about the birds and the bees with your children then to hold your sixteen-year-old daughter's hand while she gives birth. My mom took me to the library at the age of three to explain to me how "mommies and daddies made babies" (Fleming). As life went on, she talked to me about sex, rape, hygiene, pregnancy, and even homosexuality (she always encouraged me to be who I am, and not who someone wants me to be).

It hurt me to see the children of the second family denied a learning experience. The single mother used the museum as the foundation for her to let her children know about the world beyond Barbie dolls and fairy tales. Studies have shown that families that communicate are more likely to have positive results. In order to bring a people up from a desperate situation, they must first unite and educate their young ones. This museum made me want to reach out and help as many young black youths as I possibly could. It's time that we stop thinking about our own comfort zones and think about the future of our own children. When this happens for each and every family, the black community will begin to rise and finally get the respect we so rightfully deserve.

Works Cited

"Problems In The Black Community." Lewrockwell.com 2006. Lewrockwell.com. 8 August 2006. http://www.lewrockwell.com/orig7/wicks3.html

Fleming, Leticia. Telephone Interview. 1 December 2007.

"General Facts and Stats" Teenpregnancy.org. 2006. Teenpregnancy.org. http://www.teenpregnancy.org/resources/data/genlfact/asp

Holyfield, John. Homage To The Black Family.

Skelly, Ariel. Untitled. January 2007

"2007 Freshman Class Stats". Ed. National College Advertising and Marketing. 15 August 2007. http://media.www.thetriangle.org/media/storage/paper689/news/2007/09/20/News/2007-Freshman.Class.Stats-2980829.shtml

Elizabeth Rosenthal

Physician, Heal Thyself

Growing up, I was always a doctor's daughter. My dad's work as a radiologist at a major trauma center always made my life seem so different from the average lives of my peers and their families. Unlike most other kids in my school, my dad was rarely around. He almost never went to any of my sporting events or school functions, but was instead, always working at the hospital. His "call" was even worse. Imagine living in a home where breaking news on the television was a virtual guarantee that your father would soon be gone. Every car crash, every gunshot, every stabbing, his beeper blared, his phone started to ring, and my dad sprung into action. Within minutes, he would either be out the door or my house would resound with the clicks of films being sent through the computer, sometimes all night long. I blame the advancement of medical technology for this misfortune.

I was born in Allentown, Pennsylvania, and after living there for a year, my dad left to go to Pittsburgh. He went to train on the use of this new technology that was supposed to change the face of medicine, called a Magnetic Resonance Imaging (MRI) machine. To do so, he left behind me and my mom, a house that took two years to build, and a partnership in a thriving practice. My father thought this important new technology would be the future of medicine. Unfortunately, my father now realizes that there is a downside to the use of new technologies such as MRI, CT scan, or mammography machines for the practice of radiology. Patients and doctors alike are under the wrong impression that with the help of this new technology, my father and his peers are omniscient and infallible. This is not the case. My father's classic response to anyone who questions him is: "Even with the science of medicine, I am still not God. These are just machines and I am just a man."

Another problem my father encounters with the new technologies is that sometimes he knows something that he wishes he did not. I can still remember the night that I awoke to hear my normally soft-spoken father screaming at the top of his lungs as he berated his resident over the phone. "Do something, do something, help him," he shrieked over and over again. It was not until morning that I discovered the reason for my dad's unusual tirade. That night, called to read from his computer at home, he literally watched as a patient's brain split in two while his resident in the hospital panicked and did nothing. Technology was certainly no help that night as my father's knowledge only made him feel frustrated and futile.

These feelings of helplessness are even more prevalent for him when he has to deal with diagnosing something for a family member. My father has had the horrific task of telling some close family members that they have cancer, sometimes terminal. These situations render him ineffectual as a physician; he has the skill and the tools to know what is wrong, but not the ability to make things better. When I think of my father in these circumstances, I am reminded of the character of Elizabeth in Andrea Barrett's story, "The Cure." She expresses well how my dad must feel during these times when she says that "some parts of the cure never change, no matter what the doctors discover" (Barrett 219). While these new technologies have certainly helped my dad become a better doctor, I do believe that they have taken quite a personal toll on him.

My father is not the only one to suffer personally, though. While these advancements may have helped others, they have forever negatively affected my own life. To those on the outside, we have the perfect little suburban family with the perfect little suburban life. In reality, though, my father is so wrapped up in working with these new machines that he oftentimes lets my brother and me down. He doesn't mean to do so; I know that. It's just that to be a good doctor, my dad sometimes has to put his professional life over his personal life. Another physician, Matthew Foster, describes his own similar circumstances in *Medical Economics*, when he writes: "It's easy to become so devoted to your patients that you neglect the people who matter most to you" (Life in Practice).

I realize that many people think the life of a doctor's daughter is wonderful. They are under the mistaken impression that my father's enormous income and professional power can make my life perfect. Yet, this is far from the truth. Money is not time and disappointments are many. With every click of that computer, with every film that is sent through, one more piece of my heart just chips away, aching from time lost with my father.

I too now have a father who oftentimes seems dehumanized and at a loss with reality, mostly because he spends his days connected to machines instead of people. As a result of the new technology, my dad now rarely meets with patients, further depersonalizing the human interaction he once had as a doctor. This detachment and depersonalization seems to have carried over into our family life as well. Just yesterday, instead of simply calling me at college to personally discuss something he wanted to tell me, my dad instead found it more comfortable to use technology to click, click away at his computer and e-mail me instead.

In the end, while advancements in medical technology have proven to work miracles for some, they have traumatized the lives of others. I will always remember a childhood without much of my father as a result of these technological developments. Yet, who is really to blame for the misfortune and detachment I encountered with my father as a youngster? Is it the advancement of medical technology or something else? Is it the man or is it the machine?

Works Cited

Barrett, Andrea. *Servants of the Map.* New York, NY: W. W. Norton & Company, 2002. "Life in Practice."

The Doctors' Page. 2005. G.S. Nace. 9 Nov. 2007 < http://www.doctorspage.net/satisf.asp>.

Rosenthal, Richard. Personal interview. 28 Oct. 2007

Sonia Voleti

Beyond the Technicalities

Whirlwinds of anticipation twisted through me as I approached, for the first time, the dwelling of Mr. Roger L. Black. Perched in the front seat beside my mother, I still hear the sound of his gravel driveway crunching noisily under our car tires, still feel the butterflies of nervousness and excitement fluttering through my stomach, still recall the grip of my cold hands upon the strap of my black violin case. I had taken violin lessons for seven years prior to this moment, switching teachers only once. The two teachers I had had were excellent instructors and musicians, setting high standards for their students. Unfortunately, my first teacher had stopped teaching due to health-related concerns, and, after four years of studying with her, I began lessons with a new violinist. After three years with him, however, I was forced to change instructors yet again, due to persistent issues of scheduling conflict. As I climbed out of the car that day, I wondered what to expect from this new music teacher. Questions of all varieties filled my fourteen-year-old mind: Would he be an effective teacher, as patient and as motivating as my past instructors? Would he provide enjoyable music pieces? Would he yell at his students?

Upon entering Mr. Black's apartment, I found the room to be slightly cramped, though the introductions themselves went smoothly. He seemed, then, to be a friendly person, complimenting my smile and asking questions regarding my few years of prior violin experience. Beneath this amiable exterior, however, I caught a glimpse of a demanding nature: "One thing I have to say is that it's impossible for me to teach students who do not practice," he stated at one point, "so I expect all my students to practice." His words did not seem unreasonable to me. With time, however, the fluctuations in his temperament did. My lessons with Mr. Black would soon evoke within me a rollercoaster of emotion, spanning far more than the techniques of violin playing.

He was a corporeal man, typically adorned in purple corduroy pants, a button down shirt, and black-rimmed glasses. The only permanent company he had was that of his two dogs, Max and Daisy, small fluffy creatures that were accustomed to the sound of violin, and perhaps even enjoyed it. I remember watching with delight as, during one of my first lessons, Mr. Black played a G-major scale while Max howled along somberly to every note. During those first few lessons, I found that Mr. Black possessed a rather sardonic sense of humor. "Oh, yes, I once had a violin teacher who was God for all practical purposes," he recalled with a short guffaw. "Wouldn't look me in the eye when he taught, never complimented anything I did right, only criticized, and grunted grudgingly if my playing was satisfactory." Ironically enough, I later saw some of these qualities reciprocate in Mr. Black himself.

Every Saturday morning, I would assemble my music stand in front of the huge chair in which he sat. He would tune my violin as I arranged my music, and eventually I would begin to play what I had practiced that week. Before long, my lessons would be filled with blunt queries such as, "How many hours did you practice this week?" or "Did you look at this piece at all?" or "Why has your vibrato tightened up after we spent all that time working on it last lesson?" Admittedly, there were certain weeks during which I was negligent about my practicing—especially when I had been assigned to memorize a set of scales or devise a set of fingerings. Needless to say, I viewed such repetitive activities with immense disinterest. In those uncomfortable moments during lessons, his questions caused me squirming pangs of guilt and self-disappointment. However, there were many more sessions when, even after I had prepared sufficiently, my efforts would nonetheless appear mediocre in his eyes. In those situations, fright and hurt coursed through me as I struggled to respond to his skepticism. It came to a point where I began to dread and fear lessons—and it is safe to say that I was not the only one.

As I walked into lesson early one day, I saw a seven year old girl named Angela crying before his eyes after he had told her that she had not played well that week and needed to go home and practice properly. There is no doubt in my mind that after this lesson, she went home and worked to the best of her ability. Mr. Black's reprimands, therefore, ultimately did have the desired effect. Recalling that moment, I am now conscious of the duality with which I regarded Mr. Black. One part of me immensely feared and despised being subject to such a harsh and temperamental nature. The other part yearned deeply for his approval, so as to treasure it as gold, if it ever came.

My feelings can be closely correlated to a situation in "Such, Such Were the Joys," a piece in which George Orwell relates the struggles he endured during his time at boarding school. In this work, Orwell escribes the ambiguity of his interactions with his headmistress Bingo, conceding that his true feelings towards her were complete and utter repulsion:

> [...] no one was permanently in good favour, but on the other hand, even the outcasts had patches of it from time to time. Thus, although my memories of Bingo are mostly hostiles, I also remember considerable periods when I basked under her smiles, when she called me 'old chap' [...] Whenever one had the chance to suck up, one did suck up, and at the first smile one's hatred turned into a sort of cringing love. [...] And yet all the while, at the middle of one's heart, there seemed to stand an incorruptible inner self who knew that whatever one did—whether one laughed or sniveled or went into frenzies of gratitude for small favours—one's only true feeling was hatred. (Lopate 287)

I would not go as far as to say I hated Mr. Black. At the same time, however, I can say with certainty that I had little respect for him as a person.

In addition to private lessons, Mr. Black occasionally organized group performances of certain musical pieces. One of these pieces was the Bach Double Concerto, which has two violin parts: Violin I and II. Fourteen of his students were asked to play in this particular piece, and I had been delegated leader of the Violin I section. Before the actual recital, he had spent time during private lessons reviewing the respective parts with participating students. Out of these lessons, one stands out especially in my mind.

As I stood playing, he stopped and critiqued, stopped and critiqued, as always. Bowings, intonation, fingerings, vibrato, and a multitude of other technical aspects of violin playing were only a few topics of criticism. Perhaps it was overwhelming for me to hear. Perhaps I was hurt or even resented on some level his never-ending comments. All I was fully aware of, however, was that some negative feeling must have shone through my eyes as though I was challenging his opinion. All at once, Mr. Black's eyes widened in angry confrontation as he looked at me directly and snapped, "Yes that's right, you're doing it all wrong. The problem with you is that you have this dogmatic attitude towards everything. If you're not willing to change that, then there's nothing I can do to help you."

As soon as I returned home, I melted into tears at his words, because my intent had not for one moment been to challenge him. Of that I am entirely certain. What upset me most was his conviction that I played my instrument with an ego; this accusation remained as a permanent and impenetrable stain on my mind.

I practiced for an extensive amount of time that week, working very hard to learn fingerings and bowings. A tiny part of me felt that, if I did work hard, I could please him enough to make him see that I valued his advice, and would incorporate it with seriousness and humility. Ultimately, my playing did improve. It came at a high cost however, because I no longer enjoyed playing the violin. In a sense, I suppose I should have been thankful for the rawness with which he treated me, because it provided a bitter incentive for me to practice. In reality, however, there was a vast incongruity between what I should have been feeling, and what I actually felt. Motivation based on fear can only last for so long.

My circumstances in this sense parallel Orwell's feelings toward his headmasters Bingo and Sim, two rather unreasonable teachers at his boarding school, Crossgates. Orwell recounts:

> It was therefore clear that I owed them a vast debt of gratitude. But I was *not* grateful, as I very well knew. On the contrary, I hated both of them. I could not control my subjective feelings, and I could not conceal them from myself. But it is wicked, is it not, to hate your benefactors? So I was taught, and so I believed. A child accepts the codes of behaviour that are presented to it, even when it breaks them. [...] If I contrived to seem callous and defiant, it was only a thin cover over a mass of shame and dismay. (Lopate 280)

I realized soon enough that I no longer took pleasure in playing the violin. I was playing with the aim to please, to be appreciated. I cared more for what Mr. Black thought, more for the qualitative hours I put in, than for the actual love and feeling of the music I could produce. Perhaps the snarling approach did make me a better musician. Perhaps it made me a more objective instrumentalist, allowing me to improve carefully on different aspects of my playing. Focusing on such technical aspects alone, however, took away all the natural inclinations I felt when embarking upon a new piece. Music had become a meticulous endeavor in which emotion had little to no significance. All the while, I yearned for his approval. Mr. Black had instilled within me an enormous sense of fear: fear at what he would say, fear at how he would react, fear at what I was incapable of achieving. If his mood was good and his reaction was positive, I was lucky and could breathe freely until the next lesson.

Indeed, it is difficult to continue a pursuit when there is no real passion and inner-self motivation. Such was also the case with Orwell's experiences at the Harrow History Prize Contest, a competition that often brought tremendous honor to Crossgates, if its participating students were victorious: "I recall positive orgies of dates, with the keener boys leaping up and down in their places in their eagerness to shout out the right answers, and at the same time not feeling the faintest interest in the meaning of the mysterious events they were naming." Just as in Orwell's situation, where the entire purpose of obtaining an education had lost significance, music began to mean nothing more to me than the redundant practices of intonation and fingerings and loose vibrato. The students participating in the Harrow History Prize Contest had not known the significance of what they were memorizing. As children, they probably had not even cared to recognize this significance either. All they knew was that those names and dates were important to know, because such facts were presented as representations of a bigger picture. Ultimately, it was this big picture that they, and I too, missed. Just as the specific facts of history come together to chronicle the import of a historical context, the technicalities of instrumentation should come together to express a larger emotional meaning. However, becoming too consumed with such minor features causes one to lose focus on the bigger idea. When I was studying with Mr. Black, I was consumed by the "names and dates," so to speak, of violin playing. To me, these technical matters, which had once been only the minor outlying features, had become everything. I had lost sight of what the core heart of any piece of music truly represented.

After about one year, I stopped taking lessons from Mr. Black, and in doing so, rediscovered the pleasure of violin playing. Transitioning to a teacher who was immensely more reasonable in expectation and temperament, I once again understood the significance of musical experience, and valued it immensely. In all honesty, I felt the same liberation that Orwell had felt after he left Crossgates. It seemed as though a huge burden had been removed from my shoulders, an enormous pressure lifted off my chest. I was free to play with feeling and emotion, free to play for myself and no one else, free, even, to just love the violin again. As Orwell states upon leaving his despised boarding school:

> With a sense of coming out from darkness into sunlight I put on my Old Boy's tie as we dressed for the journey. I well remember the feeling of that brand-new silk tie round my neck, a feeling of emancipation, as though the tie had been at once a badge of manhood and an amulet against Bingo's voice and Sim's cane. I was escaping from bondage. (Lopate 297)

In this respect, my bondage was my desire for approval, my desire to please and be appreciated. My emancipation was perhaps the realization that what I did, I had to do for myself. Because that is the only way music can ever truly mean anything.

Works Cited

Orwell, George. "Such, Such Were the Joys... " *Art of the Personal Essay.* Ed. Phillip Lopate. New York: Anchor Books, 1995. 269-302.

Alyssa Woodman

Hatshepsut: Queen, King, and Pharaoh

The sun rises slowly over the desert, sparkling off grains of sand, snaking its way between every crevice and crack in the rocks. A slow procession of family and mourners follow the sarcophagus up the long ramp of the temple, giant, but dwarfed by the cliff rising high behind it. In the year 1458 BC, one of Egypt's greatest pharaohs was laid to rest. Her name was Hatshepsut.

There have been several great women leaders throughout history, but few have changed their image as many times as Hatshepsut. She struggled with her identity as daughter, queen, and pharaoh of one of the greatest civilizations in history. Leadership can be alienating, and many rulers find themselves separated from their people and family as they carry the burden of responsibility for their country. Hatshepsut was no exception, and her story is one of changing roles and identities, a struggle for recognition, and ultimately, being almost erased from history.

Hatshepsut was born to Thutmose, the third pharaoh of the 18th Dynasty, and his wife Ahmes. She had two older brothers who would have been next in line to the throne and she would be barely mentioned in history books today. But they both died early, leaving Hatshepsut and her half brother and husband, Thutmose II, as the successors after their fathers' death. Thutmose II ruled as pharaoh for only a few years before he died. He had a son from another wife, but because he was so young, Hatshepsut was named co-regent and so began her reign as pharaoh (Dodson and Hilton 130).

Even as a little girl, Hatshepsut underwent many big changes and gained increasing amounts of responsibility. Such responsibility is hard for anyone to deal with, no matter how old, and pressure to perform duties well can single out and isolate a person. Another intimidating truth that Hatshepsut faced was the fact that she was not first choice in the line of rule. It is hard enough to assume responsibility when it is granted to the person it was intended for; but when that person gains that responsibility through the deaths of those it was truly intended for, they are judged even more harshly on their performance. Being a woman in this position at this time in history adds to the pressure. Although women in Egypt took on many vital roles, it was still fairly uncommon for a woman to be pharaoh.

In the many years of her reign, Hatshepsut was depicted in several different combinations of clothes and royal attire, each time making a statement about her status and about who she was. When she first took over leadership of Egypt, she wore the traditional clothes of a queen, the king's wife. Later she was depicted still wearing a female dress, but a male headdress and her cartouches (ovals inscribed with the persons name, mostly for royalty) were followed by the title, "King of Upper and Lower Egypt" (Roehrig 88). It is here where she really takes on the role of the pharaoh. In another painting, she assumes the wide-legged stance of a male. By about the seventh year of her reign, Hatshepsut was depicted in a more masculine way, taking the title of king and pharaoh to a new level. Although she was co-regent with her husband's son, Thutmose III, she was always depicted in a higher standing than he. Images of Thutmose II did not appear again after this point. She no longer identified herself as the queen of King Thutmose, but as king herself. However, "she never attempted to obscure her female essence; her inscriptions consistently employ the feminine gender, maintaining the tension between male and female elements evident in almost all her representations" (Roehrig 88).

It is this tension that defines Hatshepsut and sets her apart from most other leaders throughout history. It is also one of her leading strong points, the ability to change and evolve to suit her purpose. Many leaders find their downfall in stubbornness and an unwillingness to change and accept situations. But redefining oneself can be taxing on one's self-identity and individuality. There is no way to know if Hatshepsut struggled with her changes and transformations on a personal level or if she used these purely for political purposes. But however superficial a person's decisions may be, they still affect the person to some degree, and such dramatic changes as assuming the opposite sex cannot go unnoticed.

When Hatshepsut died, Thutmose III continued his reign as sole king of Egypt. About 20 years into his reign, a defacement of many buildings and walls that had Hatshepsut's image on it took place. On many her image alone is carved out of the rock or covered over. The reason for this is still unclear to historians, and most doubt the theory of malice or jealousy on Thutmose's part (Roehrig 97), but Hatshepsut was almost wiped from the history of Egypt. Only a few depictions remain, showing her varied identities and stages of development. These many temples and constructions built during her reign, and the shear length of her co -regency (estimated around 20 years), are testament to her great leadership and ability to lead a powerful civilization. But her many roles and varied identities point to a deeper individual unlike any other in history. She stands alone as a leader willing to change her position and even her most basic identity—her femininity for—the benefit of her people.

Works Cited

Roehrig, Catherine H. (Ed.) Metropolitan Museum of Art.
    Hatshepsut: from Queen to Pharaoh. New Haven and London:
    Yal University Press, 2005

Dodson, Aidan & Hilton, Dyan. The Complete Royal Families of Ancient
    Egypt. London: Thames & Hudson Ltd, 2004

Emily Greenberg, Samantha Kats, Trevor Nederlof

The Art of Reactions at a Philadelphia Museum of Art Exhibit

This essay brings to life our group's observation of how script presentation, performance, and audience interrelate. By observing different people at the Philadelphia Museum of Art we discovered that everyone has their own way of interpreting and appreciating art. Their reactions enabled us to notice and appreciate things we never noticed before.

Walking through the heavy doors with gold metal handles of the Perelman Building, the new addition to the Philadelphia Museum of Art, we noticed security guards every few feet surrounding the valuable artwork. The museum brought on a very peaceful, relaxing tone as we made our way towards the sculpture exhibit. The only defined sounds were shoes hitting the marble floor and the woman at the desk greeting people and saying with a smile, "Tickets, please." The visitors were rather quiet and the security guards kept a close eye on each person to make sure no one was doing anything to harm the works of art or bother the rest of the people who came to admire it. By observing the people at the Philadelphia Museum of Art, specifically the exhibit *A Conversation in Three Dimensions: Sculpture From the Collections*, we discovered that different people have very different reactions to art.

The importance of the first piece, Pablo Picasso's *Man with a Lamb*, resonates with all its viewers upon entering the exhibit. It is isolated in a smaller room connecting to the rest of the exhibit. The sculpture stands tall, surrounded by white walls, allowing its dark, shiny form to really jump out at people. The texture is very rigid, bumpy and uneven which gives it a more striking appearance. This sculpture is the perfect choice to start off the exhibit.

Showcased in its own small room at the entrance, it sets a dramatic tone for the exhibit that many viewers carried with them throughout the space. *Man with a Lamb* holds a historical significance that brings deeper meaning to the entire exhibit. The exhibit's viewers all seemed to respond to this piece in similar ways. People stopped on their way in, and many stopped again on their way out. The common reaction to the sculpture was a sincere look of pondering and reflection. The piece's striking visual caused almost everyone who walked by to stop and read the description hanging on the wall which tells of the sculpture's historical significance.

In her article, *Picasso's Sentinel*, Phyllis Tuchman reports her view on the importance of Picasso's sculpture *Man with a Lamb*. The image, which is thought to be modeled after the artist's friend, Max Jacob, is one of Picasso's most important works (Tuchman 2). This sculpture is one of the few male subjects Picasso ever molded, carved, or constructed. Picasso's initial drawings for *Man with a Lamb* began when he heard that Jewish women and children living in Paris were going to be arrested and deported to concentration camps (Tuchman 4). *Man with a Lamb* reveals Picasso's unique talent for expressing his personal experiences with more universal significance.

This piece's profound impact can be linked to its creation. It was just one of many of Picasso's works that connected his personal life to the world around him. Tuchman notes that critics believe since there was a superstitious side to Picasso, it is likely that he may have imagined *Man with a Lamb* to function as if it were some sort of charm or token which conveyed hope and salvation for his friend Max Jacob (Tuchman 1). When Jacob did not respond to Picasso's warnings and pleas that he go into hiding, Picasso responded with *Man with a Lamb*. He hoped that this representation of his friend would somehow keep him alive in these troubling times. The depiction of the lamb represents the Paschal lamb. In the Old Testament, the blood of the Paschal lamb would protect Jews from being killed. Picasso hoped that his statue would do the same for his friend and his friend's family. This sculpture has continued to serve as a symbol of hope, reminding people of the troubles faced in the Holocaust. For this reason, *Man with a Lamb* is the perfect choice to start off an exhibit that showcases important pieces from the Philadelphia Museum of Art's expansive collection.

Man with a Lamb gets visitors to think about the deeper meanings in art, and more specifically, sculpture. The Holocaust is a subject that elicits very deep emotions in almost everybody. For this reason, a sculpture that symbolizes hope and struggle from that time really brings out a reaction in people. One woman said, "You can really feel the people's struggle when you look at the lamb." This woman's choice of words reveals a lot about the sculpture's impact on her. To say that she "felt" the people's struggle means *Man with a Lamb* touched her so deeply that it made her feel like she connected with the people it represents. We observed this woman as she walked from the small room showcasing *Man with a Lamb* into the Exhibition Gallery, which housed the rest of the sculptures. This woman continued to stop and reflect at every piece.

Walking into the Exhibition Gallery, one piece in particular caught visitors' attention immediately. What looked like a rainbow-colored maze of high mountains was actually Sol LeWitt's sculpture called "Splotch." The children who were dragging behind their parents were especially attracted to this piece and interested in touching and grabbing the different parts of it. One of the kids even nagged his mother by repeating, "Mommy I wanna play with it! Please, I will be careful I promise." This sculpture was made up of very bright colors, and, unlike Picasso's piece, was very smooth. The whole room was surrounded by white walls and had windows on two sides that stretched from the floor to the ceiling. This atmosphere allowed the sculptures to stick out and appear more vivid compared to the simple, tranquil setting.

Another work of art that caught visitors' attention was simply a circle design formed on the floor with a few large grey stones. This piece was *Limestone Circle* by Richard Long. The script next to the piece informed the visitors that Long was a founder of land art and always tried to incorporate nature into his art. His 32 rough-hewn limestone rocks formed a ring to represent a universal form reminiscent of ancient ritual practice. Because it is arranged directly on the floor with no clear boundaries, it appears to the audience as part of the landscape of the gallery, which was Long's intention. This circle stood out to us because it was out of the ordinary and we liked that it got the audience to appreciate nature while viewing phenomenal art. Initially, because of the simplicity of the design and materials, many people did not understand the purpose of this piece; however, when taking a deeper look, the artist's statement of valuing nature becomes very clear. Many people who walked by were very intrigued by this work of art; however, there were a few who simply walked past it without paying any attention to it. Many people shook their heads or furrowed their brows as they walked past in reaction to this sculpture.

The most important aspect of our discovery was not merely observing people's reactions, but comparing and contrasting them. Each person who walked through the archway into the exhibit had a slightly different reaction. This was a discovery in itself. However, comparing such reactions to other museum visitors' is what made our discovery so important.

One woman walked through the entrance; she circled the room and left within ten minutes of her initial entry. This woman had a hurried look on her face and she talked under her breath like she was trying to interpret the sculptures faster than her mind could process the visuals. This woman may have wanted to see a variety of art in a limited time period. Or, she may have just been uninterested in the sculptures.

In contrast to this woman, the next museum visitor we observed had a very different reaction to the art, and the museum itself. This woman was wearing comfortable clothing and taking her time at each sculpture. She stopped to carefully read the descriptions by each piece. We could see she was really absorbing the information as she looked back and forth between the sign's description and the sculpture itself. Clearly, these women had different views of and reactions to the pieces presented in the exhibit. One similarity between these two women was that they were both alone. This caused us to think that even though they were acting and reacting in different ways, they both wanted to be there. A person would probably not go to a museum alone unless he or she really wanted to be there. This fact led us to believe that even though the second woman was moving at a slower pace, it didn't necessarily mean that she had a better appreciation of art. She may have just had more time or a different way off processing the information. Also, just because the second woman took the time to read the scripture, she was not necessarily getting more out of the experience. Some people like to just look at the sculptures and make their own interpretations of them without being influenced by what is written about them.

Next, we observed and discovered the reactions of couples that entered the exhibit; these varied extremely as well. Some couples were more interested in themselves. While some couples were more interested in talking about the sculptures, and others were just more interested in silently viewing the works of art. As we stood there taking notes about how these couples were reacting to the exhibit, we discovered just how different groups of people can be. Because a couple is composed of two different people, each with different reactions, those different people make the couples' reactions even more varied than any range of reactions seen in any one person. We discovered that the couple that stood right in front of the sculpture and talked loudly for a few minutes obviously had a different way of reacting to the pieces than the couple that stayed silent. People's reactions in the exhibit were based on how they best could learn about the sculptures. The couple that seemed much more into looking at each other than any of the sculptures perhaps just liked the modern artistic atmosphere encompassing the exhibit. However, just because the couple did not look at all the sculptures does not mean that they did not benefit from the experience of being there. Each of the couples there had a unique reason for being at the exhibit and by interpreting their different expressions we were able to discover that a wide variety of people take advantage of what the Philadelphia Museum of Art has to offer.

The Philadelphia Art Museum, specifically the exhibit *A Conversation in Three Dimensions: Sculpture from the Collections*, allowed us to make a very valuable discovery about the effects that different styles of art have on people by observing their reactions to them. By making this discovery, we realized that every person has his or her own specific way of appreciating and interpreting things, and there is no right or wrong way. In fact, by observing other people's reactions, we were able to notice and appreciate things we never noticed before. Art is a beautiful thing and affects everyone in very different ways, which is what makes it special. The more open people are to innovative ideas and other people's thoughts about art, or anything else in life, the more they will learn and discover things they otherwise would not have.

Works Cited

The Philadelphia Museum of Art. 2007. 5 November 2007
    < http://www.philamuseum.org/>.

Tuchman, Phyllis. "Picasso's Sentinel." *Art in America.* 1998.
    Expanded Academic ASAP. Gale. Drexel University (PALCI).
    21 Oct. 2007 < http://find.galegroup.com/itx/start.do?prodId=EAIM>

Publishing Group
Essays

Introduction

Researching, thinking, and writing are at the core of the College of Arts and Sciences. No matter what field they're in, students must be able to research, to find and evaluate the best evidence and information on a topic. They must be able to think, to formulate original ideas and take a fresh approach to a problem or question. And, of course, they must be able to write—excellent research and thought must be communicated to others to have value. After all of their reading and thinking about the work of others, students must make their own contributions to the field by writing.

The constant exposure to accomplished works published in their field of study can intimidate students when they sit down to write. Or inspire them. It may do both as students struggle to bring their own vision to the subjects they study and find the right words. Fortunately, this struggle often yields remarkable writing. The following works, selected from student submissions to the inaugural Drexel Publishing Group writing contest, exemplify a firm grasp of subject matter and a facility with language.

The essays cover a host of subjects from a range of disciplines in the arts and sciences, including stem cell research, the challenges of trash disposal, the theme of the prodigal son in Arthur Miller's "The Prize," the art of Fascist Italy, the illusion of free will, and psychology's role in determining child custody. The topics are as diverse as the students who wrote about them, but the essays all demonstrate originality and boldness as well as great skill in researching, thinking, and writing.

Krista Lewis

Idol Minds

Today the term idol is probably, sadly, most often associated with the television show *American Idol*. However, in the seventeenth century a man by the name of Francis Bacon had a completely different association, as would be expected. At the time, numerous aspects of science, and learning in general, experienced substantial change. Many people consider Francis Bacon to have been highly influential in these changes, if not at the forefront of them. You only have to look at his published works from the time to understand their reasoning, for they intensely express the problems, or the Idols, that he felt true understanding faced. These false notions that paraded around as the truth troubled him greatly. As a result, he set out to develop what he believed to be the perfect solution and key to advancement that would surmount such problems. His quest and its consequences rooted themselves in the sciences and have persisted there ever since.

To say the very least about Francis Bacon, he took issue with many things in his life, not the least of which being the practice of natural philosophy or science. For him, it needed a complete overhaul. This attitude first surfaced while he studied at Cambridge. Here he found the existing academic approach to thought to be sterile and useless.[1] Furthermore, he felt one age of learning did not learn from another, nor did coordination exist among the various strains of scientific study. As a result, the sciences became stunted and remained "almost in the same condition, receiving no noticeable increase, but on the contrary, thriving most under their first founder, and then declining."[2] He praised learning, but only if it were done for the right reasons, for he believed, "Men have entered into a desire of learning and knowledge...seldom sincerely to give a true account of their gift of reason, to the benefit and use of men."[3] In addition, learning must be done correctly to obtain real benefits. Unfortunately, it has a number of adversaries, the most important of which is the human mind itself.[4] He articulated this nicely when he said, "For the mind of man is far from the nature of a clear and equal glass, wherein the beams of things should reflect according to their true incidence."[5]

Bacon believed human understanding to be plagued by bad habits of mind that take it off course.[6] According to him, "The universe to the eye of the human understanding is framed like a labyrinth, presenting as it does on every side so many ambiguities of way, such deceitful resemblances of objects and signs, natures so irregular in their lines, and so knotted and entangled." Some of these habits we pick up from external sources while others are innate.[7] Whatever the case may be, these Idols, as he preferred to call them, have to be removed in order for us to see nature as it truly is. Moreover, without them we develop a critical mind.[8]

The first of the four Idols he called the Idols of the Tribe. These are innate and rooted in human nature itself. He believed that the human understanding falls prey to the "false assertion that the sense of man is the measure of things," and thereby "distorts and discolours the nature of things by mingling its own nature with it."[9] For example, we tend to believe there is more order and regularity in the world than truly exists.[10] He also had little faith in our senses when left to their own devices, and saw a problem in their limitation in observation.[11] The next Idol he called the Idols of the Cave, which are part of the individual. He argued that each of us has a cave or den "which refracts and discolours the light of nature." The cave may be built out of our individual nature, our education and discourse with others, our reading of books and admiration of authorities, or the impressions that our minds must reconcile with preoccupied or predisposed ideas.[12] Since each individual is different and thinks differently from the next, it is virtually impossible to obtain a consistent, true understanding of nature.

The last two Idols are external influences introduced to the human mind. The first Bacon called Idols of the Market-place, which is derived from "the intercourse and association of men with each other." The danger with discourse is that it requires the use of words. So much of our understanding relies on our choice of words. If we do not choose wisely we can "obstruct the understanding." Furthermore, Bacon argued that attempts to define and explain the meaning of the words chosen will not rectify the issue because this in itself requires the use of more words, therefore, simply serving to compound the problem.[13] The final Idol infiltrates the human mind through "various dogmas of philosophies, and also from wrong laws of demonstration." These are the Idols of the Theater, so named because he felt, as with stage-plays, the authors of the philosophies and demonstrations represent "worlds of their own creation after an unreal and scenic fashion." For him, existing concepts are taken for granted and tradition stymies new thought. We would be negligent if we did not verify information for ourselves. These Idols are perhaps the most dangerous because they do not pertain only to current held beliefs but in beliefs yet to be presented.[14] They are like weeds in a garden: you may think you have removed them for good, but more always find a way to return.

Having pointed out the error of our ways, Bacon set out to provide the solution. The proper means to combat the Idols of the Tribe and acquire a better interpretation of nature is through the use of experiments. In this way, our senses are left only to judge the experiment.[15] To deal with the Idols of the Cave, Bacon urged "that whatever the mind seizes and dwells upon with peculiar satisfaction is to be held in suspicion," and that we should proceed with care in order to "keep the understanding even and clear."[16] The Idols of the Market-place are rather more difficult to overcome. Definitions are necessary to clarify the meaning of words; however, there exists a problem in that definitions beget more definitions. The best remedy, he argued, is to eliminate the bad theories as best we can.[17] The Idols of the Theater require constant vigilance because of their tendency to resurface. To avoid the snare of these Idols, we should pursue experience but with the stipulation that we do not take our conclusions beyond the experiment; otherwise we risk spreading more false notions. In essence, it is necessary that the mind learn to be aware of what it encounters.[18] Simply being warned about or having the knowledge of the Idols helps combat them and clear the way for the advancement of the sciences.[19]

Having recognized the hindrances we encounter in learning, Bacon sincerely sought a reformation of all knowledge and the creation of a "new learning".[20] Ultimately, he saw great potential for the sciences and he wished them to be used for the betterment of humanity.[21] In fact, he believed science to be the key to truth and empiricism to be the key to science, and indeed we see a hint of this in the solutions he provides us with in order to deal with the Idols.[22] He believed reforming the scientific method would be critical to improving all learning.[23] Out of this desire for change and advancement emerged what has become known as the Baconian method of conducting scientific work. One of the first aspects that must change, he argued, is the method of our reasoning.[24] He did not approve of deductive reasoning and syllogistic logic because he believed preconceived theories could lead an investigation in the wrong direction.[25] Furthermore, these methods are suited more toward overcoming an opponent in an argument than to real learning.[26]

Instead, he proposed we use inductive reasoning. Induction relies on experience and observation. In other words, it relies on empiricism. An analysis of what is gathered through empirical means, in combination with a system of exclusion and rejection, he argued, would lead to conclusions.[27] This, of course, means the compilation and classification of a large body of natural facts through carefully organized observation and experimentation with results that are accurately and thoroughly recorded.[28] It should be kept in mind that the experiments are not done for any use in themselves; rather they are tools to uncover causes.[29] Once enough data has been collected, the results should be placed in what he called Tables of Instances.[30] Then the process of comparison, verification and elimination may begin, and ideally a theory or general law will quickly emerge.[31] He even believed that, "The first work of legitimate induction... is rejection... "[32] However, this does not designate the end, for it is necessary to go back and perform more experimentation and observation to confirm conclusions.[33] It is worth noting that Bacon's method does not mean you simply collect all information that you come across. In fact, he compared true natural philosophers to a bee in that it gathers material from a variety of sources, but "transforms and digests it by a power of its own."[34] He found this slow, meticulous sifting of evidence to be the positive way of doing science, which resulted in the interpretation of nature. This is opposed to the anticipation of nature where, based off of few observations, you leap to a conclusion that prevents you from conducting further research.[35]

Bacon's method offered several interesting and fresh approaches to science. First of all, up until this time few had practiced experimentation as a way in which to provide proof.[36] Today, scientific work and experimentation are so enmeshed that it is rather difficult to separate the two. Furthermore, induction itself is rather flexible, open and self-correcting because the constant infusion of new experiences brings the possibility for change.[37] In fact, Bacon urged that we should record when we miss as well as when we hit.[38] This helps prevent us from repeating our mistakes, and the ability to learn from them gives us incredible flexibility. Finally, Bacon's method, in that it opposed preconceived notions, effectively erased the traditional distinction between manifest qualities and occult qualities.[39] Thanks to Bacon, subjects of study, such as heat, electricity, magnetism, and life phenomena, became legitimate in the field of natural philosophy.[40] These subjects, that had formerly been overlooked or dismissed by science, had new life breathed into them. [41]

The foundations for scientific collaboration and scientific research institutes are perhaps some of the greatest contributions Bacon made to science. Bacon felt that knowledge should be cumulative with new information continually being added and not simply a collection of old ideas gathered to prevent their disappearance.[42] In the same way, he believed, "The perfection of the sciences is to be looked for not from the swiftness and ability of one inquirer, but from a succession."[43] This played a large part in the need for experimentation, which in turn fostered the collaboration of scientists, whom he wished would give equally to the advance of science.[44] It is important that natural philosophy not be conducted by merely a few men for their own benefit, but rather by many for the benefit of all people.[45]

Furthermore, he is indeed one of the first to have endeavored into the institutional side of science.[46] This is best seen in his work entitled *The New Atlantis* in which he described a place he called Salomon's house. Salomon's house may be interpreted as the prototype of what we would call today a research institute. In it Bacon divides responsibility among several men according to his method of conducting science, so as to reach the correct conclusions while avoiding the dangers of the Idols. For example, some men collect data, others analyze and conduct experiments, others organize the findings, and some seek axioms and aphorisms provided by the data. He further describes what the house looks like and what kind of objects and instruments it contains that serve science. It is his most explicit and thorough call for the coordination of labor in the sciences.[47]

Bacon's influence is clearly shown in the rise of various scientific societies and academies during the seventeenth century, particularly in the Royal Society of London. In fact, many members of the Royal Society saw themselves as disciples of Bacon.[48] Although they may not have followed his precepts exactly, they did emphasize the collection of data and the constant development and improvement of experimental methods. During the Enlightenment, people thought of him as a hero and founder of the new science, but it did not go much further than that. Then in the Victorian era he became associated with the philosophy of inductivism and influenced the likes of John Stuart Mill.[49] He has also been credited with paving the way for scientific explanations of phenomena that are mechanistic or materialistic, which may have helped the thinking of Rene Descartes, Thomas Hobbes and John Locke.[50] Furthermore, his method has been greatly useful to the biological sciences since they deal heavily in observation, the collection of information and classification. On a number of occasions Charles Darwin professed himself to be a Baconian, though in its purest sense he did not meet the criteria.[51]

However, we should be cautious with how much praise is given to Bacon because it is all too easy to look past his shortcomings. Some have argued that Bacon's method is too narrow, in particular because it underestimates the significance that math can play in the sciences. Furthermore, without a theory it is difficult for the collection of data to produce any real results on its own. In the same vein, others have argued that his method is weak because he expected too much from experiments. He even assumed that if no satisfying conclusions were found quickly, then the process had been done incorrectly.[52] It cannot be argued that Bacon's method is useless or unnecessary; however, with time it has been proven to be insufficient and generally most useful only in the preliminary stages of scientific research.[53] During his lifetime, scientists on the Continent especially touted the former argument, believing that empiricism alone could not build science.[54] Finally, it is worth noting that in Bacon's time changes to scientific thought had already begun, though they were still rather limited. For instance, people had begun to find it essential and useful to describe things more accurately and thoroughly.[55]

In the end, Francis Bacon did not contribute any great scientific discovery of his own to the world, his method fell short of what he had anticipated, man is still plagued by the Idols, and the development of science for the betterment of all has resulted in some questionable moments in history. In spite of these failures, he remains a significant figure in the history of science. His method influenced many thinkers that followed him, he made people rethink what they knew to be true, he saw a great future for science and did his best to give that future a chance to become realized; in doing so he encouraged others to keep digging for explanations. Most importantly, he helped make people conscious of that which stood in the way of success, thereby weakening the obstructions. Though he clearly strayed far from perfection, it must be remembered that he was only human, and as he so vehemently pointed out, we humans are prone to be misled by our Idols, even if your name is Francis Bacon.

Notes

1. Marie Boas Hall, *The Scientific Renaissance, 1450-1630* (New York: Dover Publications, Inc., 1994), 247.

2. Ibid., 250.

3. Ibid., 249.

4. Ibid., 249.

5. B.H.G. Wormald, *Francis Bacon: History, politics and science*, 1561-1626 (Cambridge: Cambridge UP, 1993), 80.

6. Virgil K. Whitaker, "Bacon's Doctrine of Forms: A Study of Seventeenth-Century Eclecticism," *The Huntington Library Quarterly* 33, no. 3 (May, 1970): 209.

7. Perez Zagorin, "Francis Bacon's Concept of Objectivity and the Idols of the Mind," *The British Journal for the History of Science* 34, no. 4 (Dec., 2001): 387.

8. Peter Urbach, "Francis Bacon as a Precursor to Popper," *The British Journal for the Philosophy of Science* 33, no. 2 (June, 1982): 119.

9. Francis Bacon, *The New Organon*, ed. Lisa Jardine and Michael Silverthorne (Cambridge: Cambridge UP, 2004), 41.

10. Whitaker, 209.

11. Zagorin, 388.

12. Bacon, 41.

13. Ibid., 41-42.

14. Ibid., 42.

15. Zagorin, 388.

16. Urbach, 122.

17. Zagorin, 389.

18. Zagorin, 389-90.

19. Wormald, 82.

20. Hall, 248.

21. *Ralph M. Blake, Curt J. Ducasse and Edward H. Madden, Theories of Scientific Method: the Renaissance through the Nineteenth Century*, ed. Edward H. Madden, (New York: Gordon and Breach, 1989), 50.

22. Hall, 247.

23. Ibid., 248.

24. Ibid., 247.

25. John Henry, *The Scientific Revolution and the Origins of Modern Science*, 2nd ed (New York: Palgrave, 2002), 36.

26. Blake, 51.

27. Ibid., 51.

28. Murray G. Murphey, "The Influence of Science upon Modern Culture: The Program," *Proceedings of the American Philosophical Society* 105, no. 5 (Oct., 1961): 462.

29. Blake, 55.

30. Murphey, 462.

31. Hall, 259.

32. Murphey, 462.

33. Ibid., 462.

34. Brian Vickers, "Francis Bacon and the Progress of Knowledge," *Journal of the History of Ideas* 53, no. 3 (July-Sep., 1992): 509.

35. Vickers, 499.

36. A. Rupert Hall, *From Galileo to Newton*, 1630-1720 (New York: Harper & Row, 1963), 33.

37. Vickers, 516.

38. Florian Cajori, "The Baconian Method of Scientific Research," *The Scientific Monthly* 20, no. 1 (Jan., 1925): 86.

39. Henry, 65.

40. Vickers, 516,

41. Murphey, 461.

42. Vickers, 496.

43. Wormald, 27.

44. Hall, 253.

45. Henry, 101.

46. Murphey, 461.

47. Blake, 72-73.

48. A. R. Hall, 104.

49. Vickers, 511.

50. Ibid., 517.

51. Cajori, 87-88.

52. Hall, 255.

53. Cajori, 87-91.

54. A. R. Hall, 104.

55. Ibid., 123.

Bibliography

Bacon, Francis. *The New Organon.* Edited by Lisa Jardine and Michael Silverthorne. Cambridge: Cambridge UP, 2004.

Blake, Ralph M., Curt J. Ducasse and Edward H. Madden. *Theories of Scientific Method: the Renaissance through the Nineteenth Century.* Edited by Edward H. Madden. New York: Gordon and Breach, 1989.

Cajori, Florian. "The Baconian Method of Scientific Research." *The Scientific Monthly* 20, no. 1 (Jan., 1925): 85-91.

Hall, A. Rupert. From *Galileo to Newton*, 1630-1720. New York: Harper & Row, 1963.

Hall, Marie Boas. *The Scientific Renaissance*, 1450-1630. New York: Dover Publications, Inc., 1994.

Henry, John. *The Scientific Revolution and the Origins of Modern Science*, 2nd ed. New York: Palgrave, 2002.

Murphey, Murray G. "The Influence of Science upon Modern Culture:
The Program." *Proceedings of the American Philosophical Society*
105, no. 5 (Oct., 1961): 461-463.

Urbach, Peter. "Francis Bacon as a Precursor to Popper." *The British
Journal for the Philosophy of Science* 33, no. 2 (June, 1982): 113-
132.

Vickers, Brian. "Francis Bacon and the Progress of Knowledge." *Journal
of the History of Ideas* 53, no. 3 (July-Sep., 1992): 495-518.

Whitaker, Virgil K. "Bacon's Doctrine of Forms: A Study of Seventeenth
Century Eclecticism."

The *Huntington Library Quarterly* 33, no. 3 (May, 1970): 209-216.

Wormald, B.H.G. *Francis Bacon: History, politics and science*, 1561 1626.
Cambridge: Cambridge UP, 1993.

Zagorin, Perez. "Francis Bacon's Concept of Objectivity and the Idols of
the Mind." *The British Journal for the History of Science* 34, no. 4
(Dec., 2001). 379-393.

Anjali Sethi

Can Stem Cells Inherently Age or Is It a Result of Epigenetic Modifications?

Overview

There are many theories as to why organisms age and the mechanisms by which this occurs. Stem cells play a major role in regenerative potential of tissues and thus play a role in the ageing process as well. It is difficult to distinguish whether adult stem cells are more similar to the rest of the somatic cells in their ageing pattern or more similar to germ line cells in their immortality. There is evidence supporting the theory that stem cells do not age; they are simply epigenetically modified due to their aged environment to be less productive and efficient. However, there are also studies indicating that stem cells may inherently age by irreversible mechanisms such as the shortening of telomeres. This debate is further complicated by the fact that there are different types of adult stem cells–hematopoietic stem cells behave differently from skeletal muscle satellite cells. This research could be applied to many fields; one example is that of studies involving oncology.

Reasons for Ageing

The cells in organisms often have a predetermined lifespan. They divide a certain number of times and then die. A common attempt to explain this phenomenon of ageing is in terms of evolution. Ageing is genetically favorable because the elimination of individuals past their reproductive prime would be beneficial for the species as a whole. This would preserve resources for the most reproductively fit individuals.

Medawar's mutation accumulation theory states that this is done through mutations leading to detrimental age-related changes accumulating over successive generations if their effects were only realized well after the age of peak reproductive success. While this theory is possible, there is at this time very little evidence to support it. Another theory explaining the scheme of the ageing process is the antagonistic pleiotropy theory. This states that genes whose expression is harmful in later life accumulate in populations not because they are silent earlier in life but because they are actually beneficial to survival or reproductive fitness. Again, there is little evidence supporting this theory.

The disposable soma theory states that species have evolved with genetic programs that optimize the utilization of resources for survival and reproduction. The genetic program of any species is designed so that it resists damage long enough for organisms to reach productive maturity; thus there is a negative correlation between lifespan and offspring produced (Rando). One experiment supporting this produced a mutation in the *age-1* protein of *C elegans*, resulting in a lengthened life but at the cost of hermaphrodite fertility (Freidman). However, a study contradicting this theory induced mutations in the insulin and IGF signaling pathways, along with dietary restriction. The lifespan in these model organisms was extended with no effect on fecundity (Partridge).

Mechanisms of Ageing

There is a functional decline due to histologic and biochemical changes in tissues in organ systems with the passage of time; this is known as ageing. This declining functionality results in a diminishing capacity to respond to an injury or stress. Some molecular changes that lead to cellular dysfunction are cumulative mutations in nuclear and mitochondrial DNA, oxidative damage to cellular constituents, and the accumulation and aggregation of abnormal proteins, lipids, or other macromolecular constituents. Cellular changes that lead to tissue dysfunction are cell death, oncogenesis, and senescence. Thus with a more extensive view, tissue changes that lead to organismal dysfunction are extracellular matrix changes, extracellular deposits, and atrophy from cell loss and diminished regenerative capacity. The defense against this cellular atrophy and loss of regeneration is found in adult stem cells, which replenish tissues that have a high rate of turnover (Rando).

Many proposed mechanisms exist to explain ageing. The somatic mutation theory states that the capacity for DNA is an important determinant of the rate of ageing at the cellular and molecular levels. For example, PARP-1 is a protein that is a key player in the immediate cellular response to stress-induced DNA damage. Higher PARP-1 activity levels are associated with longer lifespans.

The telomere loss theory states that the decline in cellular division capacity with age is linked to the fact that telomeres get progressively shorter as the cells divide. This is because telomerase is not present in somatic cells; it is only found in germ cells and adult stem cells. Stress can be related to ageing in this case because oxidative stress increases the rate of telomere loss.

The mitochondrial theory states that an accumulation of mitochondrial DNA mutations with age leads to impaired ATP production. This results in a decline in tissue bioenergenesis. The altered proteins and waste accumulation theories state that the impairment of protein turnover is indicated over time by accumulation of damaged proteins. This is because the chaperones, which sequester and restore denatured proteins, and proteasomes, which recognize and selectively degrade damaged and ubiquitinated proteins, lose function. This results in the age-related problems of cataract, Alzheimer's disease, and Parkinson's (Kirkwood). It is highly likely that it is a combination of all these theories that correctly explains the exact mechanisms by which ageing occurs; there is not one exact theory that can explain the entire phenomenon.

It has been demonstrated that there are single gene mutations that could be responsible for ageing as well. For example, mice homozygous for loss-of-function mutations at the *Pit1* locus showed over a 40% increase in mean and maximal longevity (Flurkey). In another experiment, it was found that a loss of the chromatin regulatory factor Sir2 gene increases rDNA recombination and shortens the lifespan. Conversely, an extra genomic copy of Sir2 increases rDNA stability and extends the lifespan (Lombard).

Dietary restriction also plays an important role in ageing. A lower energy intake for either weanling or middle-aged mice or rats increased maximum longevity, reduced incidence and delayed the onset of several cancers and other late-life diseases, and retarded changes in terms of biologic age (Weindruch).

Germ Line Immortality, Embryonic Stem Cells, Adult Stem Cells

It has been argued as to whether adult stem cells bear more resemblance to somatic cells, cells of the germline, or embryonic stem cells. In order to determine this, properties of each of these classes of cells must be known.

Somatic cells have a limit on the amount of times they can divide. In humans, this occurs on average after 52 divisions—this is the Hayflick limit. Cells of the germ line are considered immortal; this depends on adaptive change and natural selection promoting survival and reproductive success associated with advantageous changes in the genome. They possess the ability to ensure that genetic information is passed on with the highest precision to successive generations. Germ line cells can often resist or repair damage done to the genome.

Embryonic stem cells are stem cells derived from the inner cell mass of a blastocyst; they are pluripotent. The maintenance of the genome stability is essential to the value of embryonic stem cells as tools for research and potential therapeutic vehicles.

Adult stem cells possess the capacity to resist, detect, and repair changes in the genome. This results in an ability to participate in tissue homeostasis and repair across an organism's lifespan (Rando). However, this does not necessarily mean that adult stem cells share all properties with either germ line cells or embryonic stem cells.

Evidence Against The Ageing of Stem Cells

It has been proposed that stem cells do not age; rather the changes seen in stem cells with age are due to reversible epigenetic modifications. A decline in tissue homeostasis or repair could arise from age-related changes in the numbers of stem cells present. It could also be due to the local environment or niche in which the stem cell resides; some examples demonstrating this change would be alterations in the amount and composition of the extracellular matrix, changes in the membrane proteins and lipids in cells that make direct contact with stem cells, and changes in soluble paracrine and endocrine factors that constitute the systemic milieu. The systemic milieu of an organism can result in ageing by immunological and neuroendocrine changes, and in the case of tissue injury or disease, changes in factors that are released from damaged cells and in inflammatory response that accompanies such damage (Rando).

Sometimes stem cells from aged animals show a delay in responsiveness to activated stimuli, yielding comparable results to those obtained from young stem cells. These initial responses might reflect epigenetic modifications rather than irreversible or biochemical changes.

The replicative and differentiative requirement put on hematopoietic stem cells following a bone marrow transplant also provide evidence that aged stem cells do not lose function. Here, an original small population of stem cells can produce mature progeny during a period far in excess of the original donor's lifespan. Thus it may be the environment, not the stem cells themselves, which is influenced by ageing. For example, in an experimental comparison of engraftment properties of young and old marrow in a dog, there was no decrement of stem cell function with age.

Most life-ending afflictions, such as heart disease, Alzheimer's disease, and end-stage renal failure, have etiologies that don't involve stem cells (Van Zant). Stem cells play a very small role in the ageing of tissues composing the heart and brain since these have very low cellular turnover. The aged phenotype of these tissues is controlled by mutations in the nuclear and mitochondrial DNA (Rando). Geriatric diseases involving stem cell dysfunction are very rare (Van Zant).

The ageing of stem cells may also be dependent on the type of stem cell in question. Hematopoietic stem cells display a gradual decline in function with age, but actually have an increase in numbers with age. In vitro studies have demonstrated that there is no difference between young and old cells in terms of their ability to form colonies and their proliferative potential. There is also no decline in their ability to interact with stroma. However, aged hematopoietic stem cells were less effective at homing and engrafting. A direct molecular analysis of purified hematopoietic stem cells revealed that there is a difference in gene expression between cells from young and old mice; this may be due to epigenetic modification.

Another type of adult stem cell is the skeletal muscle satellite cell. They are quiescent in adult muscle but are activated to proliferate and generate committed progeny in response to an injury or disease. With age, there is a great impairment of regenerative potential unexplained by any decline in number. The cause for this impairment may be a defect in the Notch signaling pathway. This pathway is essential for normal satellite cell activation in young animals. Regeneration mediated by aged satellite cells is highly effective when cells are transplanted into young animals as whole muscle grafts (Rando). This provides evidence for the claim that aged muscle stem cells have reversible epigenetic modifications due to their environment.

Thus the majority of the studies in which heterochronic transplantation was used came to the conclusion that stem cell functionality shows an age-related decline due to decrements in signals within the local and systemic environment that modulate the functions of stem cells or their progeny.

Evidence Supporting The Ageing of Stem Cells

It is also possible that stem cells inherently age due to the mechanisms by which other somatic cells age as well. In one study conducted, it was found that it is generally not possible to exceed five successful passages of transplant. After the second or third transplant, the few host stem cells surviving the lethal radiation dose had a competitive advantage over the serially passaged donor cells. Despite the numerical disadvantage these host stem cells had, they took over the most hematopoiesis. However, this study did not have conclusive results because it is possible that the limitation is due to manipulations associated with the transplant procedure instead of the reduced potency of the stem cell. Either way, the stem cells recovered to only a small fraction of the total number found in the unmanipulated animal (Van Zant).

More direct evidence of adult stem cells ageing can be found in experiments involving telomeres. When cells were produced in cytokine-supplemented cultures of purified precursor cells, there was a proliferation-associated loss of telomeric DNA. This demonstrated that the proliferative potential of most, if not all, hematopoietic stem cells is limited and decreases with age. In another experiment, human stem cells with CD34+ and CD38lo phenotype (indicating that they were likely to differentiate into helper T cells) were purified from adult bone marrow. They were found to have shorter telomeres than cells from the fetal liver or umbilical cord blood (Vaziri).

In yet another study conducted, it was found that stem cells accumulated intracellular damage as a result of ageing. However, as these cells were activated in response to hematopoietic stress, there was an increase in surveillance pathways leading to apoptosis, such as the p53 pathway. Compromised stem cells were removed from the pool and prevented from initiating clones with potentially dysfunctional progeny (Van Zant). This evidence supports the belief that ageing is an inherent property of adult stem cells.

A groundbreaking study conducted found that many of the features that underlie ageing of the hematopoietic system result directly from intrinsic changes that occur at the level of long-term hematopoietic stem cells. It was discovered that the aged bone marrow microenvironment only impacted B cell production from hematopoietic stem cells in the short term. Over a long term period, it was the intrinsic properties of the hematopoietic cells that caused the ageing. This provided concrete evidence that the ageing of hematopoietic stem cells is, to at least some extent, an inherent property of the cells and not due to the environment (Rossi).

Stem Cells and Longevity

Stem cells have no function in longevity. Some tissues are entirely postmitotic, so there is no tight mechanistic link between adult stem cell function and longevity. Longevity is determined by genetic variations and environmental factors (Van Zant). These factors may also influence adult stem cells, but this does not prove a causal relationship between stem cells and longevity.

Cancer as a Result of Acquired Mutations in Adult Stem Cells

The probability of acquiring cancer increases with age, and this may be partly due to stem cells. Tumors may often originate from the transformation of normal stem cells. There may be similar signaling pathways regulating self-renewal in stem cells and in cancer cells. Some cancer cells may include "cancer stem cells," which are rare cells with an indefinite potential for self-renewal that drives tumorigenesis (Reya).

One study was done in which a hypermorphic mutation in the tumor suppressor gene p53 almost completely suppressed carcinogenesis in mice but it also produced a phenotype reminiscent of ageing. This was manifested in a reduced lifespan, osteoporosis, low resistance to stress, and hematologic defects at an early age. It remains unclear how the heightened activity of a molecule normally associated with the induction of apoptosis, cell cycle arrest, or senescence of neoplastic cells would lead to the premature ageing phenotype (Van Zant). This link is one that could be crucial in both cancer and stem cell research.

Opinion and Analysis

Despite the numerous studies conducted pertaining to the same central question, whether stem cells undergo reversible or permanent changes with age remains open to debate to some extent. Only further research can elucidate the true mechanism by which age affects adult stem cells. However, with the research that has currently been done, a theory incorporating both views seems to be the most convincing.

The experiments concluding that stem cells age because of inherent changes within the cells offer valid points. Telomeres can shorten in these cells just as well as others. The cases in which old cells were transplanted into young niches clearly demonstrated that some stem cells simply do not possess the same functionality as their younger counterparts.

In the opposite respect, transplantation of old stem cells into a younger niche has been shown to result in recovery of functionality. Thus the experiments concluding that stem cells age because of epigenetic modifications due to the environment also remain valid. All that remains is to further explore these on the long term and short term basis. This has been done for hematopoietic stem cells, and it has been found that both epigenetic modification and irreversible changes in the cell play roles in the ageing of stem cells. The same needs to be done for other adult stem cells, such as skeletal muscle satellite cells.

Oncology, hematology, and regenerative medicine stand to gain much from further research in the field. A better understanding of stem cells in tumorigenesis would provide insight into the mechanisms which need to be prevented. With a better understanding of stem cell ageing and function, new techniques can be applied to regenerative medicine as well.

References

1. Flurkey K, Papaconstantinou J, Miller RA, Harrison DE. Lifespan extension and delayed immune and collagen aging in mutant mice with defects in growth hormone production. *Proc Natl Acad Sci USA* 98, 6736-6741 (2001).
2. Friedman DB, Johnson TE. A mutation in the age-1 gene in *Caenorhabditis elegans* lengthens life and reduces hermaphrodite fertility. Genetics 118, 75-86 (1988).
3. Kirkwood, TB. Understanding the odd science of aging. *Cell* 120, 437-447 (2005).
4. Lombard DB et al. DNA repair, genome stability, and aging. *Cell* 120, 497-512 (2005).
5. Partridge L, Gems D, Withers DJ. Sex and death: what is the connection? *Cell* 120, 461-472 (2005).
6. Rando, Thomas A. Stem cells, ageing, and the quest for immortality. *Nature* 44, 1080-1086 (2006).
7. Reya T, Morrison SJ, Clarke MF, Weissman IL. Stem cells, cancer, and cancer stem cells. *Nature* 414, 105-111 (2001).
8. Rossi DJ, Bryder D, Zahn JM, Ahlenius H, Sonu R, Wagers AJ, Weissman IL. Cell intrinsic alterations underlie hematopoietic stem cell aging. *PNAS* 102, 9149-9199 (2005).
9. Van Zant G, Liang Y. The role of stem cells in aging. *Exp Hematol* 31, 659-672 (2003).
10. Vaziri II, Dragowska W, Allsopp RC, Thomas TE, Harley CB, Lansdorp PM. Evidence for a mitotic clock in human hematopoietic stem cells: loss of telomeric DNA with age. *Proc Natl Acad Sci USA* 91, 9857-9860 (1994).
11. Weindruch R, Walford RL, Fligiel S, Guthrie D. The retardation of aging in mice by dietary restriction: longevity, cancer, immunity and lifetime energy intake. *J Nutr* 116, 641-654 (1986).

Ram Pathak

Light at the End of the Tunnel: Stem Cell Research

Background:

Stem cell research has taken a tumultuous path, involved in first-hand confrontation with politics, marred by critics purporting ethical/moral issues, and fueled by patients' hopes of regenerative medicine. The source of embryonic stem cells, as well as the subsequent research and experimentation on would-be zygotes, has fueled a debate ethical in origin, scientific in principle. The politics of stem cell research attempt to act as the compromiser between science and ethics. However, politics is rarely unified, as different parties hold different values. Proponents of each side have valid arguments, and it seems without further legislation, adequate funding for stem cell research will culminate to a standstill.

The cloning of Dolly opened up a door to a world without bounds. The successful transplantation of an adult mammary cell into an enucleated cell, forming an entirely new organism, invigorated scientists to explore the subject of stem cells further. If an adult cell can be reprogrammed to produce a clone, can we isolate these "reprogramming factors" to produce a fountain of youth cocktail designed to stop the aging of our cells? Moreover, is it possible to isolate cells, re-introduce them into our bodies, thereby creating new organs and replacing ones that failed or functioned incorrectly?

Recently, *Time Magazine* released an article entitled "Stem Cells: The Hope And The Hype". The article provides the reader with a detailed analysis of federal contributions to stem cell research. For example, in 2001 President Bush allowed federal funding for research on already existing stem cell lines. Unfortunately, this funding only covers twenty-one cell lines, thereby reducing genetic diversity. Moreover, these lines are too old and practices used to culture them are outdated. Kevin Eggan, principal faculty member at Harvard's Stem Cell Institute lamented the old cell lines: "They can't do what newer cell lines can do" (Gibbs). Additionally, these cell lines have undergone several chromosomal modifications resulting in subtle changes throughout the years. The government has refused funding for the creation of new stem cell lines, in effect halting the progression of stem cell research with respect to embryonic stem cells.

The political hindrances of embryonic stem cells have swayed research to focus on perfecting the technique of somatic cell nuclear transfer. However, it seems nearly impossible to attain the same totipotency as seen in embryonic stem cells. Thus, it can be seen that the issues of stem cell research have become highly personalized, concentrated on the individual. The individual must decide if the cost of sacrificing embryos is worth the reward of attaining cures to previously incurable disease. I agree that embryos do, in fact, represent life at the earliest level. We cannot simply destroy embryos in an attempt to harvest stem cells. But what if there is no cost? What if we do not have to sacrifice anything?

The purpose of the remainder of this paper is to analyze recent publications illustrating methods that bypass the need of extracting embryonic stem cells from new production lines, old production lines, or embryos altogether. Shinya Yamanaka of Kyoto University has successfully turned back the clock of cheek cells from a middle-aged woman. James Thompson of the University of Wisconsin achieved the same feat with foreskin cells from a newborn baby. The significance of this discovery eliminates the aforementioned political issues. "The achievements completely reset the boundaries of the stem cell debate, because both groups generated cells that looked and acted like embryonic stem cells, but without the need for eggs, embryos or ethical quandaries about where the cells came from" (Park 2007).

Direct Reprogramming In Mice

In October 2007, Hyun et al. published an article entitled "New Advances in iPS Cell Research Do Not Obviate the Need for Human Embryonic Stem Cells." This correspondence examined several articles demonstrating that mouse fibroblast cells can be directly reprogrammed to behave like embryonic stem cells. Recently, three different studies confirmed the production of embryonic-like stem cells from the direct reprogramming of mouse fibroblast cells (Okita et al., 2007; Wernig et al., 2007; Maherali et al., 2007). When these induced pluripotent stem (iPS) cells were injected into mouse blastocysts, they possessed the ability to contribute to all tissue types necessary for the developing embryo. Thus, this data purports that attainment of a fully reprogrammed state can be achieved by utilizing four transcription factors, as well as appropriate use of a selection procedure. In other words, with this new research it is possible to attain embryonic-like stem cells, eliminating the need for the embryo.

Direct Reprogramming In Humans

The implication of these studies on mouse fibroblast cells has generated a new way of thinking. Through extensive research in mice, Shinya Yamanaka and James Thompson have produced iPS cells in humans, obviating any need for embryos. In addition, the idea of producing human iPS cells has given hope to many patients because these cells are patient-specific/patient-generated.

Conclusion

The field of iPS research is exciting. Methods to exclude the production of tumor-associated products are being developed as we speak. Imagine the production of embryonic-like stem cells without the need for embryos or concern for tissue-specific rejection. However, this field is still in its infancy. We cannot proclaim promises without the production of more data; we still need to proceed with caution because of the natural propensity of stem cells yielding tumor cells. Hope is around the corner. The production of ES-like stem cells derived from patients themselves is intriguing and fascinating. As Dr. John Gearhart states (the biologist who first discovered human fetal embryonic stem cells), "I think this is the future of stem cell research. It's absolutely terrific."

The notion of iPS cells is quite intriguing to the field of stem cell research. As described in this paper, the ability of these cells to act like embryonic stem cells, as well as to be patient-specific/patient-generated, makes them the ultimate sought-after cure for patients suffering from terminal illnesses. By manipulating four different factors, *Oct-3/4*, *Sox2*, *c-Myc* and *Klf4*, we can successfully coax adult cells and transform them into stem cells.

The implications these findings have on our society, I believe, are tremendous. Not only can we circumvent the political hindrances and obstacles plaguing the stem cell debate today, but we also possess a real potential to treat diseases such as Parkinson's disease, spinal cord injury and diabetes. I believe this research is full of potential and it represents a new and flourishing approach to stem cell research.

Works Cited

Gibbs, Nancy. "Stem Cells: the Hope and the Hype." Time Magazine. 30
     July 2007. 21 Nov. 2007 < www.time.com>.

Hyun, I., Hochedlinger, K., Jaenisch, K., Yamanaka, S. (2007). New
     Advances in iPS Cell Research Do Not Obviate the Need for Human
Embryonic Stem Cells. Cell Stem Cell *1*, 367- 368.

Park, Alice. "A Breakthrough on Stem Cells." Time Magazine. 20 Nov.
     2007. 21 Nov. 2007 < www.time.com>.

Yamanaka, S. (2007). Strategies and New Developments in the Generation of
     Patient - Specific Pluripotent Cells. Cell Stem Cell
     1, 39-49

Ashley Landicho

Precedent Autonomy

In contemporary American medical practice, doctors believe that just as autonomy in a patient should be respected in a conscious state, so should autonomy be respected in an incapacitated state. Therefore the question arises of whether honoring patients' self-governance means treating them in accordance with their current judgment. This means doctors give patients what they used to prefer, but in a now-incapacitated state, can no longer understand. Yes, there exist methods like informed consent and advanced directives to counter this discrepancy, but this also assumes that "to respect someone's autonomy, any preferences we respect must be among that person's current preferences" (Davis 132). Yet this is not necessarily true. In order to most closely fulfill the wishes of a patient, one must imagine the patient in his or her actual debilitated condition but with complete intellectual capacity. That is, the patient must determine what values are important to him or her in an incapacitated self, not the values of his or her current cognizant self, to produce the most-informed preference.

The necessity of autonomy analysis is derived from the prevalence of its problems. "Many ill patients' experiences of pain, suffering, shock, fear, and anger prevent them from 'taking in' all of the relevant information; consequently, these negative emotional states can impair patients' ability to make informed, carefully reasoned choices about treatment" (Beste 217). This is most relevant to patients that suffer from some form of dementia such as Alzheimer's disease or any other mental deterioration in which the loss of intellectual thought is irreversible. Yet the beauty of modern medicine lies in the predictability of certain illnesses that allows patients to consciously direct the path of their physical wellbeing before the illness occurs, otherwise known as informed consent. The benefits of this includes the ability to rationally reflect on the medical situation presented and internally make judgments based on specific reasons that give value to the patient at the time. This also instills within a patient a sense of voice and independence to a seemingly inevitable fate. This supports the "widespread consensus in American medical practice that increased patient autonomy and informed consent have been appropriate correctives to the unbridled paternalism of the past" (Beste 1). But although the idea of informed consent seems almost completely beneficial, most people overlook the fact that informed consent implies that the conditions and lives of a patient are static. We must not forget that all patients and the conditions that surround them are dynamic, so therefore their preferences must parallel this and change as well.

For example, Jane Doe issues an advance directive to "Do Not Resuscitate (DNR)" in her upcoming surgical procedure because she highly values her intelligence, her professional career, and her family. Jane Doe reasons that this is her preference because she highly regards her dignity of independence and believes in the natural inevitability of the human body. She holds her dignity and these values higher than becoming entirely reliant on motorized machines in a vegetative state. Yet these things that lead her to choose this preference require Jane Doe to be in a certain state of rational and intellectual capacity. If that capacity no longer exists, then those reasons no longer pertain to her and therefore a patient loses a preference under conditional variables. In other words, "a preference does not survive a loss of the reasons behind it" (Davis 123).

A patient that devises a treatment plan in advance based on reasons made with complete mental capacity must realize that those reasons may not be viable at the time when that treatment plan is implemented. If the reasons were not pertinent anymore, then a patient would be allowing doctors to serve a former preference that serves a former self, instead of serving the preferences of the incompetent self who currently exists. Instead, autonomy should be rooted in patients that anticipate and internally digest the options and preferences he or she would later have in dementia. Once these conditions are fully understood, it is then that a more aware preference of a tentative plan of treatment can be assessed and designed.

Patients must be aware of the implications of advanced directives that are theoretically supposed to maintain a sense of autonomy by respecting that competent patient's treatment. Instead of directing preferences in a present state of mind, patients must widen the time spectrum and hypothetically envelop themselves in conditions similar to what they imagine themselves with severe mental impairment. It is only then that patients can have as close to self-governance with respect to their most-informed preferences through precedent autonomy. It is only then that patients can exhibit not only who they are now, but who they want to be.

Works Cited

Davis, John. "The Concept of Precedent Autonomy." <u>Bioethics</u>. 16.2
      (2002): 114-133. Beste, Jennifer. "Instilling Hope and Respecting
      Patient Autonomy: Reconciling Apparently

Conflicting Duties." <u>Bioethics</u>. 19.3 (2005): 215-231.

Schermer, Maartje. "Nothing But The Truth? On Truth And Deception In
      Dementia Care." <u>Bioethics</u>. 21.1 (2007) 13-22.

Karna Sura

Stem Cells: The Totipotent Truth

Stem cells are an especially taboo subject in the United States. They have been grouped with the pro-life/pro-choice debate since embryonic stem cells are grown from fertilized eggs. However, stem cells come in multiple flavors including embryonic, which are made from fertilized eggs, and adult stem cells, which are found in all humans. Each stem cell has significance in research and medicine, yet embryonic stem cells are the most favored since they are totipotent, have the ability to differentiate into any cell. On the other hand, adult stem cells are pluripotent since they differentiate into a limited number of cells. The purpose of this review is to understand different stem cells and their potential therapeutic value *in vivo*.

Embryonic stem cells (ESCs) are the most important of the stem cells since they can differentiate into any type of cells. They have the greatest therapeutic potential due to differentiating into any cell, leading to the potential ability to cure any disease or injury to tissue. Researchers have tried to inject pure population of ESCs into animals to see the therapeutic effect. Instead of any therapeutic effect, the pure population of ESCs became teratoma (literally translated as "monstrous tumor"). These pure populations differentiate into every different type of cells since they had no direction. According to Przyborski, the teratomas are actually differentiated somatic tissues when injected into *scid* mice (mice without immune systems). He believes that these tumors would provide insight in bioengineering and that the mechanism of differentiation could further help in discovering better methods of using ESCs (2005). Thus, researchers used a new method of differentiating *in vitro* and then implanting cells. ESCs have been used to differentiate into pancreatic-like cells *in vitro* using Ngn-3 (Serafimidis 2008). These cells show great promise since they are very similar to pancreatic cells but function correctly, potentially curing those who have Type I Diabetes. In addition, ESCs are used to cure tissue injury. In spinal cord injury, ESCs are differentiated into neural cells and then implanted into injured mice. The neural cells heal the spinal cord and provide electrical activity back to the spinal cord (Cui, L. et al 2008).

However, there are a couple of problems with this method. First, ESCs need specific differentiation factors that are specific to the cells wanted. Second, the differentiated cells need to be tested *in vivo* to see if these differentiated cells are viable. The differentiated cells can have different fates *in vivo* including immune response, which leads to death of the cells, or cancerous abnormalities, which can lead to the death of the animal. These possibilities need to be tested throughout *in vivo* before being tried on humans. Although ESCs require a lot of work, they offer the best therapeutic value to disease and injury since they work in a variety of circumstances, almost like a panacea. Researchers are trying to discover ways of creating ESCs from other cells due to controversy surrounding the issue of using a fertilized egg. Takahashi has developed an *in vitro* method in both mice and humans to develop induced pluripotent cells (iPS). For the iPS method, an adult human dermal fibroblast cell is infected with a retrovirus with specific embryonic transcription factors. These factors are expressed in the cell, turning them into embryonic-like stem cells (2007). These cells can be used very similarly to ESCs; however, a lot of testing needs to be completed with these cells. Although in the short-term, iPS work fine, the long-term needs to be tested for any possible problems *in vitro* as well as *in vivo*.

Adult stem cells are found in every human and are tissue-specific. These tissue-specific stem cells have importance in differentiating into cells of that tissue. Adult stem cells include adipose-derived adult stem cells (ASCs), haemtopoietic stem cells (HSCs), mesenchymal stem cells (MSCs), and neural stem cells (NSCs). Adult stem cells have importance especially in injury. Researchers have found that adult stem cells will try to heal damage by migrating to the site of damage and differentiating into the specific injured cell type. Case in point, after osteoarthritis, MSCs will migrate to the site of damage and differentiate to help cure the injury (Rollin, R. et al 2008). However, there are limitations to the total injury that can be healed by the adult stem cells since there is a low level of stem cells. In order to promote more healing and faster healing time, researchers are trying to grow stem cell *in vitro* and then implant them. One important discovery is differentiation of haemtopoietic stem cells into neurons and other cells. HSCs are part of the bone marrow, which is important in the formation of all blood cells including leukocytes, erthyrocytes, and thrombocytes. Haemtopoietic stem cells can differentiate into a number of non-blood cells including neuronal and heart tissue (Guan 2007). HSCs show great potential as a rival to embryonic stem cells since they do have the ability to differentiate into other cell type.

Stem cells are a necessary part of research and need to be investigated further. These cells offer the world a new potential cure for many diseases and problems. Both adult and embryonic stem cells need to be tested for their potential use in genetic engineering. At present time, these cells seem like the best solution to many autoimmune problems and diseases since they can differentiate into a variety of different cell types. Stem cells, as a whole, should be developed as a cure to diseases and problems, no matter the controversy surrounding them.

References

Cui, L. et al. (2008) Transplantation of Embryonic Stem Cells Improves Nerve Repair and Functional Recovery after Severe Sciatic Nerve Axotomy in Rats. Stem Cell, Epub.

Guan, K. and Hasenfuus, G. (2007) Do stem cells in the heart truly differentiate into cardiomyocytes? J Mol Cell Cardiol 43 (4), 377-87.

Przyborski, S.A. (2005) Differentiation of Human Embryonic Stem Cells After Transplantation in Immune-Deficient Mice. Stem Cell 23, 1242-1250.

Rollin, R. et al. (2008) Differential Proteome of Bone Marrow Mesenchymal Stem Cells from Osteoarthritis Patients. Osteoarthritis Cartilage, Epub.

Serafimidis, I. (2008) Novel Effectors of Directed and Ngn3-Mediated Differentiation of Mouse Embryonic Stem Cells into Endocrine Pancreas Progenitors. Stem Cell 26, 3-16.

Takahashi, K. et al. (2007) Induction of Pluripotent Stem Cells from Adult Human Fibroblasts by Defined Factors. Cell 131, 861-872.

Ahmed Zahra

Aid for AIDS Struck African Nations

"There are people who make miracles in this world. One of them lives right here in the U.S. He realized that vital elements could be harvested from the stalk of the wheat. In his hands, India, which at the time had been ravaged by drought and overpopulation—in his hands, the wheat crop increased from 11 million tons to 60 million tons annually. His name is Norman Borlaug"(In This White House, The West Wing). What Norman Borlaug did for India and Pakistan in the 1960s was nothing short of a miracle, and a miracle is exactly what developing nations across the world need to be able to supply medication to all those who have been infected. Since its discovery in the early 80's, the disease has spread manifolds across the globe infecting over millions of people each year while killing millions as well. The state of affairs now seems just as helpless as it was before the Green Revolution, forty years ago. The spread of the disease, however, has taken its greatest toll in the African subcontinent, where developing nations that were already struggling to strengthen their economies are now facing the possibility of losing an entire generation of people due to HIV/AIDS. But, while the world waits for another Norman Borlaug, what is required is the strengthening of the global endeavor on part of the First World countries in alliance with world organizations such as the United Nations to tackle the AIDS crisis.

Worldwide, in 2006, 4.3 million new infections were recorded, as were 2.9 million AIDS-related deaths—more than in any previous year. Today, 39.5 million people are living with HIV, with the worst of the epidemic centered in sub-Saharan Africa (UNAIDS Annual Report 2006, p. 5). What makes the situation in these countries even more disturbing is the prevalence of this disease coupled with destitution and a frail economy. Average prevalence in sub-Saharan Africa is 8.8% in the adult population (15–49 years old). The upper bound for prevalence is yet to be established, but Botswana has the highest rate so far with 36% adult prevalence, followed by Swaziland, Zimbabwe and Lesotho, which all have prevalence between 24 and 25% (Piot et al). The impact of the AIDS epidemic on these countries has taken a toll on their social capital. The life expectancy rates that took decades to rise are once again falling and in worst affected countries a possible reversal of the population pyramid is already taking place. In *The End of Poverty*, Jeffery Sachs talks about Nthandire, a village in Malawi where not a young man or woman was in sight. The scene is similar in such places where AIDS has wiped out adults leaving more in their 60s than those in their 30s and 50s. The demographic impact of AIDS is distinct. HIV infection is the highest in men and women in their productive years and more importantly, unlike other diseases, the number of people dying from AIDS will continue to rise in the years to come. The confluence of these problems has set many poor African nations in an inescapable economic dilemma. If an entire people of a country were incapacitated how would the country ever get out of the deathtrap of a depressed economy?

An important step towards undertaking the AIDS problem is providing access to drugs for the millions who are infected. And here is where the problems begin. All the drugs in the market are patented under intellectual property rights, and hence cannot be reproduced and sold at different prices by anyone except for the rightful owner. However, in the end of 2001, the World Trade Organizations ministerial meeting at Doha declared that the Trade-Related Aspects of Intellectual Property Rights (TRIPS) Agreement should not stand in the way of AIDS response (Galvão, Para. 10). A war of prices between pharmaceutical companies and generic manufacturers ensued, which has led to lowering of prices of the required drugs. Several triple-therapy regimes can be provided (combining drugs from GlaxoSmithKline, Merck & Co., and Bristol-Myers Squibb Co.), each for less than $1330 per year per person. The World Bank has used an estimate of $500 for complementary treatment costs in Africa, but this appears very high (Binswanger, Para. 2). Even after the lowering in prices and the aid, the costs come up to be around $1800 per year. A large majority of patients would be unable to afford treatment. The per capita purchasing parity in Malawi, for instance, is $290 (U.S. Department of State, 2008), and the numbers are similar for other countries where people are affected. With geographical constrictions, a burdened economy and lack of infrastructure weighing these nations down, governments of developed economies will have to finance large-scale programs directed at highly affected countries.

For this endeavor to be made possible it is imperative that the monetary needs and expenditures for these countries be calculated and then be appropriated from all possible sources. Help from officials from organizations such as the United Nations Economic and Social Council and the World Bank to keep track of expenses will make it easier to assess the needs of each country individually. Presently, the largest contributions to AIDS response have been through the Global Fund to

Fight AIDS, Tuberculosis and Malaria (UNAIDS Annual Report 2006 Pg. 51). However, the process to get funding is complex and requires the submission of a proposal. Of the US$ 6.6 billion approved, only US$ 2.9 billion has been distributed on account of the need to submit proposals. It seems strange that even though the money has been appropriated it has yet to be put to use. Unfortunately, in many of these countries misallocation due to bureaucracy is an issue and therefore there is inhibition on the part of such organizations to provide absolute funding. But this should not be allowed to obstruct aid from reaching the needy. Official assistance to monitor expenditure will help evaluate need and increase allocation effectively.

There are many other problems that are connected to AIDS and need to be addressed. Some of them include education programs, prophylaxis, treatment for diseases that people are more likely to contract with a suppressed immune system, etc. Also, even with funding available for access to drugs, the problem of drug administration is a matter of concern. It is necessary that adequate infrastructure in the form of health clinics, hospitals and health officials be accessible. Developed nations need to invest in the building and overhaul of the current infrastructure in these nations to better aid the ongoing initiatives. In 2006, there were 2.9 million AIDS-related deaths (UNAIDS Annual Report 2006, Pg 5). Last year GlaxoSmithKline, a pharmaceutical company, recorded an outcome profit of 15.2 billion US dollars (GSK Business Performance, 2007). Half the money could be used to provide antiretroviral drugs for 4 million people in Africa for one year. There is so much to be done but what could be more important than getting medication to those who would die without it?

References

1. "In This White House" The West Wing P.O.V. Dir. Ken Olin. 25 October 2000
2. "Making the Money Work" UNAIDS Annual Report 2006
3. Piot et al. "The global impact of HIV/AIDS." Nature 410 (2001): 968-973 8th March 2008
   http://www.nature.com/nature/journal/v410/n6831/full/410968a0.html
4. Galvão J. "Brazil and Access to HIV/AIDS Drugs: A Question of Human Rights and Public Health" American Journal of Public Health (2005) 8th March 2008
   http://www.pubmedcentral.nih.gov/articlerender.fcgi?artid=1449327

5. Binswanger "HIV/AIDS Treatment for Millions" Science
    292(2001) : 221-223 8th March 2008
    http://www.sciencemag.org/cgi/content/full/292/5515/221
6. U.S. Department of State "Background Notes" 18th March 2008
    http://www.state.gov/r/pa/ei/bgn/
7. GSK Business performance 2007 18th March 2008
    http://www.gsk.com/investors/reports/q42007/q42007.pdf

Krista Lewis

The Art of Fascism

When thinking about the history of the Italian peninsula, the presence and the significance of art in its development is impossible to ignore. Anyone who has studied Western history is familiar with Michelangelo, Raphael and daVinci. Yet the history of the peninsula is not solely in distant eras. Italy's experiences during the first half of the 20th century are not insignificant in the long arc of history, and as with all prior periods, art played no small part in their unfolding. The adoption of Fascism by Italy in 1922 marked a new direction for the peninsula and its people. Art very quickly became a tool to foster this change. However, the relationship between the new regime and this tool failed to be as straightforward as one might guess. The obvious conclusion that the regime controlled the arts is true in many respects, yet the opposite is just as accurate.

To better understand the setting that gave rise to art produced in Fascist Italy, it is necessary to look at the dominant ideological beliefs of the time. The 1932 "Doctrine of Fascism," written by Benito Mussolini and Giovanni Gentile a decade after the beginning of Fascist rule, is a good place to start. Here they explain that "Fascism is action and it is thought... it sees not only the individual but the nation and the country [and] there can be no conception of the state which is not fundamentally a conception of life."[1] These statements show that the state is everything in fascism. Individuals are absorbed by the state and life is the state. The document reveals the basic fascist values of action, struggle, discipline, culture, education, and work when it further explains that:

> Fascism wants man to be active and to engage in action with all his energies... It conceives of life as a struggle in which it behooves a man to win for himself a really worthy place, first of all by fitting himself (physically, morally, intellectually) to become the implement required for winning it. As for the individual, so for the nation, and so for mankind. Hence the high value of culture in all its forms (artistic, religious, scientific) and the outstanding importance of education. Hence also the essential value of work, by which man subjugates nature and creates the human world (economic, political, ethical, and intellectual).[2]

Certain beliefs the authors expressed about the purpose of a state and particular aims of the fascist state itself are also worth noting. First, "A nation, as expressed in the State, is a living, ethical entity only in so far as it is progressive. Inactivity is death."[3] Furthermore:

> The State is not only the present; it is also the past and above all the future... The State educates the citizens to civism, makes them aware of their mission, urges them to unity; its justice harmonizes their divergent interests; it transmits to future generations the conquests of the mind in the fields of science, art, law, human solidarity; it leads men up from primitive tribal life to that highest manifestation of human power, imperial rule.[4]

These statements demonstrate fascism's propensity to look to the future and the importance of the future to the regime. Fascism itself, "aims at refashioning not only the forms of life, but their content – man, his character, and his faith," and "it does not allow itself to be deceived by mutable and fallacious appearances."[5] These last statements expose the contradictory nature of Italian Fascism; the former talks of the desire for transformation while the latter disparages such abilities.

Finally, the document discusses the fascist stance toward life, war, and peace. "The Fascist disdains an 'easy' life," and "does not believe in the possibility of 'happiness' on earth." For a fascist, "Life as he understands it means duty, elevation, conquest... it must be lived for oneself but above all for others, both nearby and far off, present and future." Furthermore, "Fascism does not... believe in the possibility or utility of perpetual peace... War alone keys up all human energies to their maximum tension and sets the seal of nobility on those peoples who have the courage to face it."[6] Clearly, action, struggle and sacrifice are what make a person worthy of greatness.

Mussolini's personal view of the regime and its relationship to the Italian people is seen in interviews conducted by Emil Ludwig in the spring of 1932. During one interview, Mussolini explained that "the masses are nothing but a herd of sheep as long as they are unorganized." They are unable to rule themselves and must be led by enthusiasm and interest.[7] He desired a strongly disciplined nation with masses that would be taught "to live, to work, and to fight in a great fellowship—but in a hierarchy, not in a mere herd."[8] Furthermore, the masses should believe rather than know, for "it is faith that moves mountains, not reason." For Mussolini, everything depended on "one's ability to control the masses like an artist."[9]

Prior to the fascist takeover in Italy, the futurist art movement espoused many beliefs that echo fascist beliefs. As a youthful and aggressive movement, futurism recognized the dynamism of societies based on technology and it supported Italian nationalism.[10] Artists fought against subjugation to the past, wanted man to be assertive, and viewed the modern world as one in motion, fast and intense.[11] Above all, they insisted on their uniqueness and pure Italian origins.[12] According to the "Futurist Manifesto," futurists wanted "to sing the love of danger, the habit of energy and rashness." They believed "Beauty exists only in struggle. There is no masterpiece that has not an aggressive character." They wanted "to glorify war—the only cure for the world."[13] Obviously, futurism and fascism shared beliefs in the power of conflict, the importance of the future, and the desire for action and movement. Though futurism could have been the dominant state art for the fascist regime, it never received official sanctioning. In fact, several artistic movements vied for the top spot, and like futurism, never gained the coveted position. The Novecento movement competed first.[14] These artists were characterized by their use of blocky, solid forms and depicted images of women, landscapes, still lifes, or mythological scenes. Novecento won favor because it managed to be experimental without being too avant-garde; it was modern but recognizable.[15] As the politics of the fascist regime changed, the movement also tried to change. However, by the mid-1930s Novecento lost favor for being too "internationalist."[16]

Considered Stracittà, or "super city" movements for their emphasis on modern, urban activities of life and technology, followers of both Futurism and Novecento believed they best epitomized Fascist motives and desires.[17] Another artistic development, the Strapaese movement, opposed every aspect of the Stracittà. Artists, such as Giorgio Morandi, captured everyday objects and idealized the life of hard-working peasants. The movement represented the traditional values and customs of regular Italian citizens, characterized Fascism in its early years, and felt Italian society could be improved by being linked to the past.[18] This movement fit the ideas of discipline, simplicity, hard work, and tradition. However, its steadfast emphasis on rural, autonomous life did not sit well with the regime's promotion of Rome, centralization and expression through spectacle.[19]

Several smaller artistic movements, such as Scuola Romana and Concretisti, coexisted with Futurism, Novecento, and Strapaese, but did not receive similar attention.[20] The fact that so many artistic movements sought the approval of the government and thrived is curious since Fascism in Italy intended itself to be authoritarian if not totalitarian.

As one historian characterized it, "the regime practiced repressive tolerance" when dealing with the arts.[21] Part of the reason they faired so well is due to Mussolini's recognition that they could aid "in giving form to ideology and rhetoric."[22] He understood life to be partly an aesthetic experience; therefore, art could help promote his goals. Nonetheless, Mussolini needed greater incentive than toleration if he wanted artists to be involved in his regime. The most effective proved to be patronage. Under the State's generous sponsorship, artists could work without censorship so long as their work refrained from being explicitly anti-Fascist.[23] With the combination of toleration and patronage, few artists felt the pressure to emigrate from Italy.[24] They did, however, feel pressure to show conformity to the regime. If they wished to exhibit their work or enter in competitions, they had to join a Fascist trade union.[25] Not surprisingly, this offer proved difficult to refuse. [26]

The support of the arts allowed Mussolini to project his ideology to the masses, but he had ulterior motives. Plurality created an image of all-inclusiveness and unity, which Mussolini desired for the country. Furthermore, the support of all the various artistic movements prevented an artistic underground from forming, which gave the regime "intellectual and moral leadership" that helped gain the consent of other groups.[27] He also believed that a diversity of expression led to the production of good art, and hoped for a cultural[28] regeneration that would rid Italy of its old bourgeois culture. Finally, arts promotion served to erase the image of Fascists as merely a group of "Philistine ruffians."[29] These many side effects legitimized Fascist rule, and proved it intended to be more than a passing fancy. With the creative world willingly leashed, Mussolini made sure that it conveyed the right beliefs.[30] This generally resulted in images and projects that flattered Italy by showing its power and embrace of modernity while neglecting to show any inkling of its flaws. Mussolini believed this self promotion gave Italy's society the boost it needed to make it a successful rival to other states.[31]

Since Fascism looked to the future, its art had to symbolize the regime's image as a revolutionary, dynamic force. This came through, particularly in the early years. But it also had to show that Fascism did not abandon Italy's roots and traditions.[32] As the regime aged, this became increasingly emphasized. Mussolini believed that tradition could organize people and spread an understanding of Fascism.[33] He saw Italy's potential to be a powerful, admired nation again, but felt it needed a push to get there. Thus, the regime intended to reinvigorate Italians through the juxtaposition of a decadent and corrupt present with an honorable past.[34] The city of Rome itself, and the images of the past it provoked, became a major influence on Fascist ideals. Indeed, Rome became an exhibition in its own right. Mussolini, the consummate persuader, did not want to overtly force the Italian people into anything. He needed them to transform of their own volition, ignorant of their herd mentality. In a 1924 speech, Mussolini showed that he knew the manipulation of antiquity, art and the people's pride in both could help him direct their lives. In his speech, he declared:

> Art, together with law, has marked with its stamp the unifying expansion of the Latin world. In Rome, and wherever Rome arrives in the world with its legions and its powerful spirit, we feel we are in front of a force of beauty that is not only a manifestation of a state of the spirit and civilization, but has in itself the brilliant germ of Italian art... The style is the eternal and luminous characteristic of the race and will... give to man the standards for creating the future cities... "[35]

Mussolini successfully highlighted parts of Fascism and historical pride that appealed to individuals, which enabled everyone to find something to relate to in Fascism.[55]

Tradition found expression most often through the use of triumphal arches, columns and equine portraits and statues. The imagery connected Fascist Italy to an imperial and civic past.[37] This served as a way to exhibit the legitimacy of the present regime, and project a desire not only to follow in the footsteps of a glorious predecessor but surpass it.[38] Mussolini recognized that supporting the arts could renew a desire in Italians for historical importance.[39] At the same time, he made sure not to neglect the modern attributes that made Fascism and its leadership unique.[40] He needed public loyalty if Fascism were to follow his vision.[41] Therefore, art had to reflect the needs and hopes of society so that it could be appreciated by the masses.[42] These efforts to orchestrate the peoples' experience and view of the past aimed to create a sense of community and build a unified Italian people of the present and the future.[43] Association to such a unifying force would then help the regime gain and deepen consent from the people.[44] Even though the people were supposed to live for the State, the State really lived for the people.

For art to unify, however, it had to reach all levels of Italian society. Furthermore, unity necessitated one interpretation of historical fact. Most importantly, the art had to be Italian. With these requirements, much of the art produced under the regime showed devotion and heroism for Italy, and often depicted "ideal men." Dedication to cleanliness, purity, and health through outdoor activities also found expression, as did portrayals of motherhood and the glorification of strength and hard work illustrated through scenes of peasantry. Despite their poverty, peasants had stability in their rural origins, something that could not be found in the turbulent, growing urban areas of Italy. These themes all suggested security in an unquestioned hierarchy. To increase their visibility, the regime used public art in the traditional fresco form. The constant presence of frescoes, akin to the regime's constant reference to previous epochs, solidified the beliefs they embodied.[45]

Institutions and organizations meant to guide the development of Fascist culture in Italy took shape early in the regime's history. Most consisted of syndicates or unions, such as the Fascist Syndicate of the Fine Arts. These institutions believed culture should be the culmination of social, spiritual, and historical action from within a nation, and art should not be separated from social and political conditions.[46] The Fascist party and government involved themselves in these organizations as a means to show their support and prove that Fascism meant action. Their involvement in art reform flaunted the power and wealth the new regime possessed, and the actual streamlining and centralization of the arts proved that Fascism kept its word and worked toward a unified Italian national culture.[47]

As time progressed, the regime's attitude toward the arts showed signs of change so that by 1940 the Fascist government itself created the Department of Contemporary Art. Out of fear for the potential art had in fostering individuality, the State became more directly involved in the art world.[48] By the mid 1930s, the acceptance of plurality as a way to unify Italian culture and dispel unrest began to backfire. Anti-pluralists felt the treatment of Italian culture did not reflect the authoritarian structure of state and society that Fascism meant to produce. Instead it weakened the State and resembled liberalism and social internationalism. Therefore, they sought an art that represented Fascism.[49] By 1936, Fascism in Italy had clearly become less revolutionary and far more settled. This shift, in combination with pluralist critics and the incessant conflicting visions of Fascism, resulted in what has been termed the "Battle for Culture."[50] Art became less modernist and exhibited an imperial flair.[51] Political and imperial content became much more apparent, which became particularly evident when Mussolini set the themes to several artistic competitions.[52] In 1939 it would be "States of Mind Created by Fascism." "The Battle for Grain," "Italian Fascist Youth," and "Out of Blood, the New Europe" followed in subsequent years.[53]

One of the most important aspects related to the arts under Fascism is the way in which the regime brought the arts to the public. The fact that Fascism wanted all Italians to be included in cultural activities is important to remember.[54] Fascism's early anti-museum sentiment made exhibitions and festivals the prevailing formats for presentation.[55] Exhibitions, being temporary, moved beyond what galleries and museums could provide because they expanded artistic content and reached more people. They adapted to shifting tastes so people did not have to stray from the State for artistic and cultural needs. The regime wanted its people to be cultural consumers, and the more they consumed the better the State could support its artists.[56]

In its effort to reach more people, the regime succeeded in changing the accepted understanding of high culture since exhibitions included styles and techniques associated with popular and mass culture, such as film and public art. In order to make exhibitions even more attractive, the State subsidized train fares and offered group rates. Heavy advertising also spread the word far and wide.[57] Exhibitions brought the dictatorship, artists, and citizens under one roof, where the dictatorship projected its history of Fascism and concept of society onto the people. The more citizens that experienced these exhibitions the better because it meant more people absorbed and shared the culture of Fascism.[58]

Mussolini stated in a 1926 speech to the Italian people that, "We mustn't remain solely contemplatives. We mustn't simply exploit our cultural heritage. We must create a new heritage to place alongside that of antiquity. We must create a new art, an art of our times: a Fascist art."[59] In retrospect, this reveals both the success and failure of Mussolini and the Fascist regime. They certainly succeeded in making Italy an active state. Nonetheless, they did everything they could to exploit the cultural heritage of Italy, and as a variety of artistic styles flourished, no single Fascist art form ever truly developed. The regime's handling of the arts during its years in power exposed its superficial and contradictory nature. It created links to a gloried past where none existed and tried to convince its people of a destined greatness. The regime could not support itself on its own merits. It relied on abstract, fictitious notions and the strengths of others to create a façade to gain support and consensus. By all appearances, Fascism in Italy showed a great ability to adapt to changing circumstances, yet such ability is only effective when there is a stable core of values and beliefs to rest on.

Notes

1. Benito Mussolini and Giovanni Gentile, "The Doctrine of Fascism,"from World Future Fund: A Research Institute for the Study of Global Future Trends [electronic bulletin board] (Alexandria, VA, 2007 [cited 2 December 2007]); available fromhttp://www.worldfuturefund.org/wffmaster/Reading/Germany/mussolini.htm; INTERNET.

2. Ibid.

3. Ibid.

4. Ibid.

5. Ibid.

6. Ibid.

7. Emil Ludwig, *Talks With Mussolini* (London: Unwin Brothers Ltd.,1932), 122.

8. Ibid., 125-126.

9. Ibid., 128.

10. Joshua C. Taylor, *Futurism* (New York: Doubleday, 1961), 109.

11. Ibid., 9-11.

12. Ibid., 54.

13. F.T. Marinetti, "Futurist Manifesto," from University of Michigan, Center for the Study of Complex Systems [electronic bulletin board] (Ann Arbor, MI, 1997 [cited 2 December 2007]); available from http://cscs.umich.edu/~crshalizi/T4PM/futuristmanifesto.html; INTERNET.

14. Edward R. Tannenbaum, *The Fascist Experience* (New York: Basic Books, Inc., 1972), 260-262.

15. Marla Susan Stone, *The Patron State: Culture & Politics in Fascist Italy* (Princeton: Princeton University Press, 1998), 47.

16. Ibid., 49.

17. Mark Antliff, "Fascism, Modernism, and Modernity," *The Art Bulletin* Vol. 84, No. 1 (March 2002): 100.

18. Emily Braun, "Speaking Volumes: Giorgio Morandi's Still Lifes and the Cultural Politics of Strapaese," *Modernism/Modernity* Vol. 2, No. 3 (1995): 91.

19. Ibid., 93.

20. Stone, 52-53.

21. Tannenbaum, 300.

22. Stone, 3.

23. Ibid., 4-6.

24. Tannenbaum, 263.

25. Silvia Barisione, Matteo Fochessati, and Gianni Franzone, Under Mussolini: *Decorative and Propaganda Arts of the Twenties and Thirties from the Wolfson Collection, Genoa* (Genoa: Fondazione Regionale, 2002), 29.

26. Stone, 6.

27. Ibid., 65.

28. Ibid., 67.

29. Ibid., 76.

30. George L Mosse, "Fascist Aesthetics and Society: Some Considerations," *Journal of Contemporary History* Vol. 31, No. 2, Special Issue: The Aesthetics of Fascism (April 1996): 245.

31. Tannenbaum, 269.

32. Mosse, 251.

33. Diane Yvonne Ghirardo, "Citta Fascista: Surveillance and Spectacle," *Journal of Contemporary History* Vol. 31, No. 2 (April 1996): 367.

34. Antliff, 149-150.

35. Jan Nelis, "Constructing Fascist Identity: Benito Mussolini and the Myth of the Romanità," *Classical World* Vol. 100, No. 4 (Summer 2007): 413.

36. Antliff, 165.

37. Ghirardo, D.Y., 358.

38. Ibid., 367.

39. Kate Flint, "Art and the Fascist Regime in Italy," *Oxford Art Journal* Vol. 3, No. 2 (October 1980): 49

40. Ghirardo, D.Y., 349-350.

41. Ibid., 349.

42. Mosse, 246.

43. Nelis, 394.

44. Mosse, 246

45. Flint, 51-54.

46. Diane Ghirardo, "Architects, Exhibitions, and the Politics of Culture in Fascist Italy," Journal of Architectural Education (1984) Vol. 45, No. 2 (February 1992): 67.

47. Stone, 23-24.

48. Flint, 50.

49. Stone, 93.

50. Ibid., 178-179.

51. Ibid., 227.

52. Borden W. Painter, Jr., *Mussolini's Rome* (New York: Palgrave Macmillan, 2005): 69.

53. Flint, 51.

54. Stone, 95.

55. Jeffrey T. Schnapp, "Epic Demonstrations: Fascist Modernity and the 1932 Exhibition of the Fascist Revolution," in *Fascism, Aesthetics, and Culture*, ed. Richard J. Goslan (Hanover:University Press of New England, 1992), 32.

56. Stone, 95-99.

57. Ibid., 97-98.

58. Ibid., 17-18.

59. Schnapp, 1.

Bibliography

Antliff, Mark. "Fascism, Modernism, and Modernity." *The Art Bulletin*
Vol. 84, No. 1: 148-169. March 2002.

Barisione, Silvia, Matteo Fochessati, and Gianni Franzone. *Under
Mussolini*: Decorative and

*Propaganda Arts of the Twenties and Thirties from the Wolfson
Collection, Genoa.* Genoa: Fondazione Regionale, 2002.

Braun, Emily. "Speaking Volumes: Giorgio Morandi's Still Lifes and the
Cultural Politics of *Strapaese.*" *Modernism/Modernity* Vol. 2,
No. 3: 89-116. 1995.

Flint, Kate. "Art and the Fascist Regime in Italy." *Oxford Art Journal* Vol.
3, No. 2: 49-54. October 1980.

Ghirardo, Diane. "Architects, Exhibitions, and the Politics of Culture in
Fascist Italy." *Journal of Architectural Education* (1984-) Vol. 45,
No. 2: 67-75. February 1992.

Ghirardo, Diane Yvonne. "Citta Fascista: Surveillance and Spectacle."
Journal of Contemporary History Vol. 31, No. 2: 347-372. April 1996.

Ludwig, Emil. *Talks With Mussolini.* London: Unwin Brothers Ltd., 1932.

Marinetti, F.T. "Futurist Manifesto," from University of Michigan, Center
for the Study of Complex Systems [electronic bulletin board].
(Ann Arbor, MI, 1997 [cited 2 December 2007]). Available from
http://cscs.umich.edu/~crshalizi/T4PM/futurist-manifesto.html;
INTERNET.

Mosse, George L. "Fascist Aesthetics and Society: Some Considerations."
Journal of Contemporary History Vol. 31, No. 2, Special Issue: The
Aesthetics of Fascism: 245-252. April 1996.

Mussolini, Benito and Giovanni Gentile. "The Doctrine of Fascism," from
World Future Fund: A Research Institute for the Study of Global
Future Trends [electronic bulletin board]. (Alexandria, VA, 2007
[cited 2 December 2007]). Available from
http://www.worldfuturefund.org/wffmaster/Reading/Germany/
mussolinihtm; INTERNET.

Nelis, Jan. "Constructing Fascist Identity: Benito Mussolini and the Myth
of the *Romanità*." *Classical World* Vol. 100, No. 4: 391-415.
Summer 2007.

Painter, Borden W., Jr. *Mussolini's Rome*. New York: Palgrave Macmillan,
2005.

Schnapp, Jeffrey T. "Epic Demonstrations: Fascist Modernity and the
1932 Exhibition of the Fascist Revolution." *In Fascism, Aesthetics,
and Culture*, ed. Richard J. Goslan, 1-37. Hanover: University
Press of New England, 1992.

Stone, Marla Susan. *The Patron State: Culture & Politics in Fascist Italy*.
Princeton: Princeton University Press, 1998.

Tannenbaum, Edward R. *The Fascist Experience*. New York: Basic Books, Inc., 1972.

Taylor, Joshua C. *Futurism*. New York: Doubleday, 1961

Barkha Patel

Trash Talk

Introduction

The environment has become a prevalent subject in the 21st century. Popular newspapers and magazines seem to always print at least one article in every issue about a current environmental problem. Television news, talk shows, and commercials try to generate possible solutions to the destruction of the environment. And schools all over the nation are trying to educate children and young adults about the problems and almost effortless ways to make a difference. The environment is definitely the talk of the town.

In the past decade, several environmental issues have been impacting daily standards of living. The most prevailing issue in both America and the rest of the world is the effect called global warming. Some people do not even believe that the climate is changing. Yet, scientists have determined possible causes of global warming and also many solutions. But the effectiveness of this research depends on how it is utilized. Furthermore, air pollution and water pollution have caused great controversies in many countries to the extent that large corporations have been sued billions of dollars for harming the environment. Some cases have even led to the passage of some successful environmental policies. Also, the oil and other energy supplies have been drastically decreasing. Schools everywhere are teaching children to switch off the lights whenever they leave the room. Car dealers are constantly advertising the feature of more gas mileage per gallon as a way to increase sales. Unfortunately, the topic of solid waste is often overlooked by many citizens, probably because any discussion of waste is unappetizing. Nevertheless, it is a very important issue and must not be ignored.

It must be understood that every object that is thrown "away" is considered trash. It must also be understood that this "trash" is not discarded out of an area, but rather moved from one place to a landfill. Local landfills are being so drowned with solid waste that in time there will be no more places to keep our trash. "The EPA reported that there was more than 209 million tons of municipal solid waste generated in 1996" (4.3 pounds per person per day!); now, more than a decade later, the amount has doubled (Kubasek, 297). A solution may be to dig more landfills for the trash, but there must be unoccupied terrain for that. All our trash can not be shipped to Wyoming (no offense). Plus, no one wants to live anywhere near a landfill because of the smell and unsanitary air. This makes property surrounding landfills very cheap. Worst of all, the solid waste in landfills usually seeps into the ground, contaminating both the soil and the water. Recently, toxic chemicals and other hazardous wastes have been improperly disposed of, causing health risks through the drinking water or the air we breathe for all those in proximity. Clearly, the exponentially increasing amounts of solid waste and the unavailability of landfills is a problem that needs to be a priority in our country.

No matter how many people may acknowledge the existence of environmental problems, there must be policies that correlate. To make effective policies, every branch of government and numerous administrative agencies have impacted environmental policy. Congress has passed a significant number of laws to encourage the recovery and reuse of wastes as resources. Presidents have appointed environmentally friendly leaders to high positions in government. The Judicial Branch has supported the clean up and active regulation of private businesses who abuse their permits. The EPA has created successful programs to regulate the proper disposal of hazardous and non-hazardous wastes. However, it is the local and state governments that must be merited for their more aggressive role in policies. The federal government has set nationwide standards and provided funds, but the active management of solid waste is controlled by municipal programs. Specifically, the state of New Jersey has taken numerous measures to regulate the never-ending waste problem. Let us examine the current policies, standards, and programs set by each branch and level of government, taking a closer look at the bills from the state of New Jersey, and propose other possible resolutions for the trash problem.

Federal Government

Most of the advancements toward solving the improper waste disposal problems have been initiated by the Federal Government. This is because waste disposal is a transboundary problem, apparent in all regions of the United States, not isolated in only one area. Therefore, all the branches of the Federal Government affect environmental issues, specifically waste management. First of all, Congress has passed several policies to regulate the overwhelming trash Americans create. The first legislation that Congress ever funded for waste management was the Resources Recovery Act of 1970. This Act, approved by President Nixon, "provided grants to state and local agencies in developing resource recovery and waste disposal systems" (Vig and Kraft, 395). These systems were encouraged to find innovative solid waste management. Even though this Act was extremely vague and lax, it was a valuable step towards environmental protection. Chiefly, Congress affects the solid waste problem through agenda setting and budget appropriations.

After the Environmental Protection Agency was established in 1970, it took over the formulation of most environmental legislation. This agency, initially under the executive branch, is now also considered an independent agency that has the power to research problems, create legislation, and enforce laws. With such powers, it began passing statutes that were more specific and effective. For example, the Marine Protection Act of 1972 regulated the dumping of waste materials into the oceans and coastal waters, and the Resource Conservation and Recovery Act of 1976 allowed "the EPA to set regulations for hazardous waste treatment, storage, transportation, and disposal" (Vig and Kraft, 396). But most importantly, the Superfund Amendments and Reauthorization Act of 1986 sponsored the clean up of the nation's most harmful chemical waste dumps. Congress, now focused on funding programs rather than creating programs, allocated more than eight billion dollars to clean such sites in local communities. The EPA prioritizes its legislation to make sure Congress adopts the policies and apportions money for them.

Along with Congressional and agency influence in waste management, the President also plays a role in the process. The most critical role of the President in environmental policies is the appointment of EPA heads and other high positions. If the President is concerned about environmental issues, he will appoint strong, active leaders hoping for change and accomplishments. This would be the case for Nixon's appointment of the first EPA head, William Ruckelshaus. Ruckelshaus is still alive and working for environmental programs. In 1983, Reagan appointed him to serve as the interim director for the Superfund project. However, our current President Bush considers environmental problems to be frivolous compared to terrorism and the economy. For that reason, he has appointed Stephen Johnson the head administrator of EPA. Unfortunately, Johnson is more concerned about pesticides than solid waste, so there has not been any recent legislation for the waste problem in America. Therefore, Presidential appointments are important to environmental protection.

The third branch of the government, the Judicial Branch, is also vital to setting standards for proper waste disposal. It is widely acknowledged that many corporations blindly dispose chemicals into the water or litter public grounds, which leads to harmful contamination of the environment. The most common way of punishing such careless acts is through filing lawsuits. The state will sometimes sue large corporations to penalize them for their catastrophic actions. The main standard that the judiciary sets is the liability issue. The main question is who is to blame for the pollution from the corporations. In many cases like *United States v. Mottolo,* "the court held the president of the chemical company personally liable, stating that those persons who actually arranged for or disposed of a hazardous waste under the Act did not need to be owners to be held responsible" (Kubasek, 323). Most people would assume that the employees or owners of the corporations who actually threw away the chemicals would be liable, but the CEO or president is to be charged as well. It is their responsibility to make sure all the workers are educated on how to dispose the waste properly. In many cases like the one above, the judiciary has set a valuable standard for proper waste disposal. Furthermore, the courts have enforced environmental policies by taking away permits. All waste treatment, storage, and disposal facilities (TSDFs) need permits that designate the region in which they will do so. Some courts have revoked their permits if the waste disposal was unacceptable. This punishment has been more effective than the painless fines. Basically, the judicial branch, along with the other branches of the federal government, has helped improve the nation's waste dilemma.

New Jersey State and Local Government

Along with the helpful steps the federal government has taken to reduce solid waste, state and local governments across the nation have taken measures as well. While the federal government may generate policies and standards to abide by, state and local governments are responsible for enforcing them. Enforcement is the most important task because it is easier to oversee a small district than it is to oversee the entire nation. State and local governments are encouraged to implement detailed policies to reduce environmental destruction in their communities. One of their main priorities concerns waste management.

Specifically in New Jersey, waste management is a big issue. First of all, trash is most abundant in places with larger populations. New Jersey has nearly nine million residents. It is very heavily populated compared to a state like Vermont that has a little more than 600,000 residents. New Jersey shelters the millions of people in about seven thousand square miles, whereas Vermont has more than nine thousand square miles for the same amount of people living in Jersey's three most populous cities:

Newark, Jersey City, and Paterson. Furthermore, New Jersey used to store other states' waste. For example, the densely populated New York City used to send its trash to New Jersey's landfills. It has stopped now, but some of New Jersey's landfills are filled with trash that does not even belong to its state. With the lack of space to dig more landfills, and the growing population in New Jersey, the reduction of solid waste is a huge priority.

Recently, New Jersey senators and representatives have been fighting for a new federal law—The Clean Railroads Act. It has been discovered that many corporations dump waste along railroad lines as a loophole in the waste disposal permits. In particular, a two-mile stretch of railroad tracks in North Bergen are surrounded by nearly two stories worth of solid waste. Representative Frank Pallone, disgusted by such findings, says that "our legislation ensures that new waste facilities sited near rail lines comply with the same regulations as every other trash facility" (US News Fed Service, 2007). The Senators are especially concerned with the health risks at hand. New Jersey residents that live near these unregulated sites are highly in risk of serious illnesses due to "fire hazards, groundwater contamination, and debris... that can contain elevated levels of arsenic and mercury" (US News Fed Service, 2007). New Jersey is pushing for solid waste regulation near railroad lines to ensure the safety of its residents.

Moreover, toxins in New Jersey landfills have been detrimental to the environment. First of all, the presence of arsenic and mercury has not been a big concern for the federal government because of the lack of "sound science" related to such issues (Vig and Kraft, 178). But New Jersey had found this to be a major concern. For that reason, Assemblyman Herb Conaway of the 7th District has proposed Bill No. 1839 to not only end the sale of mercury batteries, but also to regulate their disposal. By January of 2011, mercury batteries should no longer be offered to consumers and no longer be disposed with the rest of Jersey's solid waste. Scientists have determined mercuric oxide in mercury batteries to be toxic. It therefore needs to be eliminated from landfills. Along with arsenic and mercury, paint has been deemed toxic as well. Both oil-based and latex-based paint is toxic to animals and fish, human skin and lungs, and plants and trees. Paint has been an overwhelming source of waste in New Jersey landfills and must be regulated with the other toxins listed above.

Overall, the New Jersey legislature has been evaluating the gravity of solid waste management. Currently, there are nearly 20 bills pending to be reviewed relating to bulky waste, landfills, and recycling. It is a relief to see this state stepping forward to handle such an ignored issue in the United States. It is important to realize that space is limited to store the trash and the American population is exponentially growing. That means that trash will continue to generate, but there will be no place to put it. For the state of New Jersey, it could be sooner than foreseen. That is why the state legislature needs to take drastic measures to protect its residents and the environment because current measures are not enough. Reforms need to be made, and enforcement must be more effective.

Possible Solutions

New Jersey has realized that the amount of the solid waste produced by residents needs to be reduced tremendously. Assemblyman John E. Rooney of District 39 has taken some steps to aid waste management. In Bill No. 1122, he has revised the Solid Waste Management Act to remove obsolete parts of the bill and plug in new reformations. For example, he recognized the problem with enforcement and has proposed a plan. First of all, he wishes for the New Jersey Department of Environmental Protection to give districts the control over the rates, fees, and charges of solid waste processing. Most importantly, he wants greater charges to be put on for the out-of-state facilities that bring in solid waste into New Jersey landfills. New Jersey should impose "a landfill closure and contingency tax of $0.50 per ton of solid waste accepted for disposal" by other facilities. With taxes, solid waste will be reduced in the long-run because no one wants to pay extra money for something they can essentially reduce.

In addition, recycling has been further encouraged by current pending bills. Each county in New Jersey was required to supply recycling bins for plastic, bottles, and paper to all households about five years ago. But this step was not backed by enforcement. The garbage collectors did not enforce recycling with the use of the provided bins. Assemblyman Rooney in Bill No. 502 simply advocates "that the solid waste collector will not collect the contents of the solid waste container containing designated recyclable materials until the resident removes the recyclable material." If the garbage is not collected, the residents will have to recycle properly. This enforcement will most likely be successful to diminish the presence of bottles, cartons, and jugs in New Jersey landfills. Solid waste collectors must be strict and properly trained if this bill becomes law.

In my opinion, recycling is the best solution to manage the overwhelming solid waste production in New Jersey. Beginning in elementary school, children are taught to recycle in the classrooms. With this knowledge, they go home and pressure family members to do the same. But it is disappointing to see big institutions rejecting the concept of recycling. My high school in Edison, New Jersey, did not recycle. This school has over 2000 students and 200 faculty members that create tons of trash every day. In the classroom and cafeteria, there are recycling bins for paper and bottles. But at the end of the day, the janitors dump all the trash into one bag. Instead of sorting it all out, the janitors quickly clean up the school and head home. Worst of all, college students waste large amounts of food daily in their dining halls. Because of the buffet style set-up in the cafeterias, students get one of everything to eat. However, they only eat about half of the food on the plate. All this solid waste piles up in one of the 13 active sanitary landfills in New Jersey. Students must either eat all their food or pack it to eat another day. If large institutions like public schools and colleges firmly recycle, the amount of solid waste generated would be greatly reduced.

All in all, New Jersey is suffering from improper waste management. The amount of solid waste is increasing along with the increase in population. Unfortunately, there is no space to dig more landfills to store more waste. Therefore, other measures must be taken to lessen the amounts. Senators and assemblymen have suggested several bills to revise current policies and clean up areas that are contaminating neighborhoods. I have proposed the enforcement of recycling in all schools and colleges across the state. But the pending bills and propositions are still being reviewed by the New Jersey Legislature. These bills should be enacted and enforced as soon as possible to save the deteriorating environment. Undoubtedly, solid waste is a serious issue that cannot be ignored in the United States of America.

Works Cited

Conaway, Herb. New Jersey. Assembly. No. 1839. 24 Jan. 2008. 14 Feb. 2008.

Kubasek, Nancy K., and Gary S. Silverman. Environmental Law. 6th ed. Upper Saddle River, NJ: Pearson Prentice Hall, 2007.

New Jersey Department of Environmental Protection. 2006. < http://www.nj.gov/dep/dshw/>.

"New Jersey." Information Please Database. 2007. 21 Feb. 2008 < http://www.infoplease.com/>.

"New Jersey Members Comment on Court Decision on Solid Waste
Processing." US State News. Washington, D.C.: US Fed News
Service, 2007. 15 Feb. 2008
< http://proquest.umi.com/pqdweb?did=1336446011&Fmt=3&cli>.

Programs/Special Topics." Division of Pollution Prevention and
Environmental Assistance. 29 Jan. 2008. 17 Feb. 2008
< http://www.p2pays.org/>.

Rooney, John E. New Jersey. Assembly. No. 1122. 2006. 14 Feb. 2008.

Rooney, John E. New Jersey. Assembly. No. 502. 2008. 14 Feb. 2008.

Sens. Lautenberg, Menendez, Rep. Pallone Introduce Measure to Protect
New Jersey Residents From Unregulated Solid Waste Stations
Along Rail Lines. US State News. Washington, D.C.: US News Fed
Service, 2007. 15 Feb. 2008
< http://proquest.umi.com/pqdweb?did=1228291111&Fmt=3&clientId=18133&R
QT=309&VName=PQD>.

Vig, Norman J., and Michael E. Kraft. Environmental Policy. 6th ed.
Washington, D.C: CQ P, 2006.

Amanda McArthur

Atheists, Fools and Madmen: Nietzsche in O'Neill's Life and Works

Though his plays continue to be revered as classic American literature, Eugene O'Neill neither drew his inspiration from his compatriots, nor did he portray life in his country to be as idealistic as many of the time supposed. As he rejected his dysfunctional childhood family life and its traditional Catholic ideals, he gravitated toward the likes of August Strindberg and Friedrich Nietzsche, in whose works O'Neill found existentialism as a replacement, pseudo-religion. Though while many existentialists derive a resigned complacence from the philosophy, O'Neill, with the help of Strindberg's plays, found—and embraced—only despair and hopelessness in Nietzsche's theories. At the turn of the nineteenth century, in a country where people were excited to witness of what man was capable, O'Neill began to see only a natural and disheartening inevitability for man to fail. This desperate and often nihilist attitude toward life led O'Neill to move to existentialism and feel a deep, personal connection with it. The relationship between O'Neill and Nietzsche's existentialism appears throughout O'Neill's works, particularly his autobiographical play *Long Day's Journey into Night*. Elements of the play present specifically Nietzschean ideals, such as the intellectual rejection of Christianity, the doctrine of eternal recurrence, and the notion of tragic suffering, though all are O'Neill's own distinct translation of the existentialist philosophy.

Published by his wife three years after his death, *Long Day's Journey into Night* is essentially an autobiography written in the form of a play. It is set within the time frame of one day, which represents and alludes to thousands exactly the same. The four characters—James, Mary, Jamie, and Edmund Tyrone—represent O'Neill's father, mother, brother and self, respectively. The opening scene is set in the living room after breakfast, and the family is in forcedly high spirits. As the day progresses, the characters' flaws are revealed and rehashed: Mary is a morphine addict trying, albeit unsuccessfully, to hide her drug abuse from the family; James is a tyrannical, stingy, alcoholic father who has failed both himself and the family; Jamie is a waste of life, a drunken whoremonger and family leech who is obsessed with his brother's failure; and Edmund is an existential, atheistic poet-of-sorts with tuberculosis ("consumption") and no support from his family, despite admitted suicide attempts and an overall sense of despair. As the hours pass, each of these shortcomings is addressed in arguments and drunken/drug-induced tirades between the family members, until at the end the four are each in their own altered state, no farther from their real world for all their attempts at leaving it.

As can be seen in arguments between Edmund and his family, the chief reason for their attacks on his philosophy is the rejection of Christianity that necessarily comes with it. In following the chronology of O'Neill's life, though, we see that he was already gravitating away from the Christian faith by the time he read *Thus Spake Zarathustra*, Nietzsche's book that is famous for the line "God is dead" and for the introduction of his doctrine of eternal recurrence. Thus, rather than driving O'Neill from his religion, Nietzsche's intellectual argument against Christianity in the book may have been what drew O'Neill so compellingly to him in the first place. In his article titled "O'Neill's Philosophical and Literary Paragons," Egil Törnqvist says of this relationship, "[i]t was in 1907, five years after he had given up on Catholicism, that O'Neill became acquainted with Nietzsche's writings, and it is likely that it was above all as a meaningful substitute for his shattered faith that Nietzsche's philosophy appealed to him" (18).

Through Zarathustra, Nietzsche describes Christianity as an escape mechanism which believers use to rationalize suffering, the one thing he believes to be inherent in human life. However, in the statement "God is dead" lies an implication that God, at one point, was. In the book, Nietzsche is not holding that God does not exist, but rather that he no longer exists—that he is no longer necessary in modern society. Nietzsche says,

> confronted with morality (especially Christian, or unconditional, morality), life *must* continually and inevitably be in the wrong, because life *is* something essentially amoral—and eventually, crushed by the weight of contempt and the eternal No, life *must* then be felt to be unworthy of desire and altogether worthless. (cited in Higgins 32) [italics in the original]

Seen here, Nietzsche never truly discusses whether or not there is a God, but rather that the Christian faith ignores the realities of modern life, and provides a way for people to escape from the idea of unexplained suffering. Suffering, Nietzsche says, should be embraced and accepted; trying to rationalize it in any way, including the way of the Christian church, will only result in failure. Thus O'Neill embraced Nietzsche's rejection of Christianity, but never grasped the full message, as we can see in his attempt (in writing the play) to rationalize suffering.

Throughout the play, O'Neill makes a point of showing the family's dismissal of Edmund's philosophy and concurrent rejection of the religion into which he was born and raised. Nietzsche, among others, is referenced already in the first scene of the play, where O'Neill's stage directions place his books on the family's bookshelf. Throughout the following scenes, each family member reprimands Edmund for his choice in reading material. His father is his worst critic, calling Edmund's opinions "[m]orbid filth...despair and pessimism" (O'Neill 136), and his philosophers "[a]theists, fools and madmen" (138). He adds that both Jamie and Edmund have "flouted" the Catholic faith, bringing "nothing but self destruction" (79). Jamie, too, calls Edmund's Nietzsche his "pet with the unpronounceable name" who is merely "a lot of bunk" (Ibid). Even Mary, usually nervous and subdued, exclaims:

> [s]uch morbid nonsense! Saying you're going to die! It's the books you read! Nothing but sadness and death! Your father shouldn't allow you to have them. And some of the poems you've written yourself are even worse! You'd think you didn't want to live! A boy of your age with everything before him! (93)

The family as a whole, and each member in his or her own way, attacks and rejects the very foundation upon which Edmund's personality is based.

Another Nietzschean ideal that appears in the play is the doctrine of eternal recurrence. Also known as the doctrine of eternal return, it says that every moment in time—every conversation, every relationship, etc.—has happened before, and will happen again, eternally. Thus, the future is already the past and vice versa, and the only moment that truly stands out is the present. Rather than a device that can change our lives, eternal recurrence "represents an 'existential imperative,' a heuristic tool that illustrates 'a particular attitude toward life.' Specifically, this attitude is 'the expression of nihilism overcome'" (Higgins 162). This "attitude" is more important than the actual content of the doctrine, and has "practical implications for our lives" (164). In their article about eternal recurrence in O'Neill's plays, Albert Kalson and Lisa Schwerdt say of eternal return, "however long a time may pass, according to the eternal laws governing the combinations of this eternal play of repetition, all configurations which have previously existed on this earth must yet meet, attract, repulse, kiss, and corrupt each other again" (134). For many existentialists, this cycle of uncontrollable, endless repetition provides a freedom from fault and the ability to truly live in the present, which is the only thing, according to the doctrine, that we can truly enjoy.

True to his fatalistic self, though, O'Neill found only despair associated with an endless repetition of suffering and failure, which becomes apparent in the play. As the day moves toward night, Mary carries her family to "a past that is at once the present and the future for them all" (Kalson and Schwerdt 144). The rest of the family is aware of this process as well: Edmund says to his mother of her recurring bouts with morphine, "it's bad for you to forget. The right way is to remember. So you'll always be on your guard. You know what's happened before" (O'Neill 46). Mary also calls attention to the perpetual repetition of the men's alcoholism when she says, "[y]ou will be drunk tonight. Well, it won't be the first time, will it—or the thousandth?" (72). Edmund, then, exclaims for what seems to be the last time he has experienced happiness, "I was set free!... I belonged, without past or future, within peace and unity and a wild joy, within something greater than my own life, or the life of Man, to Life itself!" (156). The structure of the play also follows the pattern of eternal recurrence, most notably because it surrounds one day that represents thousands of others before and after it. As the day progresses into night, so too does the family approach the past while it moves into the future.

The most significant Nietzschean ideal present in the play, though, is also the one with which O'Neill presumably struggled the most—tragic suffering. A sub-aspect of this is Nietzsche's Apollonian/Dionysian duality as described in *The Birth of Tragedy*. In the book, Nietzsche uses the gods Apollo and Dionysus to represent two opposing perspectives on life within every individual. Kathleen Marie Higgins, in her book called *Nietzsche's Zarathustra*, explains these two representations through defining the gods themselves:

> Apollo is the god of sunlight and thereby of illumination and vision, and also the god of order and restraint.... Dionysus is appropriately the patron of dithyrambic music, along with wine, revelry, and sexual frenzy. He emblemizes the various potencies that take us outside of ourselves. (25)

Higgins suggests that Nietzsche means to imply that both orientations toward the self and the world are distortions, but that they are also necessary to every individual (30).

Throughout *Long Day's Journey into Night*, O'Neill introduces this duality within the family's dynamics. In the beginning of the play, each character attempts to believe that theirs is a happy family—they try to force a sort of Apollonian objectivity, and actually believe that they are being honest with each other (which, according to the allusions to eternal recurrence, must happen every morning). As time progresses, though, the truth emerges—Mary returns to her morphine, and her husband and sons to their drinking. With each scene, each character is further removed into their drug-induced world in an attempt to escape the truth, yet the truth comes out more strongly than when they were sober. While Jamie recognizes the veracity of *in vino veritas* (O'Neill 168), Edmund embraces the idea that distortion of reality provides escape from the eternal repetition of life. Towards the end of the play, he quotes Baudelaire to Tyrone in an attempt to explain this: "Be always drunken. Nothing else matters: that is the only question. If you would not feel the horrible burden of Time weighing on your shoulders and crushing you to the earth, be drunken continually... "(135). By the end of the play, it becomes apparent that the Apollonian perspective never existed for the family, and that even when they are sober, theirs is a Dionysian family. While this opposing perspective seems to have provided clarity for the family, readers know that the same cycle is destined to recur the following day, ad infinum.

Just as Nietzsche's Apollonian/Dionysian duality stems from the ancient Greeks, so too does his philosophy of the necessity of tragic suffering in human life. The notion of tragic suffering itself is characteristically pessimistic; Higgins describes Nietzsche's "tragic perspective" as

> undeceived about the murky facts of human life. It recognizes that the individual is constantly exposed to no-win situations, hideous pains that are not compensated with the resulting greater satisfactions, and insecurities whose only certain resolution is death. (37)

Though while the concept provides no solace in overcoming incomprehensible suffering, its inevitability can bring comfort in resigning oneself to mere acceptance. Doris Falk, in her book on tragic tension within O'Neill's works, says that Nietzsche feels "that tragedy is an affirmation—a 'symbolic celebration'—of life. The death of the hero [in a tragic play] must reveal the dignity, nobility, and the universality of his struggle, even though from the beginning it has been a futile one" (44). Nietzsche's philosophy, however, is less *because* of Greek tragedy, and more in *accordance* with it. He contends that real tragic plays are successful because of their ability "to move the individual audience member to identify with someone else" (Higgins 34), so that "the audience recognizes the hero's predicament as its own, and their surrender of individual distance in identifying with the hero makes them literally vulnerable to tragic suffering, although in this case vicariously" (36). Thus, tragic suffering exists in plays in order to emphasize and portray the suffering inherent in human life.

Agreeing wholeheartedly with Nietzsche's idea of tragic suffering in both life and drama, O'Neill still never embraced its potential to comfort those who accept it. In tragic suffering, as in other Nietzschean ideals, O'Neill only found despair. With this perspective, he wrote *Long Day's Journey into Night* and other plays as "attempts to explain human suffering and, somehow, to justify it....As a twentieth-century man, [O'Neill] had to interpret the ancient idea [of Greek tragedy] in twentieth-century terms and symbols" (Falk 5). He accomplishes a portrayal of human suffering, although according to Nietzsche, once one attempts to justify suffering, he or she is doomed to fail. Despite his personal failure to accept tragic suffering, though, O'Neill manages, in the play, to force his audience to not only view but also *feel* his family's suffering. He does this in a number of ways; for example, the play, when performed, is nearly four hours long, and its repetitive nature (in both dialogue and plot), combined with its length, pushes the audience to nearly despise it and long for relief. In the context of a tragedy, this feeling makes the play a success. Also, Falk says, *"Long Day's Journey into Night* is tragedy—not melodrama or 'slice of life'—because each of its protagonists is partly responsible for his own destruction and partly a victim of the family fate" (194). By the end of the play, the audience, with O'Neill, understands that "the world is just as meaningless and disordered as ever, even if the hero survives" (Ibid).

Overall, Nietzsche's philosophy is hopeless and tragic, but is meant to (and often does) bring those who come to understand it a feeling of existential acceptance. O'Neill, however, never made it to this end point of comfort in the meaninglessness of life. Part of this has to do with O'Neill's own desire to search for a meaning in life—a reason for his suffering—and his despair when it cannot be found. Another reason for his interpretation of Nietzsche's works, though, can be attributed to another of O'Neill's self-proclaimed idols: the Swedish playwright August Strindberg. Strindberg, too, accepted Nietzsche's philosophy with pessimism comparable to O'Neill's, though never quite as despairingly. Kalson and Schwerdt say the difference can be seen in their plays, but is inherent in their own life perspectives;

> [l]ike the absurdists who ignore the positive
> implications of existentialism... Strindberg and O'Neill
> too eventually turned from the joy and triumph
> inherent in Nietzsche's philosophy to the futility it
> holds....For Strindberg, who for a time believed in the
> power of his will, recurrence led to passive acceptance
> and resignation; for O'Neill, who as a young man
> exalted in its promise of renewal, it finally meant
> despair. (135)

Essentially, Strindberg took the philosophy a step down to hopelessness. The appearance of this translation of Nietzsche's works in his plays then provided a bridge that O'Neill could metaphorically cross, taking the philosophy a step further—to his final despair.

In the end, "tragedy meant many things to [O'Neill]," says Edward Shaughnessy in his book *Down the Nights and Down the Days:* "'the force behind life,' the knowledge that we are exiles, the need to connect but the inability to do so" (51). For many existentialists, these realizations bring a resigned comfort—an acknowledgment of the beauty in human suffering. O'Neill, though, clung to these ideals as a pseudo-religion to replace his rejected Catholicism, yet still found no answer to his despair. As an autobiography, *Long Day's Journey into Night* was his final attempt at understanding the O'Neill family's suffering that they seemingly did nothing to deserve. While this effort to rationalize tragedy was a failure for O'Neill (which, according to Nietzsche, is no surprise), he managed to create a tragic drama in every definition. Readers and audience members come to feel Edmund's despair, subsequently understanding O'Neill's own misery. The play, expressing Nietzsche's views (albeit the negative side of them), may even give others comfort that they are not alone in their meaningless suffering. Because of this (and possibly unintentionally), O'Neill's play is a successful venue through which Nietzsche's message of consolation in the solidarity of human suffering can reach the world. Either that, or the play itself is pointless, along with any attempt to explain, understand, or even differentiate between, suffering and happiness. As Nietzsche says through Zarathustra, "All is alike, nothing is worth while, the world is without meaning, knowledge strangleth" (ch. 62).

Works Cited

Falk, Doris V. *Eugene O'Neill and the Tragic Tension: An Interpretive Study of the Plays*. New Brunswick, NJ: Rutgers UP, 1958.

Higgins, Kathleen Marie. *Nietzsche's Zarathustra*. Philadelphia, PA: Temple UP, 1987.

Kalson, Albert E. and Lisa M. Schwerdt. "Eternal Recurrence and the Shaping of O'Neill's Dramatic Structures." *Comparative Drama* Ed. Clifford Davidson and John M. Stroupe. 24.2 (1990): 133-147.

Nietzsche, Friedrich. *Thus Spake Zarathustra*. New York, NY: The Penguin Group, 1978.

O'Neill, Eugene. *Long Day's Journey into Night*. New Haven, CT and London, UK: Yale UP, 2002.

Shaughnessy, Edward L. Down the Nights and Down the Days: Eugene O'Neill's *Catholic Sensibility*. Notre Dame, IN: Notre Dame UP, 1996.

Törnqvist, Egil. "O'Neill's Philosophical and Literary Paragons." *The Cambridge Companion to Eugene O'Neill*. Ed. Michael Manheim. Cambridge, UK: Cambridge UP, 1998. 18-32.

Ryan Cooper

Free Will

To believe that humans are in some way superior to all other sentient beings is a pompous and ill-informed belief. There is nothing inherently special or supreme about being a human. There are several theories that place man as the ruler and protector of the Earth, but these theories are vague and unsound. The belief in God and his creation of man in his image is one theory, but this requires the assumption that God exists. Discounting this assumption, the existentialists' critique of science claims that the humans are superior to other objects and beings because of the free will and consciousness that humans have. This "free will" is held on a pedestal because humans are aware that it is available to them. "Free will" is nothing but a pretentious label for the randomness associated with all things in the world. If humans truly possessed this "free will" then there would be no way of predicting any actions that humans perform. This simply isn't true. Humans are very predictable, just like everything else in the world. There are governing forces that have forced the evolution of humans and all creatures and even all objects throughout time to conserve energy. These forces create predictable interactions in all creatures, objects and even humans.

Philosophers scoff at the science of psychology and claim that science cannot predict the actions of a human because of the existence of free will. Free will is defined as the ability of man to choose one action over another. The critique of science that philosophers have is that a human is not a science project; it cannot be pieced together or predicted by the scientific method. Science may try to predict human behavior, but due to the ability of a human to exercise free will there will never be an exact understanding of human behavior. Existentialists further clarify this claim by contending not only does a human possess free will, but also a human is conscious of this free will and of his or her surroundings. This, existentialists claim, is what separates man from an object or a creature, the ability to exercise free will and be conscious of the decisions. For these reasons, existentialists assert that science will never understand a human.

Labeling the unpredictability of man as "free will" is a desperate attempt to hold man above other creatures in the world. There is nothing inherently special about a human; a human is a collection of cells that grow in a symbiotic relationship that strive to maintain a temperature of 98° Fahrenheit. This is the same goal as all other mammals. Other creatures such as fish, reptiles and so on may not maintain a temperature of 98°F, but the overall goal is to maintain optimum-growing conditions for the cells associated with the organism. This goal of maintaining body temperature makes all creatures, including a human, predictable. In order for a human to maintain a temperature of 98°F for one hour approximately 50 Calories are required.[i] This is a sufficient amount of energy to maintain 98°F. This amount of energy consumption requires the amount of energy a pound of pasta provides every 32 hours or a serving of pasta (one eighth of a pound) every 4 hours. This energy consumption does not account for any work being done by an average human, but only considers the maintenance of 98°F. With this information, one can predict that a person, or creature of a similar size, will eat at least once per day and will consume 1200 Calories. No amount of "free will" can change this fact. A person, in order to continue existing as a person, must consume this energy to maintain body temperature and prevent cell degradation. As simple of a conclusion this analysis may have discovered, "humans must eat," the point is that the behavior of humans is as predictable as any other creature in the world.

Most sentient beings have a sense of touch, smell, taste, sight, and hearing. These are all evolutionary devices to help control energy losses. The sense of touch helps to distinguish between energy releasing items and energy sinks; meaning that a creature uses touch to discover if something is hot or cold. Using touch as feedback, a creature can discover where to go if it is cold or what to do to cool off in case of over-heating. The ability to sense hot or cold items is a very direct way of sensing the transfer of energy in and out of the body. A human can notice a difference in temperature down to almost 1°F. This transfer of energy due to a difference in temperature of 1°F is approximately the same amount of energy lost per second as it takes to maintain a temperature of 98°F approximately 50 Calories per hour[ii] per square meter exposed to the temperature difference. This is no coincidence; this is most likely a quality that has evolved over the past few millennia in all creatures. The ability to sense when energy consumption has doubled due to a change in temperature is an important survival tool for a creature. A human uses a sense of touch to determine when he or she feels comfortable; meaning he or she uses the ability to monitor energy losses to discover a resting place that minimizes the amount of energy lost. This is the reason a person will use a blanket at night or wear a sweatshirt in the cold; it is an evolutionary mechanism that all mammals share. It is fair to say that any person that feels cold will either wear more clothing, or turn on a heater. A person that ignores this loss of energy is not practicing "free will." In fact, if the person deliberately ignores the sense of touch, then the person will become ill in some way. No conscious, reasonable person would choose to become ill. Therefore, it is safe to assume that a conscious, rational person will prevent energy loss whenever possible. This is a trait that all creatures share; there is nothing special about the energy conserving principles of humans.

The senses of smell and taste are also feedback mechanisms that have evolved over the past few millennia. Smell and taste are used to determine the difference between not only edible/potable and non-edible/non-potable substances, but also a means to determine the energy density of food and drink. There is a reason that low-fat cookies are not as flavorsome as regular cookies; it is because the original cookies offer more energy-rich substances to fuel the body. This is a survival mechanism that has developed the taste buds of modern-day humans. Creatures survive in many different environments. These environments all have different fuel sources available. The creatures that consume low-energy foods or substances that will not easily convert the stored energy to useable energy will die and the creatures that consume high-energy foods and foods that are easily converted to useable energy will survive. Humans will not consume foods that do not provide enough energy because humans have developed a taste for high-energy and easily converted energy foods. This is why humans prefer the taste of sweets; sugars are easily broken down into useable energy to be used by the body. Fatty foods are palatable because fat is an extremely energy-dense substance; a gram of fat stores 9 Calories of energy[iii], 1 pound of fat stores enough energy for a human to maintain 98°F for over 80 hours. It is no mystery why fried foods are tempting; evolution has molded creatures into energy-seeking and energy-conserving devices. A human that eats fried foods and becomes fat is merely succumbing to an evolutionary energy-seeking system of the body, *not* exercising "free will."

The energy preservation of creatures has evolved brains into control devices over the body to minimize energy loss. The senses are all inputs for the brain to determine the return on energy invested. The return on energy invested refers to the analysis of comparing how much energy was consumed and how much was either saved or gained. As an example, assume that a creature has the option of dragging a 50 kg rock 20 meters or carrying the rock ten meters drop it from a ledge onto a container to open it for a chocolate bar. To push the rock would require approximately 1 Calorie and to lift the rock and carry it would require 0.1 Calories[iv] plus the energy required to move 20 meters. This wasn't calculated, but it will be much less than the energy required to overcome the friction between the rock and the ground. The chocolate bar contains approximately 200 Calories. The decision of the creature would be to lift the rock and carry it because this process requires less than half of the energy of the other option and therefore the return on the energy invested is 199.9 Calories as compared to 199 Calories. By using sight, the distance can be estimated; if the distance were shorter, it may not be worthwhile to pick up the rock to move it. This is an extremely simplified example of a decision to use energy to gain food, but the conclusion is that creatures can be predicted to choose the process that requires the greatest return of energy invested.

Where humans stand apart is in the ability to calculate and predict the outcome of actions on a far greater range than most other creatures. Most creatures have certain preventative measures to reduce energy lost. Examples of this are bears that hibernate for the winter to prevent heat loss, the migration of geese, or chipmunks and squirrels that store nuts for consumption during colder months. This act of energy conservation is seen in all creatures in one way or another. Humans have extrapolated this principle of energy conservation with technology. There is a long history of technology, but all ideas in technological development involve either decreasing the energy used by humans or making use of an alternate form of stored energy. This started with the use of clothing to reduce heat loss, and then fire was used to produce heat instead of the human metabolism. Continuing this line of technological development, humans now use fossil fuels as a stored energy source to drive cars, heat housing, etc. By utilizing other forms of stored energy, besides the human body, humans have been able to reduce the energy used for survival considerably. Although the process of energy conservation has changed from bodily energy conservation to the conservation of energy-rich resources, humans are still driven by an evolutionary desire to reduce energy losses. Applying the theory that humans will conserve energy-rich sources, human behavior can be predicted. It is predictable that humans will work to obtain money to spend on energy and energy-conserving devices. Energy can be bought in the form of fossil fuels and food. Energy-saving devices are found in almost every store and include, but are not limited to: bicycles to decrease the work required to travel a distance, drugs to alleviate the metabolic stress in the body, clothing to limit heat loss, and so on. Even computers are a means of saving energy. A recent study found a correlation between mental computations and glucose levels in the blood [1]. The study found that over 10 minutes of mental work, glucose levels dropped by approximately 1 mmol/L. By observing this result in the same manner as mentioned beforehand, this is approximately 400 Calories[v] for every hour of mental computation, or one pound of pasta for every four hours of mental work. By employing a computer to achieve these mental calculations, the amount of time spent thinking is greatly diminished. This leads to the conclusion that computers will be popular because it helps to conserve human energy. Each individual will have a certain approach to obtaining the money for these items or obtaining the items directly, but the overall goal is to obtain the items for the purpose of energy conservation.

A human is a product of his surroundings due to the long evolution of man. The surroundings of man are the world; the world is unclear and unpredictable. Therefore, a human is unclear and unpredictable because it is a product of something unclear and unpredictable. "Free will" is a haphazard term assigned to the unpredictability of man, it has no more meaning than the randomness associated in the weather.

Science is used as an attempt to predict events that occur in nature. Probability is an integral part of developing scientific theories. If a theory or equation can be validated through 95% of the experimental results, then the theory is generally accepted as a well-constructed theory. The only way for a scientific theory to become infallible would be to create and execute an infinite number of experiments with an infinitely larger number of results. This simply is not possible in the time frame of scientific activities. There are many factors that affect scientific theories and the process of drawing conclusions is done by isolating one or a few factors and looking for a trend between different factors and the results of the experiments. As an example, there is an atomic radius associated with all atoms. This atomic radius is accepted to be the radius in which the atom's electrons will remain. This theory is true 95% of the time; the other 5% of the time the electron could be anywhere. This does not mean that the electron experiences "free will." According to existentialists, the electron has no conscious to know and decide where it will be. Humans are products of evolution; therefore this "free will" associated with humans is as much a result of human freedom as the electron's path outside of its atomic radius. There are many theories on the behavior of humans. If these theories can be proven correct in 95% of the experiments, then the theory is valid regardless of "free will." As many forces that exist that change the path of the electron, there are even more factors that affect the behavior of creatures, including humans. The inability to comprehend all of these factors does not mean that there exists an ambiguity for humans to exist without the same bounds to the world that all other creatures and objects experience.

The conclusion that must be retained by existentialists is that humans are not above natural laws because science cannot predict the behavior of a person. To claim that humans are completely unpredictable by science is a gross misunderstanding of the world and nature itself. Humans are compositions of the same matter and energy as all other creatures and objects. All of these creatures and objects interact in certain ways and result in certain trends. Scientific theories can only be proven to a certain extent; in this regard, there is nothing that can be predicted. Humans are not above the laws of nature due to some mystical force deemed "free will" just because humans analyze these laws of nature.

References

[1] Scholey, Andrew, Harper, Susan, and Kennedy, David O. *Cognitive Demand and Blood Glucose*. Physiology and Behavior 73 (2001), pp 585–592.

Calculations

i. Energy to maintain 98 °F:

$$W_h = 200 lbs = 907 kgs$$
$$V_h = 907 kgs \frac{1 m^3}{993 kg} = 0.09 1 m^3$$
$$r_h = \sqrt[3]{\frac{V_h 3}{4\pi}} = 0.2794, = 4\pi r_h^2 = 0.98 m^2$$
$$Q_{out} = A_h(h(T_h - T_\infty) + \varepsilon\sigma(T_h^4 - T_\infty^4)) \approx 60 W$$
$$Q_{out} = 60 W \approx 50 \frac{Calories}{hour}$$

Where Wh is the weight of an average human, Vh is volume of the human, rh is the estimated radius of an estimated human sphere, Ah is the estimated human surface area, Qout is the heat loss due to convection and radiation, h is the convective heat transfer coefficient estimated as 5 W/m2K, ϵ is the emmissivity of a human assumed to be 1, σ is the Stefan-Boltzmann constant, 5.67*10-8 W/m2K4, Th is the temperature of a human 98°F, T∞ is the temperature of ambient air assumed to be 25°C.

ii. Energy loss of 1 °F:

$$q_{transfer} = \frac{k(\Delta T)}{L}$$

Where qtransfer is the heat transfer flux, meaning that it is measured per unit area in this case per square meter, between an object and a human hand. The value ΔT is the difference in temperature between blood and the object. The value was estimated as 1 °F from the assumption that a human can sense a fever on another human even if the fever is just above 99°F. k is the heat transfer coefficient of the skin estimated as 0.37 W/K

iii. Energy storage of fat found from The Physics Factbook:
http://hypertextbook.com/facts/2004/PingZhang.shtml

iv. Energy return of rock:

$$E_{1,required} = \mu F_{n,rock} d = 3920 \approx 1 Calorie$$
$$E_{2,required} = mgh \approx 490 \approx 0.1 Calorie$$
$$E_{return} = E_{chocolate} - E_1 = 199 Calories$$
$$E_{return} = E_{chocolate} - E_2 = 1999 Calories$$

Where E1,required is the energy required to drag the rock, μ is the coefficient of friction between the ground and the rock approximated as 0.4, Fn,rock is the normal force of the rock in this case equal to the weight of the rock, mg, d is the distance the rock is being dragged, E2,required is the energy required to pick up the rock estimated to be equal to the amount of energy needed to pick the rock up, m is the mass of the rock, g is the acceleration of gravity 9.8 m/s2, h is the height to carry the rock estimated to be 1 meter, Ereturn is the return on energy invested, Echocolate is the energy available from the chocolate.

v. Converting glucose level to energy consumed:
Assumptions: the drop in glucose is directly related to brain activity, the drop in glucose is used directly to "power" the brain functions, a person is 91 L of blood, the 600 seconds of mental activity was free of other energy consuming factors, the full 600 seconds was used for rigorous thought processes.

Given: glucose energy storage= 686 Calories per mole

$$1 \tfrac{mmol}{L} \cdot \tfrac{1mol}{1000 mol} \cdot 686 \tfrac{Cal}{mol} = 0.686 \tfrac{Cal}{L}$$
$$V_h = 9 L$$
$$E_{mind} = \frac{9 L \cdot 0.686 \tfrac{Cal}{L}}{600 seconds} = 0.1 \tfrac{Cal}{s} = 360 \tfrac{Cal}{hour}$$

Madeline Olsen

The Price of a Prodigal Life

The story of the prodigal son is a well-known parable in the Bible that tells of two brothers, one of whom chooses to squander his inheritance in riotous living; the other remains at home to labor with their father. When the profligate son returns, poor and needy, the father throws a celebration in his honor; this angers the other son, who slaved by his father's side, for his brother has been improvident and troublesome. As we know, however, things are not always what they seem. What if the prodigal son had a more genuine motive for his actions than did his hard-working brother? And what if the hardworking brother, who one expects to be virtuous and good-hearted for his charity towards his father, is only naïve and in denial? Arthur Miller asks just these questions and displays both sides in his 1968 play *The Price*. He places the two brothers' stories side-by-side, leaving the reader to make the judgment of whose actions were more justifiable. It is a story of perspectives, resentment, and regrets, as Victor and Walter, two estranged brothers, convene for the first time in sixteen years. From Victor's perspective, Walter's actions seem selfish and greedy, but once the reader is able to see the motive behind this "prodigal" son's actions, it seems as if Walter's neglect of their father was justly provoked.

After their father lost both his significant fortune and his confidence following the crash of the stock market, Walter and Victor were forced to make decisions that would affect the rest of their lives. Similar to the events portrayed in the parable, Victor remains at home to morally and financially sustain their father while his brother sets off to pursue independent goals. Though Walter refuses to give in to his father's pleas of helplessness, Victor entirely abandons his dreams of becoming a successful scientist to support his father. Left financially drained and out of hope, Victor asks his brother, now a successful surgeon, for a loan to continue his education. Walter refuses him. At this point, one might assume that Walter simply is a self-centered, greedy character, but it is soon revealed that their father was not as helpless as he seemed. Despite the fact that Victor was giving up the little he had to provide for him, his father was silent of the significant amount of money he had hoarded, which was capable of supporting them both. Walter was knowledgeable of these actions, but said nothing directly of it to his brother, however, Walter is convinced that Victor was aware of this truth but chose to ignore it.

Though it is subtle, one of the points the parable of the prodigal son touches on is the courage it takes to go out on one's own and risk failure. The prodigal son takes this chance and fails, but when he returns his father still commends him, despite his loss. Walter had this bravery, but his brother lacked it. After he was denied the loan from his brother, Victor gives up on his dream, though he had many other means of obtaining the money he needed for his schooling. Victor could have easily sold some of his father's expensive possessions or simply asked his father about his hoard of funds, however, Victor was too afraid of how his father would respond to these actions. Though he did not need his son to support him financially, Victor aided him anyway, giving up his dreams in the process. If he truly wanted to pursue a scientific career, Victor could have readily acquired the funds to support his education, but his fear of failure held him back. He used his compassion for his father to shadow this fear, avoiding the possible failure that he was so afraid of but also resulting in a life full of regrets.

Though the prodigal son squanders all of his money and soon becomes destitute, Walter, who represents the prodigal son in *The Price*, is in contrast very wealthy. The underlying similarity between the affluent Walter and the impoverished prodigal son is that they both did not capture what they set out to find. In the parable, the prodigal son sought wealth, but ended up even poorer than when he started. Walter did not venture out to specifically obtain wealth; he left to find stability and happiness but is now divorced and barely speaks to his children. Victor, on the other hand, with a lowly career as a police officer, obtained just what Walter aimed for: he has a stable life with a loving wife and a successful son. This addresses one of the central themes of the play: everything comes with a price. Walter believed that having more money would make his life stable, and the price he paid for focusing on this was the degradation of his family relationships. Victor focused on the opposite, preserving family relationships, and the price he paid was the opposite as well: he cared for his father and as a result lost his opportunity for a promising career.

One significant difference between the parable of the prodigal son and *The Price* is that in the parable the father serves as a sort of idealistic figure through his forgiveness and understanding of his prodigal son while in *The Price*, the father's actions are central to the conflict. The most practical and sensible character is also the oddest individual, an old salesman named Solomon whom Victor called to sell his father's furniture. Solomon is the life force in the play, and though he is an outsider to the problem at hand, he seems to understand it more than any other character from the beginning. Not only does he serve as comic relief in the play, but he also serves to convey the theme of the story—sometimes one just must let go and move on. Frequently, he laments his daughter who committed suicide, but since he cannot understand the situation, he comprehends that he must move on and let it go, though it is a very hard thing to do. Essentially, this is what Victor and Walter must do at the end of the story.

This conclusion is ironic considering the play's similarities to the prodigal son. While the parable emphasizes forgiveness, this is essentially what the ending of the play lacks; instead, *The Price* accentuates moving on from an irresolvable issue. Both brothers are unable to truly understand each other, and their problems and differences go unsettled. Neither brother can see the story through a different perspective and instead of working towards accordance, it is symbolized that they both move forward with their lives despite the troubling burden of their past.

Pearl Mathew

Credit Cards: A "Boon" or "Bane" for College Students

Abstract

The purpose of this paper is to show that credit card usage/behavior of individuals in college towns differs from individuals in non-college towns. These differences may make people in college towns an attractive demographic for credit card companies. I collect data on individuals in college counties and non-college counties from 3 different sources. I then perform univariate and multivariate tests to address the hypothesis. The analysis shows that individuals from college counties are risky as customers. Further, individuals in college towns tend to own more cards than people who don't live in college towns. Univariate tests show that active balances on credit cards for people in college towns tend to be lower, but when controlling for variables such as population, unemployment and per capita income this relationship changes. As these variables increase, the active balances also increases. People in college counties are more likely to be 60 days past due and less likely to be 90 days or 120 days past due on their credit card bills than individuals in non college counties

Introduction and Background

Compared with previous generations, students today have greater accessibility to credit cards, and they also have higher levels of disposable income.[1] Students in colleges are an important demographic for credit card companies since most students tend to work part-time or full-time during school and upon graduation they tend to have higher levels of personal disposable income as compared to non-students.[2] In addition, Americans are very loyal towards their first credit card and tend to keep it for an average of 15 years,[3] which could prove to be immensely profitable for credit card companies that can generate revenue in the form of overdraft and late fees.

One advantage credit cards offer students is that they can be of service in case of emergencies or if unexpected payments come up. Further, they can help students establish a credit history while in school.[4] But for many students this is their first encounter with handling money and making payments, which may result in paying of late fees on overdue bills.[5] Also, since this is the first time many students use credit cards, they fail to realize that the interest rate applied by credit card companies on debt is cumulative.[6] Debt owed can be so overwhelming that it could affect the normal course of study and students may end up delaying graduation.[7] A University official at Louisiana University claimed that more students tend to drop out because of the credit card debt as compared to failure in studies.[8]

The student loan provider Nellie Mae reports that 76% of undergraduate students had at least one credit card in 2004. The agency also reports that the average outstanding balance on credit cards held by students was $2,169. Thirty-four percent of students got their first credit card through direct mail solicitation, 18% got their first credit card through vendors and booths on campus, and 26% received a card through parental referrals.

Review of Literature

Previous research has been done on gender differences in usage and management of credit cards by college students by Hayhoe, et al. (2000). They find that women on average use credit cards more often than men. Also they find that women tend to make use of credit cards to buy clothes, whereas men use credit cards to buy appliances and electronics. Palmer Pinto and Parente (2001) show that those students whose parents help them acquire a credit card tend to carry lower credit card balances than students who acquire a credit card without the help of their parents. Taylor and Overbey (1999) delve into the mind of college students and their findings suggest that students often accumulate high loans and credit card debt because they have expectations of higher future income. Their research also points out that non-students have higher credit card debt as compared to students. In a study done by Roberts and Jones on college students (2001) the authors suggest that credit card usage is emotionally driven. College students with high levels of stress and anxiety tend to make more credit card purchases.

Research Idea

College students seem to be very risky as customers and yet credit card companies actively pursue them. In this paper I attempt to quantify the differences in credit card usage and behavior between individuals in college towns versus those in non-college towns. In this way I hope to shed some light on how college students behave as credit card customers and why they may be seen as attractive applicants for credit card companies

Data and Methodology

I collect data spanning 10 years (1997-2006) from three sources: The U.S. Census Bureau, TrenData (TransUnion), and Haver. I collect the number of college students as compared to the general population in every county of every state from the U.S. Census Bureau (2000). I use Haver to collect the following quarterly variables by county: the number of people employed in the total labor force, the unemployment rate, and the number of people.

From TrenData, variables are calculated by randomly sampling 27-28 million consumers. Trendata uses the term "bankcards" synonymously with credit cards. I collect the following variables by county: number of active bankcards per consumer, number of active bankcards per bankcard borrower, ratio of borrowers who have an active bankcard, ratio of bankcard borrowers currently 120 days or more past due, also 60 and 90 days past due, average balance of new bankcards, average balance of bankcards currently 60 days or more past due, number of new bankcards per consumer, number of new bankcards per bankcard borrower, ratio of new trades which are bankcards, ratio of new bankcards, average balance of active bank revolving trades, total bank revolving debt per bank revolving borrower and total bank revolving debt per consumer.

Data from Haver and TrenData are merged on the basis of county and state for every county and state and every quarter of every year in the sample period. The U.S. Census Bureau data is replicated throughout all the quarters for all the years from 1997 to 2006 since data was only available for the year 2000, since Census Bureau data is only collected every decade. The data obtained from the Census Bureau is then merged with Haver and TrenData on the same basis of county state and quarter.

Take in Table 1

Univariate Analysis

The sample is divided into "college towns" and "non- college towns" by the percentage of college students in each county. College towns are defined as counties where at least 15% of the population is made up of college students and counties with less than 15% of college students are classified as non-college towns.

Table 1 contains descriptive statistics. There are 118,916 county-quarter observations for non-college towns and 4,600 observations for college towns. The average balance on new bank cards (BCABN) is $1,330.73 for non-college towns and $1,250.08 for college towns. The difference between the means is statistically significant at the 1% level. The reason for this could be that when credit card companies first issue credit cards to students, they give them a small credit limit to start with because students have limited credit histories as compared to non-college students.

Variables such as active bankcard per consumer (BCNAC), active bankcards per bankcard borrower (BCNARB), number of new bankcards per bankcard borrower (BCNNRB), and number of new bankcards per consumer (BCNNC) are all higher for college towns than for non-college towns, the reason for this may be that credit card companies aggressively target college students through a variety of sources such as on-campus solicitation, direct mail, parents, telemarketing and TV. Even if colleges ban credit card solicitation on campus, credit card companies find alternative places that students frequent.[9]

Take in Table 2

Multivariate Analysis – Logistic Regression

I next analyze the data in a multivariate setting so as to control for other factors that may impact credit card usage. I also create a variable "percent_stud" which is the percentage of college student in each county as compared to the general population. I use this variable as well as unemployment rate and per capita income to explain the average balance of active bank revolving trades (BRAB), active bankcards per borrower (BCPBA) and bankcard borrowers 90 days past due (BCPB90).

The results of the regressions are reported in Table 2

Univariate statistics show that college towns have lower average balances as compared to non college towns, but when controlling for the economy this relationship changes. Here we see that as the percentage of students in a county increase, the average balance also increases. This result supports the idea that college students may be riskier borrowers than non-college students.

In Model 1 of Table 2 as the per capita income goes up, the balance also increases. The reason for this could be that as incomes goes up, consumers are more confident of holding higher levels of debt. Also, as the unemployment rate goes up, the average balance goes up. This may be because the spending continues to remain the same while the source of income is not there anymore and it takes time to either cut back on the current level of spending or find a new job.

In Model 2 of Table 2 I show that when the percentages of college students rise, the number of active bankcards increases. This is consistent with the univariate results and also is consistent with the idea that students are risky borrowers. As the per capita income goes up the number of active bankcards also increases. Further, as the unemployment rises, the number of cards goes down, which is logical since when people do not have jobs, they are less likely to sign up for new bankcards and may get rid of cards they already own.

In Model 3 of table 2 I use the percentage of borrowers who are 90 days past due as the dependant variable. When the percentage of students rises in the county, the percentage of cardholders 90 days past due also rises. The reason for this may be that for most students this is their first time dealing with credit cards and as students are a major constituent of the population in college towns, the delinquency rate also rises. As per capita income goes down, individuals who are 90 days past due on credit card bills increases which is logical since when income goes down, percentage of the payments consumers will make towards their outstanding credit cards may decline. Unemployment rate and past dues are positively related. I also used 60 days past due and 120 days past due as the dependant variable. I found that the results were even stronger for 60 days past due but weaker for 120 days past due. In each case increase in student population was directly related to the proportion of the population that was delinquent in paying their credit card bills.

Conclusion

The univariate and multivariate tests show that college students are indeed riskier than a normal consumer. They tend to own more bank cards on average but have smaller balances on their cards and tend to be delinquent on outstanding balances. Thus, students in college towns are a very important demographic for credit card companies even though they are risky; the reason for this is that is individuals in college towns generate revenue in the form of late fees and pay high interest on outstanding balances.

Table 1: Descriptive Statistics

This table presents tests for difference in means and medians between college towns and non –college towns for different credit variables. Non college towns (n=11, 8916) and college towns (n=4,600). BCABN represents Average Balance of new bank cards. BCAB60M represents average balance on bankcards 60 days or more. BCNAC represents active bankcard per consumer. BCNARB represents the Active bankcard per bankcard borrower. BCNNC represents the number of new bankcards per consumer. BCNNRB is the number of new bankcards per bankcard borrower. BCPBA is the Active bankcards per borrower. BCPB120M represents Bankcard Borrowers 120 days past due. BCPB90M is the Bankcard Borrowers 90 days past due. BCPB60M is the Bankcard borrowers 60 days past due.BCPN is the ratio of new trades which are bankcards. BCPN is Ratio of new trades which are bankcards. BCPN is the Ratio of new trades which are bankcards.
BCPNR is the Ratio of new bankcards. BRAB is the Average balance of active bank revolving trades. BRTDB is the Total bank revolving debt per bank revolving borrower. BRTDB is the Total bank revolving debt per bank revolving borrower. BRTDC is the total bank revolving debt per consumer. Percentage is the population of students/ total population. *,**,*** indicate the significance at the 10%,5% and I% levels respectively

TrenData Variables	Non College town N =118916	College Town N=4600	T-statistic
BCABN	1330.73 (1201.69)	1250.08 (1182.20)	80.65 8.34***
BCNAC	1.63 (1.58)	1.75 (1.71)	-0.14 21.19***
BCNNRB	0.12 (0.12)	0.13 (0.13)	-0.01 23.43***
BCPBA	0.66 (0.67)	0.70 (0.70)	-0.04 (36.29)***
BCPB120M	0.0093 (0.0078)	0.0076 (0.0065)	0.001 20.36***
BCPB90M	0.0136 (0.0118)	0.0114 (0.0099)	0.002 17.74***
BCPB60M	0.0217 (0.0193)	0.0188 (0.0166)	0.002 16.04***
BRAB	1946.36 (1829.76)	1890.56 (1790.30)	40.65 6.58***
BRTDB	5773.80 (5617.87)	5617.87 (5237.36)	79.212 4.92***
BRTDC	3527.41 (3114.66)	3651.70 (3316.39)	-182.3 (5.16)***
Unemployment rate (%)	5.33 (4.90)	4.18 (3.93)	1.08 46.04***
Percentage (population of students/ total population)	0.05 (0.04)	0.23 (0.21)	-0.18 (172.95)***
Labor force	45.72 (11.33	50.00 (31.20)	-8.668 (4.72)***
Population	5112.17 (779.00)	16408.42 (10816.00)	-11917 (48.21)***
Per capita income	27294.07 (26313.00)	27978.97 (27395.00)	-684.9 (6.48)***

Table 2: Regressions

BRAB-Average balance of active bank revolving trades. BCPBA -Active bankcards per borrower. BCPB90M-Bankcard Borrowers 90 days past due. *,**,*** indicate the significance at the 10%,5% and 1% levels respectively

	(BRAB)	(BCPBA)	BCPB90M
Percentage	566.88 (12.52)***	0.002 (4.49)***	0.00246 (4.23)***
Per Capita Income	0.037 (115.19)***	0.00 (168.93)***	(3.060) (-74.93)***
Unemployment rate	35.52 (37.65)***	(0.0093) (-96.79)***	0.00 (65.56)***
Constant	720.18 (62.25)***	0.54298 (425.64)***	0.018 (124.49)***
Obs	98003	122513	122513
Overall R-sq	0.1257	0.3142	0.1082

References

Hayhoe R.C, L.J.Leach, P.R Bruin, M.J.Lawrence, C Frances "Differences in spending habits and credit use of College students" Journal of Consumer Affairs. Vol.34, Issue 1, 2000

7,8. Johnson, Creola, "Maxed Out College Students: A Call to Limit Credit Card Solicitations on College Campuses". New York University Journal of Legislation and Public Policy, Vol. 8, p. 191, 2005

6. Lawrence F.C, R.C Christofferson, S.E. Nester, E.Barry Moser, J.A Tucker and A.C Lyons "Credit Card Usage of College Students" Evidence from Louisiana State University, 2003

3. Marcus, David L., "Students start early and charge often" U.S News & World Report, Vol.130, Issue 11, 2001

1,9. Palmer S.T, M. B Pinto, and D.I.I. Parente"College Students' Credit Card Debt and the Role of Parental Involvement: Implications for Public Policy "Journal of Public Policy and Marketing V.20 (1) 105-113.2001

4 Smith, Frances B., "Students and Credit Cards" Consumers' Research Magazine, Aug 99, Vol.82, Issue 8

Taylor, S.D. and G. Overbey (1999) "Financial practices and expectations of student and non-student consumers" Journal of Family and Consumer Sciences V.91, No. 4.

2,5. United States. General Accounting Office College Students and Credit Cards.Congress. Washington, 2001.

Anjali Sethi

Shattering the Illusion: A Critical Analysis of A Doll's House

A Doll's House by Henrik Ibsen was revolutionary in its time. In the Victorian era, when women were seen but not heard, Ibsen made the radical claim that women were more than shiny display pieces. Nora represents a new type of woman that breaks out from the norm of compliancy and submissiveness. Her husband, Torvald, treats her as a precious ornament instead of truly loving and valuing her as a person. Thus, at the climax of the play in Act Three, Ibsen uses the conflict between illusion and reality to portray the final change that needs to take place for the emancipation of a suppressed woman. It takes a true conflict to break the illusion of happiness and elucidate the reality of a suppressive relationship.

Torvald and Nora Helmer keep up the illusion of happiness and prosperity for all those around them. In his times of need, Torvald will never admit to the world that he has weaknesses. For example, when he needs money, he doesn't ask for help. Instead, he lets his family's condition deteriorate so much that his wife has to resort to illegal means to save it. Torvald is not the only one who lies to the world. When Nora takes the loan, she tells nobody until she divulges her secret to Mrs. Linde three years later. Until then, she keeps up the farce of affluence.

Even worse than lying to the rest of the world, Torvald and Nora lie to each other. Their love is false, yet neither of them realizes this until the climax of the play. Their relationship is superficial and lacks depth. He treats her as his prize and possession, and values her only for her beauty. "Why shouldn't I look at my dearest treasure?—at all the beauty that is mine, all my very own?" (Ibsen 55). However, Torvald doesn't realize that beauty is ephemeral while a connection between two souls is eternal. He even admits to himself that he is playing make believe when he courts Nora. "Do you know why I never talk to you much, why I always stand away from you and only steal a quick glance at you now and then... do you know why I do that? It's because I am pretending we are secretly in love, secretly engaged and nobody suspects there is anything between us" (Ibsen 55). Whenever Nora tries to speak seriously with him, he dismisses her as incompetent. "Just listen!—little Nora talking about scientific investigations!...Little featherbrain!" (Ibsen 55-57). Although he sometimes teases her and sometimes reprimands her, the message is always the same: she is inferior and thus whatever she says is insignificant.

Torvald and Nora live under the illusion of equality in matrimony, but in reality, they define patriarchy. Torvald manipulates Nora to feel more confident about himself. "... She has in a way become both wife and child to him. So you shall be for me after this, my little scared, helpless darling" (Ibsen 62). He exerts his control over her to emphasize his masculinity. "I should not be a man if this womanly helplessness did not just give you a double attractiveness in my eyes" (Ibsen 61). Torvald is a man trapped in the idea that he will always be dominant, and he is unwilling to ever change.

Torvald's fear of reality is shown through the use of symbolism in Act Three. "She has danced her Tarantella, and it had been a tremendous success, as it deserved—although possibly the performance was a trifle too realistic—a little more so, I mean, than was strictly compatible with the limitations of art" (Ibsen 53). Torvald is afraid of reality and avoids it at any cost. He knows that if Nora is exposed to life outside the illusion in which they are trapped, a storm will ensue. Therefore he takes all efforts to keep her away from it, whether it is in a dance or in any other form. Torvald's exertion of control in the dance is symbolic for his control in all other aspects. Nora is his trophy wife who will twirl when he signals her to do so. She is obedient, and any time she comes close to stepping out of bounds, Torvald reminds her of her place in the household. Nora's frenzied dance is also symbolic of the "torment in her mind" (Goonetilleke, par. 7) as she unknowingly prepares herself for the transition that she will soon undergo. It is seen as an attempt to stop time (Pearce 3).

The letter sent to Torvald detailing Nora's illegal loan acts as a symbol from the outside world. It represents how it only takes one external influence to topple the delicate glass relationship Torvald and Nora share. The letter serves as a dramatic connection between the doll's house and the world outside. It makes decisions irrevocable (Pearce 4). When Torvald reads the letter, all the illusions carefully maintained for so long are shattered. At the very first minute Torvald finds that his wife has disobeyed him, he repudiates everything he has said to her in the past eight years. He takes back all his "love" and replaces it with hate. His illusion of love is shattered because he never really loved Nora, but instead viewed her as a possession. It is finally revealed that Torvald's priorities have always placed Nora last on the list. Everything else in his life has taken precedence over her.

First is his reputation. "Helmer: But no man would sacrifice his honor for the one he loves. Nora: It is a thing hundreds of thousands of women have done" (Ibsen 67). Torvald cares more for what other people think of him than what she who is closest to him, his wife, thinks. He is willing to give up his whole relationship, or illusion of a relationship, with his wife in order to keep up appearances. "No religion, no morality, no sense of duty" (Ibsen 60). He conforms with the values of society rather than agreeing to those of his wife. "To him the man is the superior being, holding the economic reins and thereby concentrating in his hands all power and responsibility in the household, making the woman his slave" (Goonetilleke, par. 2). When his "slave" disgraces him and his so-called pristine morality, he is quick to judge. He acts to preserve the illusion of his family for outside viewers, rather than stand by his wife.

Torvald also prizes his wealth more than he does Nora. Throughout the play, he forbids Nora from spending money and chides her for partaking in simple pleasures. He criticizes her spending habits to be much like those of her father—even before the conflict is revealed, he playfully accuses her of financial incompetence. When Torvald discovers that Nora has borrowed money illegally, he only contributes to her problems instead of helping her solve them. "Oh, what a terrible awakening this is. All these eight years... this woman who was my pride and joy... a hypocrite, a liar, worse than that, a criminal!" (Ibsen 59). A man that truly loved his wife would support her through any financial hardship, yet Torvald does the opposite.

Even his children take precedence over his wife. He calls Nora unfit to raise the children when he finds out about her loan. "But I shall not allow you to bring up the children; I dare not trust them to you" (Ibsen 60). He decides to leave the children motherless rather than have a mother who does not conform to his unattainable standards of perfection. Torvald lives under the illusion that he loves his children and knows what is best for them. He is a complete failure as a father. Whenever the children are present, Torvald turns them over to their mother, but when they are not present and he is upset with Nora, he rashly takes full responsibility for them. Also, "when Nora's crime is revealed, he gives in to Krogstad's demands, making him even more hypocritical than Krogstad. He too becomes a father of lies and disguise, polluting his own children" (Rosefeldt, par. 6). Thus Torvald chooses his children, who he does not truly care for or ever communicate with, over his wife.

The way Torvald treats Nora in her time of need elucidates her reality. She went to great lengths to help solve his financial difficulties. Now when she needs him, he alienates and condemns her. Earlier, he had said "many's the time I wish you were threatened by some terrible danger so I could risk everything, body and soul, for your sake" (Ibsen 55). Yet when the time has come to do just that, he abandons her instead. In doing so, sets off the volcano that has been dormant inside Nora for so long. All the problems in their relationship have been pushed into a dusty corner for eight long years. Thus at the first time they discuss a new issue, all the old problems quickly resurface, so fast and so plentiful that they create a distance between Nora and Torvald that can never be filled. It is too late.

Instead of discussing an issue as two equals would do, Torvald condemns Nora and treats her like a child. His behavior is reminiscent of Nora's father. "You and papa have committed a great sin against me. It is your fault that I have made nothing of my life... He called me his doll-child, and he played with me just as I used to play with my dolls" (Ibsen 63). Nora's commentary on her father reveals that she has lived her whole life in an illusion. First, her father kept her sheltered and protected, never learning by experience. Then she was transferred to Torvald, who continued the trend by treating her as a doll rather than as a partner and confidante. Their relationship has been a farce, a game. She is a trophy wife who is pretty but empty, just like a doll. Nora lived under the illusion that those who took care of her loved her as much as she loved them. When Torvald is unwilling to sacrifice anything for her as she has done for him, Nora realizes that she has wasted so much potential trying to appease those who control her (Goonetilleke, par. 3). This is when she makes her drastic decision to abandon her duties towards her husband, her children, and society. "You have never loved me. You have only thought it pleasant to be in love with me... I must now try and educate myself—you are not the man to help me in that. I must do that for myself. And that is why I am going to leave you now" (Ibsen 63-64). Nora is not just a woman, a doll. She is a symbol of the suppressed woman, and by confronting reality, she sets an example for all those who try to hide behind illusions and live an empty life.

Ibsen makes a great social and political statement with Nora's dramatic exit and the slam of the door behind her. It has been cited as the beginning of the women's liberation movement (Goonetilleke, par. 3). Had she closed it softly, it would have represented the meek escapes other women of the era made. But Nora is strong in her decision; she is unlike Mrs. Linde who waited for her husband to pass away before fulfilling her duty towards herself. Therefore some critics have stated that he is an idealist, that he believed "beauty, truth, and goodness are one" (Moi 2). The play ends with "clarity," "artistic harmony," and "beauty" (Moi 6). Marriage has become a caricature of what it once was, and so a cleansing of souls has occurred in the dissolution of a bad relationship.

However, Ibsen's idealism has been successfully argued against. For every woman who paves the way towards equality, there are thousands more who hinder the progress of equality between the sexes. Ibsen portrays this through the use of Mrs. Linde. She is a very weak character who married not out of love but out of necessity. "There was nothing else I could do... You mustn't forget I had a helpless mother and two young brothers" (Ibsen 50). She, like Nora, felt suppressed by her husband, but unlike Nora, she did nothing about it. She instead remained passive and waited for him to die. Even after his death, she did nothing to better herself or improve conditions. She remained a pawn in society's manipulation of women. When Krogstad proposed a return to the life of patriarchy by offering marriage, Mrs. Linde gladly accepted. "There is not the least pleasure in working for one's self. Nils, give me someone and something to work for" (Ibsen 51). With Krogstad's history as an unsavory character involved in blackmail, his supposed change in heart seems short-lived. As most men of the era, he will probably return to his sordid lifestyle, and his wife and ornament, Mrs. Linde, will have to comply. Thus for every woman who takes a step forward into reality, many women seem to take steps backward and retreat into illusions. Ibsen thus argues that social justice takes many people and many years to achieve.

Also, Nora's success after her dramatic exit is never ensured. She is "merely acting out an alternative doll's role. The roles derive from the sentimental and escapist imagination of her society" (Pearce 2). Mrs. Linde has succeeded in the real world using the qualities and values completely opposite to those of Nora. Mrs. Linde is mature, economical, and calm. Meanwhile Nora is sheltered, easily excited, and a compulsive shopper. Ibsen's realism can be seen in the possibility that Nora is just walking from one illusion into the next.

His realism is also displayed in his lack of reconciliation between Nora and Torvald. Therefore, there is "no ultimate victory of the ideal" (Moi 5). The reader is not uplifted by the play; rather, he or she feels a sense of loss and some argue that this signifies a loss of faith in divine power (Moi 5). Ibsen is currently thought of as an avid realist, one who portrays human beings as they are. In Act Three of *A Doll's House*, he shatters the ideals and illusions held up by society.

Henrik Ibsen has proven himself to be a social and political harbinger of change through his masterpiece *A Doll's House*. In Act Three, the conflict of illusion versus reality for Nora becomes the conflict of illusion versus reality for all those who have ever been suppressed. Whether Ibsen's message contains idealist or realist values, it cannot be argued that the emancipation of woman and the dissolution of inequality were his main goals. Nora slamming the door behind her represents her full emergence from the world of illusion to the world of reality. What fate she holds after that is uncertain. However, slamming the door of a doll's house only opens infinite doors of possibility beyond that one.

Works Cited

Goonetilleke, D.C.R.A. "A Doll's House: Overview" in Reference Guide to World Literature, 2nd ed., edited by Lesley Henderson, St. James Press, 1995. Literature Resource Center Gale Group Databases. Hagerty Lib., Philadelphia, PA. 4 June 2007 < http://galegroup.com>.

Ibsen, Henrik. "A Doll's House." *Four Great Plays by Henrik Ibsen*. Ed. John Gassner. New York: Bantam Books, 1981. 2-68.

Moi, Toril. "First and Foremost a Human Being: Idealism, Theatre, and Gender in a Doll's House." Oxford: Oxford UP, 2006, *FirstSearch* OCLC. Hagerty Lib., Philadelphia, PA. 4 June 2007 < http://newfirstsearch.oclc.org>.

Pearce, Richard. "The Limits of Realism." *College English*, Vol. 31, No. 4. (Jan., 1970), pp. 335-343. *JSTOR*. JSTOR. Hagerty Lib., Philadelphia, PA. 4 June 2007. < http://jstor.org >

Rosefeldt, Paul. "Ibsen's 'A Doll's House'." *The Explicator* 61.2 (Wntr 2003): 84(2). *Expanded Academic ASAP*. Gale Group Database. Hagerty Lib., Philadelphia PA. 4 June 2007 http://find.galegroup.com/itx/infomark.do?&contentSet=IAC Documents&type=retrieve&tabID=T002&prodId=EAIM&docId= A99398770&source=gale&srcprod=EAIM&userGroupName=drexel_ main&version=1.0>.

Amanda Dovidio Zelechoski

Child Custody Determinations: The Role of Psychology in Historical Context

This essay briefly traces the history of child custody law and examines previous and current roles played by psychology in child custody matters. The historical evolution of decision-making about child custody provides an essential context for understanding the current involvement of mental health professionals in child custody determinations.

Historical Overview of Child Custody Determinations

The earliest known recorded statute related to the parent-child relationship was the Code of Hammurabi (Marafiate, 1985). According to Marafiate (1985), the Code, which is believed to have been written in 2150 B.C., specified that children owed their parents a certain degree of respect, in return for which they would receive minimum care. Essentially, it was up to the father whether to accept the child. If accepted, the father could punish the child however he saw fit including, for example, cutting off the child's hands if they were used to strike him or removing the child's eyes or tongue as punishment for disrespect to his parents (Marafiate, 1985). In addition, because children were considered property, a father could also use his child to pay a debt. If a father chose not to accept his child, he could opt to kill the child or deprive the child of any status as a family member (Marafiate, 1985). As will be highlighted throughout this discussion of child custody doctrine, the concept of children as chattel or property belonging to parents, typically the father, is often the basis on which the judicial system made child custody determinations.

Over 2000 years later, under Roman law, most perceptions of parental rights and procedures for determining child custody remained unchanged (Marafiate, 1985). Fathers continued to have absolute power over their families and it was common practice for a father to mutilate, abandon, or sell his children (Marafiate, 1985). Because women were also considered property at this time, mothers did not have any rights related to their children (Kelly, 1994)

In later English common law, fathers continued to have supreme power over their children. However, fathers also gradually became legally obligated to protect, support, and educate their children (Kelly, 1994). Case law during this time repeatedly affirmed the father's indisputable right to the custody of his children. For example, in 1804, Leonard DeManneville forcibly entered his ex-wife's home and "snatched his naked child from the bosom of its mother," and later left the child lying naked in severe weather (Firing, 2007, p. 225). However, the English court refused to interfere with the rule that a father was legally entitled to the custody of his child (Rex v. *DeManneville*, 1804)

An interesting exception to these standard English common law practices involved legitimacy of the child. In the case of an illegitimate child, the father had no legal right to the child and the child's natural mother was given custody (Marafiate, 1985). This issue was essential because the child's legitimacy was linked to land ownership and subsequent entitlement to familial land through inheritance.

As English Courts continued to award custody to fathers (except in cases of illegitimacy or death of the father), basing their decisions on property interests, American common law followed identical practices throughout the latter part of the eighteenth century and into the nineteenth century (Firing, 2007). However, the paternal preference was gradually applied less strictly as in English common law (Kelly, 1994). For example, in a landmark Pennsylvania case, Commonwealth v. Addicks (1815), the court introduced the principle of making child custody determinations based on a child's best interests. Specifically, the court stated,

> In a controversy for the custody of an infant of tender years, the court will consider the best interests of the child, and will make such an order for its custody as will be for its welfare, without reference to the wishes of the parties, their parental rights, or their contracts" (Commonwealth v. Addicks, 1815, p. 1).

This was one of the first instances in which a court considered the question of parental fitness a major issue, as well as eliminated the former automatic preference for the father as custodial parent.

Another major change came with the passage of Talfourd's Act in 1839. Under this English law, courts were directed by the British Parliament to award custody of a child under the age of seven to the mother, and to award visitation rights to mothers for children seven years and older (Kelly, 1994). Many states subsequently adopted statutes modeled on this

Act, which eventually became known as the "tender years doctrine." Accordingly, judicial opinions related to child custody matters began to reflect a maternal bias into the early part of the twentieth century (Firing, 2007).

As American society progressively became more industrialized, fathers became primary wage earners in factories, and women took over as the primary child care providers in the home (Hodges, 1986). This division of family responsibilities understandably influenced subsequent custody decisions (Kelly, 1994). The presumption in favor of the father gradually began to shift, not only at the result of industrialization, but also because women's rights and the women's movement emerged (Kelly, 1994). An increase in the legal status of women in the United States during the nineteenth and twentieth centuries influenced the movement toward a maternal preference. These factors, in conjunction with society's increasing concern for children's welfare and growing knowledge about children's development, began to loosen the long-standing paternal preference (Kelly, 1994).

In 1925, Judge Benjamin Cardozo endorsed what is now known as the "best interests doctrine" in his opinion in *Finlay v. Finlay*, arguing that "[equity's]... concern is for the child" (p. 626). While Judge Cardozo is credited with introducing this notion that custody should be determined based on what is in the best interests of the child, it has been argued that the idea of deciding custody by primarily considering the child's welfare was established long before *Finlay v. Finlay* (Marafiate, 1985). In *Chapsky v. Wood* (1881), a father was attempting to gain custody of his five year old daughter from the child's maternal aunt who had raised the child since birth due to the impoverished circumstances of the parents. The judge denied the father custody, citing the welfare of the child as "the paramount consideration," (pp. 653-654).

As the predominant view in the United States became the best interests perspective in the early to mid-twentieth century, there concurrently materialized a presumption that young children, or children of "tender years," are best served by remaining with their mothers. The social movements progressing at this time, such as the women's movement, and increasing interest in child development were fundamental in the dominance of this tenders years concept (Marafiate, 1985). The emergence of Freudian psychoanalytic theory and its emphasis on the mother's role in subsequent development of attachments was also influential in supporting the maternal preference (Kelly, 1994). Consequently, the paternal preference was definitively replaced by a maternal preference. This maternal presumption for custody remained unyielding for many decades.

This paradigm was challenged after the divorce rate began to rise dramatically in the 1960s and fathers began to assert sex discrimination and constitutional equal protection claims (Kelly, 1994). Also, both the feminist movement and women increasingly entering the work force weakened the image of maternal caretaker and ensuing preference. Consequently, by the mid-1970s, most states had abandoned the maternal presumption in favor of gender-neutral laws (Kelly, 1994).

Although a consensus has never existed among the legal, judicial, and mental health communities regarding what is in the best interest of children as applied to custody disputes (Kelly, 1994), the Uniform Marriage and Divorce Act of 1970 (amended in 1987) explicitly delineated the elements of the best interests standard and was eventually adopted in various forms by most states (Kelly, 1994). The current best interests standard requires the court to consider the following factors in determining custody:

1) the wishes of the child's parent or parents as to his custody;

2) the wishes of the child as to his custodian;

3) the interaction and interrelationship of the child with his parent or parents, his siblings, and any other person who may significantly affect the child's best interest;

4) the child's adjustment to his home, school, and community;

5) the mental and physical health of all individuals involved

(Melton, Petrila, Poythress, & Slobogin, 2007). While this standard appears facially explicit, it has proven very difficult to apply due to the lack of consensus among all involved professional disciplines as to the specific nuances of each of these factors (Kelly, 1994).

Throughout the last fifty years, several other standards have been proffered. The "primary-caretaker standard" was presented as a seemingly more objective and gender-neutral alternative to both the tender years presumption and the best interests standard. Similar to the tender years presumption, the primary caretaker rule presumes that "young children generally are better off when their primary attachment is preserved," (Melton et al., 2007, p. 545). Another suggested position was the "least detrimental alternative," in which the psychological parent, or the parent most connected to the child's emotional and physical needs, would have physical custody and authority over all decision-making on behalf of the child, including how much to allow the other parent's involvement in the child's life (Goldstein, Freud, & Solnit, 1973).

Although the best interests standard is generally applied in most United States jurisdictions in some form, several jurisdictions implement the primary caretaker standard and several use the least detrimental alternative method of analysis. However, it is important to recognize that, in practice, maternal presumption still remains the norm and that, in some jurisdictions, the tender-years presumption is still given substantial weight (Firing, 2007).

In making determinations about what it in the best interest of children, the current trend among courts is to conduct an equivalent examination of the child's relationship with each parent (Melton et al., 2007). Accordingly, the utility of clinical input and the constantly evolving role played by psychology in the child custody determination process have undergone numerous changes.

The Evolving Role Played by Psychology in Child Custody Determinations

It has only been in the last century that psychology and social science have begun to play a prominent role in child custody determinations. Because the trend has moved toward determining the best interests of the child by examining the relationship with both parents (as opposed to either an inherent maternal or paternal preference), clinical input has been increasingly sought in recent years in a number of ways, the most prominent of which are discussed below.

Research

Research on the effects of divorce on children has had increasing influence on decision-making at parental, judicial, and legislative levels (Kelly, 1994). However, there remains controversy regarding the extent to which social science should be used to influence legislation and judicial practices in custody determinations due primarily to inadequate, inconclusive, or contradictory research methodology (e.g., Melton et al., 2007; Kelly, 1994). Although much is known about the effects of divorce and conflict on children (e.g., Wallerstein, 1991; Cummings & Davies, 1994), there exists scarce valid and reliable research about the effects of different custody arrangements on children and families experiencing varying circumstances (Melton, et al., 2007).

Assessment of Psychological Parenthood

The notion of assessing "psychological parenthood" was one of the first ways psychologists began to participate in the child custody process. Coined by Goldstein, Freud, and Solnit in 1973, this term was defined as a child's emotional attachment that results from "day-to-day attention to his needs for physical care, nourishment, comfort, affection, and stimulation" (Goldstein et al., 1973, p. 17). This concept, and the part it played in best interests determinations, was often criticized for its intrinsic subjectivity (Marafiate, 1985). Even after attempts were made to operationally define and assess the elements of psychological parenting and what is in a child's best interests, vast subjectivity remained in a judge's decision-making process about custody. Consequently, the assistance of psychologists was increasingly requested to aid the judicial fact-finder in evaluating psychological parenthood. Today, factors related to psychological parenthood are only some of the many factors considered in determining what is in the best interests of a child (Melton et al., 2007).

Evaluation

Over the last thirty years, the judicial system has increasingly relied upon psychologists to aid in determining what is in the best interests of children. As the presumption shifted from paternal preference to maternal preference to no preference and now to holding the child's welfare paramount, judges are called upon to consider substantially more factors than were historically required. The Uniform Marriage and Divorce Act (1987) requires the court to consider, among other things, such factors as: the interaction and interrelationship of the child with his parent or parents, his siblings, and any other person who may significantly affect the child's best interest; the child's adjustment to his home, school, and community; and the mental and physical health of all individuals involved.

Although there remains debate as to the extent to which a psychological evaluator can contribute to this consideration, as well as the utility of those contributions, psychologists are being relied upon more frequently as court dockets become increasingly crowded (Melton et al., 2007). Melton and colleagues (2007) noted that "clinical impressions about alliances and conflicts within the family and their bases might present judges with a useful framework for consideration of which child goes where" (p. 541); however, they caution mental health professionals against the temptation to overreach the limits of their knowledge and provide unwarranted opinions.

Mediation

Along with a recent movement toward mediation of child custody disputes as a compulsory first step in the divorce process (Katz, 1994), mental health professionals are now regularly called upon for the unique combination of skills they can bring into a mediation context. The role of the mediator in child custody mediation is to assist the parents in reaching mutually acceptable agreements. Cooperative problem-solving and a focus on addressing each family member's needs are emphasized, as opposed to the adversarial nature of typical divorce and custody proceedings (Kelly, 2000). Mental health professionals are often considered more effective and useful facilitators in the negotiation process than are standard mediators because of their ability to clarify points of agreement and disagreement in an emotionally charged environment (Kelly, 2000).

Future Directions

Melton and colleagues (2007) pointed out that in the overall area of child custody determinations, "relevant empirical knowledge is especially limited and that prevailing legal standards are especially problematic," (p. 561). It is clear that society has a come a long way from the Code of Hammurabi which deemed children property and without any rights, to the now current practice of considering the child's welfare as the paramount concern in any custody determination proceeding. However, substantial progress still needs to be made.

With respect to the involvement of social science and psychology, many advances and improvements have been made in how studies are conducted, increasing both reliability and validity in methodology which, in turn, increases the legal system's confidence in the results. Substantial findings have emerged with respect to what is known about the effects of divorce on children, and the surface has yet to be scratched regarding the impact of various custodial arrangements (i.e., joint or sole custody) on children. In addition, there are few specialized tests in existence that specifically assess components related to custody and visitation. The few measures that do exist have not been empirically validated either at all or for use in child custody matters. Advances in psychological testing specific to child custody determinations would be not only useful to psychologists conducting evaluations, but would increase the judicial system's confidence in social science evidence presented to the court in child custody matters.

As has been the case throughout history, societal trends will continue to influence the way in which child custody determinations are made. Because children's constitutional rights continue to be examined and expanded, children may begin to play an increasingly larger role in the decision-making about their own custody arrangement. In addition, as the makeup of American families continues to change, such as the emergence of same-sex couples and intentional single-parent homes, what is considered an acceptable and beneficial custodial or living arrangement will likely transform as well. As such, it is vital for mental health professionals to stay informed about empirical research findings regarding what is in the best interests of children.

References

Chapsky v. Wood (1881). 26 Kan. 650.

Cummings, E. M. & Davies, P. (1994). *Children and marital conflict: The impact of family dispute and resolution.* New York: Guilford Press.

Custody of Infants Act (1873). 36 & 37 Vict. C. 12.

Finlay v. Finlay (1925). 148 N.E. 624.

Firing, M. B. (2007). In whose best interests? Courts' failure to apply state custodial laws equally amongst spouses and its constitutional implications. *Quinnipiac Probate Law Journal, 20,* 223-259.

Goldstein, J., Freud, A., & Solnit, A. J. (1973). *Beyond the best interests of the child.* New York: Free Press.

Guardian of Infant's Act (1925). 15 & 16 Geo c. 45.

Guardianship of Infant's Act (1886). 49 & 50 Vict. C. 27.

Hodges, W. F. (1986). *Interventions for Children of Divorce: Custody, Access, and Psychotherapy.* New York: Wiley.

Katz, S. N. (1994). Historical perspective and current trends in the legal process of divorce. *Future of Children,* Spring 1994.

Kelly, J. B. (1994). The determination of child custody. *Children and Divorce*, 4, 121-142.

Kelly, J. B. (2000). Issues facing the family mediation field. *Pepperdine Dispute Resolution* Journal, 1, 37-42.

Marafiate, R. A. (1985). *The Custody of Children: Behavioral Assessment Model*. New York: Plenum Press.

Melton, G. B., Petrila, J., Poythress, N. G., & Slobogin, C. (2007). *Psychological evaluations for the courts: A handbook for mental health professionals and lawyers* (3d ed.). New York: Guilford.

Rex v. Manneville (1804). 102 Eng. Rep. (K.B. 1804).

Talfourd's Act (1839). 2 & 3 Vict. C. 54.

Uniform Marriage and Divorce Act § 402, 9A U.L.A. 561 (1987).

Wallerstein, J. S. (1991). The long-term effects of divorce on children: A review. *Journal of the American Academy of Child and Adolescent Psychiatry*, 30, 349.

First Place – Graduate

Monica Pace

Urban Environmental Education: Voices, Motifs, and Models in Philadelphia, PA

The practice of environmental education, or EE, in an urban setting may seem unnecessary—or even paradoxical—at first. Traditional educational models have focused on the environment as "Other," as a natural landscape that exists apart from human beings but is constantly threatened by their actions. This paradigm may be responsible for the sense of hopelessness, apathy, or complete ignorance that arises in even the well-educated citizen faced with environmental issues. An emerging definition of environmental education, however, challenges the traditional ideas of both "environmental" and "education." Urban environmental education reflects a shift in focus from the rural to the urban landscape, and a commitment to learning as a lifelong process that continues well beyond the classroom. In Philadelphia's environmental education programs, as in EE programs found in other cities, three powerful motifs continue to surface: interconnectedness, empowerment of the citizen, and hands-on experience. This paradigm localizes the environment—bringing it to the doorstep and the city street—and proves that environmental education is, by its very nature, urban.

Influences

It would be impossible to discuss Philadelphia's urban EE programs, in definition and in practice, without first exploring three major influences at the international, national, and state levels. At the international level, the Tbilisi Declaration of 1977 was a starting point in both historical and conceptual terms. While it may seem remote from Philadelphia in terms of time and distance, this USESCO conference on environmental education, held in Tbilisi, Georgia in the former Soviet Union, solidified environmental education's authenticity, definitional clarity, and modern context. Emphasizing an interdisciplinary approach, the Declaration maintains that the environment consists of both natural and manmade constructs, and should, "Consider the environment in its totality—natural and built, technological and social" (*The Tbilisi Declaration Intergovernmental Conference on Environmental Education*). For environmental education to be truly interdisciplinary, incorporating the natural and the artificial, the scientific and the social, it must also be available to every citizen, and not just the pupil. This is another hallmark of the Declaration: "Environmental education should cater to all ages and socio-professional groups in the population" (ibid). Finally, as set forth in the *Tbilisi Declaration*, any successful educational program, whether for adults or for children, should meet the following criteria. It should raise *awareness* of the environment and its issues, equip citizens with *knowledge* of the facts surrounding the issues, instill a proactive *attitude* and arm them with *skills* to solve environmental problems, and finally should provide a means of active *participation*. This last criterion, that of activism, figures prominently into the models of urban environmental education to be explored below.

On the national front—slightly closer to home—a second major influence upon EE programs in Philadelphia is the National Environmental Education Act of 1990 (http://www.epa.gov). Placing the U.S. Environmental Protection Agency in charge of supporting and funding formal educational initiatives, it provides a strong argument for EE to be offered in all schools. To facilitate this process it created the Office of Environmental Education, which provides grants and offers educator, media, and student training in environmental issues. Several individuals and institutions in Philadelphia have received grants from the Office of Environmental Education, including the Schuylkill Center for Environmental Education, Temple University, and the School District of Philadelphia ("EE Grants Awarded in Pennsylvania"). True to the tenets of environmental education, particularly in the urban setting, the grants promote higher learning—on the university level and beyond—and underscore the importance of active participation in the local environment. For example, a grant awarded to the Schuylkill Center for Environmental Education for its *Manayunk Watershed Education & Protection Program*, eventually enabled students to "become teachers [themselves] to educate family members and members of the community" (http://www.epa.gov).

A third influence upon EE in Philadelphia is the Pennsylvania Center for Environmental Education, or PCEE (http://www.pcee.org). The center was established in 1996 to form partnerships with several stakeholders in Pennsylvania's natural resources, including the Department of Environmental Education, the Community of Economic Development, and the State System for Higher Education. Two of its main goals match those found in all urban EE programs: to empower the citizen (in this case, "all PA citizens") and to consider the interconnectedness between land- and city-scapes by "Integrating environmental education into higher education" (http://www.pcee.org). PCEE facilitates both formal education in an academic setting and "nonformal" education in a less-traditional setting. Sponsored programs in the Philadelphia area, for example, have been held at the Morris Arboretum of the University of Pennsylvania, the Academy of Natural Sciences, The Schuylkill Center for Environmental Education, and even the Philadelphia Zoo. In its publication, *The Essentials of Environmental Education for Pennsylvania* (http://www.pcee.org), PCEE defends its interdisciplinary approach, and in so doing, challenges the learner to expand upon the concept of environment: "Environmental solutions are not only scientific, but also include historical, political, economic, and cultural perspectives." Urban areas and their environmental decisions would inherently be included.

While the Tbilisi Declaration can be viewed as a seminal voice legitimizing environmental education in general, a study published in *Environment* documents a decision by the National Science Foundation (NSF) as a key factor in establishing EE in a decidedly urban context. As Thomas M. Parris writes in "Urban Ecology," when the NSF opted to headquarter its new Long-Term Ecological Research sites in the hearts of Baltimore and Phoenix in 1997, it "broke with a long established ecological-science tradition that sought out 'natural' or 'pristine' settings" and "ushered in a new era of institutional recognition for urban ecology'" (3). The "new era" of urban EE continues as environmental centers spring up in major cities across the country. In perhaps the true test of a subject's scholarly legitimacy (courses in Elvis studies, perhaps, notwithstanding), urban EE is now included in university curricula worldwide.

Motifs

As noted in the introduction, the three main elements of urban EE as detailed in current literature are empowerment of the citizen, interconnectedness (or integration) of themes, and hands-on experience. Interconnectedness is the single-most recurring idea. It refers to the relationship between citizen and environment and between city and nature; and, especially in an educational setting, it refers to the breaking down of boundaries, or blurring of distinctions, between all subjects studied. In "Becoming Environmentally Literate Citizens," for example, Susan L. Groenke and Randall Puckett describe EE as a subject-holistic, rather than subject-specific, style: "Environmental citizenship cannot be developed fact-by-fact... but rather, through a sophisticated understanding of interconnected systems" (23). Joseph Fail, another educator of urban environmental studies, developed a program with "unifying themes" that eventually become the "basis for other concepts taught later in the course" ("Teaching Ecology in Urban Environments," 20). The program, which includes field trips to a local power plant, watershed, sewage treatment facility, and forest, also emphasizes the similarities and symbiotic relationship between city and natural resources. As Fail notes during the forest lesson, "Our final reflections concern how cities mimic this natural ecosystem" (20).

In urban environmental education, the themes of hands-on experience and empowerment share a cause and effect relationship: the latter is contingent upon the former. For students accustomed to learning primarily from books, experiential learning could be a welcome change. It has the added potential to motivate students to become involved not only in their studies, but also in their communities. As Joseph Fail so succinctly puts it: "Nothing teaches like experience" (22). However, because this is no passive sitting in the classroom style of learning, it may also present a challenge to students who are already reluctant to participate in an academic setting. Denice Haynes, a middle school teacher in Indianapolis, writes in "Introducing Urban Children to Environmental Activism" that students' response to the less-orthodox teaching methods that characterize EE was initially one of "disregard and powerlessness" (*Urbana* 24). Interestingly, the study points out, once students grasped how their actions influenced the environment, they developed a "sense of agency" or empowerment, and went on to develop plans to improve their school environment.

Urban EE in Philadelphia

In terms of environmental resources, Philadelphia has a lot to be proud of. Home to both Fairmount Park (one of the largest urban green spaces in the U.S.) and the Schuylkill Center for Environmental Education (one of the oldest EE centers in the country), Philadelphia has also recently earned the distinction of being named one of America's "Greenest" cities by MSN's "City Guides" (http://cityguides.msn.com). The article cites careful urban planning, the increasing incorporation of wind energy, and the use of public transit by about a third of the population, as three attributes other cities should emulate. Noticeably absent in the article, however, is any mention of Philadelphia's EE programs and opportunities, and how they play a deciding role in the overall "greenness" of the city. Environmental education in Philadelphia, like in the models studied above, displays a diverse mix of the formal and informal, occurring in both likely and unlikely places—from the classroom to the outdoors to even the TV set. The Schuylkill Center for Environmental Education (http://www.schuylkillcenter.org) is perhaps the most well known EE facility in Philadelphia. It is not so much a center as a collection of distinctive environments native to the region: originally established on farmland in 1965, it has expanded to include wooded areas, wetlands, and meadows. Although its location (northwest of the city in the Roxborough neighborhood) and its emphasis on the conservation of natural surroundings may make it easy for a visitor to forget they are in a major metropolitan area, certain elements of cutting-edge technology place the Center in a distinctively urban environment. The Green Roof on the Education Building, for example, consists of living, growing grass, which serves as an energy-efficient way to keep a building cooler in the summer and reduces runoff from rain.

The Schuylkill Center, as with other facilities providing urban EE, assumes an interdisciplinary, hands-on approach to learning. This is evident in the many programs, both formal and informal, offered to children and adults. For students, the annual Envirothon integrates science and current social and political events; and for adults, the "Green Living" workshops combine health and environmental impact issues.

While the Schuylkill Center offers extra-curricular environmental learning, another environmental education facility in Philadelphia incorporates EE directly into the school curriculum. The Wissahickon Charter School, founded in 2002, dedicates its entire curriculum to the empowerment of the student using the Wissahickon Valley as an extension of the classroom. All subjects, not just environmental studies, are carefully chosen for their emphasis on direct, experiential, "active" learning. The Service Learning project, for example, puts students at the helm of exploring social and environmental issues in their communities. Ultimately, the school aims to impart a sense of "ownership" of learning itself (*School Curriculum and Design*, http://www.wissahickoncharter.org). As detailed in the Tbilisi Declaration and the other EE models above, the more engaged a child is in academic issues, the more engaged he or she will become in all aspects of his or her environment. Empowerment, the idea that what one does makes a difference, results from this activism.

Formal environmental education in Philadelphia does not exist solely within the setting of environmental centers or schools. This spring, for example, two Temple University students made headlines—and won accolades—for their dedication to urban environmental issues. Vincent Gasper, the winner of an Udall Foundation scholarship for environmental careers, describes his project as educational: "I want to transform brownfields and urban blight from negative spaces that detract from their surroundings to positive areas where the public can be educated about natural issues such as water management, while also enjoying an esthetically beautiful landscape" ("Two Students' Environmental Work Earns Udall Recognition," http://www.prnewswire.com). In demonstrating that his work serves several purposes, Gasper's study seamlessly integrates social justice issues (improving one's total environment) with education on the environment as a valuable resource. In April, students from another school, West Philadelphia Achievement Charter Elementary, were chosen by the P.A. Department of Agriculture to participate in an environmental program called The Growing Connection ("Earth Day Celebration Brings Agriculture to Philadelphia Students," (http://www.prnewswire.com). While the primary purpose was to increase agricultural awareness through hands-on experience in an urban setting, the program also integrated cultural studies, as students networked with Growing Connection Groups in other countries. The "growing connection," then, could be used to describe the students' increasing awareness of connections between local and world issues.

While the least orthodox urban EE program in Philadelphia is broadcast on a university television station (Drexel's DUTV), it itself has no specific academic ties. Elizabeth's Fiend's interdisciplinary *Big Tea Party: A Little TV Show* (http://www.bigteaparty.com) nearly defies description: no small feat for a broadcast that, at three minutes a segment, more resembles a commercial. A blend of "cooking, crafts, and anarchy," with a healthy dose of recycling and conservation, the program ultimately demonstrates the empowerment of any individual—child or adult—who embraces the hands-on DIY (do it yourself) lifestyle. In an interview with the author for a previous article, *Big Tea Party's* Elizabeth Fiend describes how the group's new urban EE DVD, *Green Tea Party*, filled a void in the environmental experience of inner-city students. Educators, she mused, had been "desperate for a high-quality educational video that will really entertain the kids" ("Garden Varieties: Big Tea Party's Elizabeth Fiend" http://www.philadelphiawriters.com). What makes *Big Tea Party* and its companion *Green Tea Party* so vital to the canon of urban EE is its use of immediate surroundings: Philadelphia is recognizable as its cinematic backdrop. The advice and demonstrations it offers, such as how to conserve water by placing an empty soda bottle in the toilet tank, work with inexpensive materials that the participant already has. The results are immediate and satisfying, and prove that anyone can live an ecologically friendly lifestyle, no matter where they live. "This lifestyle is all about choice and empowering the individual," Fiend maintains in the companion booklet to the film, *A Study Guide to Green Tea Party*.

Conclusion

Because the environment encompasses both natural and city-scapes, and because all environmental and social systems impact one another, the study of urban EE is not only possible, it is essential. As the programs in Philadelphia have indicated, if environmental education is to maintain any sort of relevance for the city dweller, it should include elements of both natural and urban ecosystems. Like a natural setting, an urban setting, too, holds enormous potential. If one can be defined by its resources, then urban EE challenges the other to be defined by its resourcefulness.

Sources

Big Tea Party: A Little TV Show. http://www.bigteaparty.com

"Earth Day Celebration Brings Agriculture to Philadelphia Students." PRNewswire http://www.prnewswire.com.

"EE Grants Awarded in Pennsylvania." *EPA (Environmental Protection Agency)* http://www.epa.gov/enviroed/grants/PA02.htm#NE97303201 0).

Fail, Joseph Jr. "Teaching Ecology in Urban Environments." *The American Biology Teacher.* Nov 1995: Vol. 57. 522

Groenke, Susan L. and Randal Puckett. "Becoming Environmentally Literate Citizens." *The Science Teacher.* November 2006: 23.

Haines, Denice and Beth Berghoff. "Introducing Urban Children to Environmental Activism." *Primary Voices K-6. Urbana.* Oct 2000: Vol. 9. 23-29

"National Environmental Education Act of 1990." EPA. http://www.epa.gov/enviroed/pdf/neea.pdf

Pace, Monica. "Garden Varieties: Big Tea Party." *Philadelphia Arts Writers* http://www.philadelphiawriters.com/articles/08_2004/ bigteaparty.htm

Parris, Thomas M. "Urban Ecology." *Environment.* June 2004: Vol. 46. 3

Pennsylvania Center for Environmental Education http://www.pce.org

"School Curriculum and Design." Wissahickon Charter School http://www.wissahickoncharter.org/curriculum/overview.shtml.

Schuylkill Center for Environmental Education
http://www.schuylkillcenter.org

The Tbilisi Declaration Intergovernmental Conference on
Environmental Education
(https://innoserv.library.drexel.edu/search/pStein/
pstein/1,3,5,B/l962~1628122&FF=pstein+susan&1,,2,0)

"The Ten Greenest Cities in America." *MSN City Guides*
(http://cityguides.msn.com/citylife/greenarticle.aspx?
cp-documentid=4848625&page=4).

U.S. States News. "Two Students' Environmental Work Earns Udall
Recognition," PR Newswire http://www.prnewswire.com.

Sondra A. Schreibman

Awesome Minutia: How the Smallest Organisms on Earth May Provide Solutions to Humanity's Biggest Problems

Turn on the television, flip through the channels and before long you are bound to catch a glimpse of that familiar pie chart illustrating how many germs will die if you use the sanitizer, soap or spray being advertised. At the beginning the circle is filled with dark, worm-like creatures writhing on a blue background. Once the product is applied a wiper races around the circle, erasing all but a tiny sliver of the creatures, leaving behind an otherwise radiant blue background. Flip down a few more channels and you might see children walking blindly into the invisible danger than lurks in every sandbox or play structure, on every table, door handle or toy. The camera catches these everyday objects at unusual magnification and from perverse angles, giving common scenes a foreign, vaguely threatening feel. The children laugh and play, innocently oblivious to the malice surrounding them. "Children don't understand the invisible dangers they face," a sweet yet firm voice informs you. "That's why it's so important that you protect them as best you can." The camera pans back, light fills the room and Mom bounds forward, the warrior hero in yellow rubber gloves, wielding a new and improved, extra-safe household cleaner. "Finally," intones the voice with a sense of relief, "a cleanser that's both easy to use and effective enough to satisfy even the toughest critic." Day in and day out we are flooded with a barrage of information proclaiming the danger of the microcosm that surrounds us. In an environment like this it's no wonder so many people are revolted by the word 'bacteria' and think of microorganisms collectively as "germs."

Because they cannot be seen, and because they are most often mentioned in the context of disease-causing parasites, many people think of microorganisms as a fairly uniform group of creepy troublemakers. Multicellular organisms, on the other hand, display traits that are easily recognized by the human eye and so these organisms seem very diverse to us. A cat, for instance, is clearly different from an apple, which in turn is rarely mistaken for a bumblebee. Although they may not look different, even when magnified one hundred times by a microscope, bacteria are the most diverse organisms on Earth, comprising two of the three domains which make up the broadest scheme of taxonomical classification. Evolutionarily speaking, archaebacteria are as closely related to eubacteria as they are to you or me.

Life on earth began about 4 billion years ago, and the last common ancestor of archaebacteria, eubacteria and the multicellular organisms such as plants and animals lived a little over 3 billion years ago.[1] As the organisms on our branch diversified in size and appearance the bacteria diversified in other ways. The archaebacteria became the daredevils of the invisible world, colonizing dangerous places ranging from boiling volcanic vents at the bottom of the sea to the ice sheets of the Antarctic. Eubacteria, on the other hand, spread across the rest of the land, coating every surface, swimming through every waterway and even colonizing the bodies of animals as they evolved. In addition to occupying a staggering array of spaces bacteria have developed a range of appetites, feeding on every imaginable substance. While multicellular organisms are limited to photosynthesis, predation or scavenging, bacteria can fuel their systems using any of those three methods or by feeding on rocks, gasses and a variety of soluble chemicals.

Although some species of bacteria have evolved to wreak havoc on our bodies and cause illness upon exposure, the invisible world of microbes is a diverse one and the vast majority of organisms are harmless, or even potentially helpful. Many researchers focus on combating the threats posed by invasive, destructive microbes that produce toxins and cause disease, and many of us would not be alive today without their contribution to medicinal science. Today, however, I ask you to turn your attention away from those malevolent microbes and consider instead the potential of the rest of the invisible world to work with us, providing valuable services to humanity simply by being themselves.

Detoxifying the Oceans

The indulgences and conveniences of modern life have come at a price that may not be readily apparent to most people living in the developed nations of the world. To others the problem is abundantly clear. Joan Davis of San Francisco first realized that something was wrong with her ten-year-old son when his fifth grade teacher called her in for a meeting. Matthew Davis had always been a good student and had shown particular enthusiasm for creative writing, so Ms. Davis was deeply disturbed to hear that her son was suddenly struggling to compose simple sentences. At home she noticed another troubling symptom: Matthew had begun to curl his fingers as if gripping something and could no longer catch a ball while playing outside. Ms. Davis wasted no time in taking her son to a neurologist where a blood test revealed that Matthew was suffering from mercury poisoning. After listening to the boy's eating habits the doctor suggesting a surprising solution: Matthew should give up his favorite food—albacore tuna.[2]

Heavy metals such as mercury enter the oceans in a variety of ways, and so are considered non-point source pollution.[3] In other words, heavy metals enter the water from a variety of sources ranging from active mines to logging sites to litter. There are many, many small amounts entering the ocean, so no one source deserves a lion share of the blame. Metal, such as mercury, accumulate in the flesh of fish to varying degrees dependent on a number of factors including how efficiently the fish is able to excrete the metals, how easily metal can diffuse through the skin of the fish and what the fish feeds upon.[4] Predators such as tuna tend to accumulate more heavy metals in their tissue than herbivores because the metals have accumulated in the smaller fish that they eat, and they therefore receive a concentrated does with every meal. When people then eat those predators their dose of toxic metal is more concentrated still. Two years after his diagnosis and his last meal of canned tuna Matthew Davis has recovered fully and his blood level of mercury is well within the safe limit. Unfortunately countless other children remain at risk. A study of canned albacore tuna sold in New Jersey between 1998 and 2003 found that 25% of cans sampled contained mercury levels exceeding the safe limit set by the FDA.[5]

Decreasing the levels of heavy metals that flow into the ocean would prevent an escalation of the dangers posed by some seafood, but cannot decrease the levels already present. In order to do that we would need some type of filter that takes up the metals from the water and sequesters them so that fish don't ingest them and pass them on to us. The cyanobacteria *Spirulina* is able to act as such a filter, absorbing a variety of toxic metals into their bodies while alive and even after death.[6] Another potentially useful microbe that may be able to sequester heavy metals in the ocean is found miles below the surface surrounding hydrothermal vents.[7] Bacteria that congregate around these extremely hot volcanic vents are able to withstand high temperatures in addition to being able to process heavy metals, and both *Spirulina* and the deep sea hydrothermal bacteria may be useful both in their natural habitat, sequestering metal already in the ocean, and as aids in the battle to keep more metals from washing out to sea. By creating pools of runoff at the site of a mine or other industrial source and populating them with heavy metal-sequestering microbes the metals could be stopped before they reached the ocean, and at a very low cost.

Improving Food Safety

A food-based threat that is more widely known than heavy metal toxicity is food poisoning. Most people have experienced the effects of food-borne illness, and although healthy adults generally recover quickly, young children, the elderly and those people with a compromised immune system can become seriously ill or even die when exposed to microbes or microbial toxins on food. Although it may seem unlikely or even illogical, one of the safest and most ancient means of combating food-borne pathogens is by sending in other, helpful microbes. After people began living close together in cities but before waste water treatment had been developed contaminated drinking water posed a serious threat to humanity. In Europe people avoided drinking raw water by brewing weak alcoholic beverages such as beer with the help of microscopic yeast. Another challenge of early civilization was that of food storage. In order to prevent mass starvation during times of shortage or drought people had to find a method of preventing stored food from being contaminated by harmful pathogenic organisms. Once again a solution came from other microbes in the form of lactic acid bacteria.[8]

Lactic acid bacteria (LAB) are a group of related organisms that are often used as starter cultures in fermented foods such as cheese, and which produce anti-microbial compounds known as bacteriocins. Meats exposed to LAB have 99% less pathogenic staff bacteria as compared to untreated meat, and the presence of a particularly competitive strain of LAB has been correlated with an extended shelf life in refrigerated ready-to-eat meat dishes.[9] The compounds produced by LAB are harmless to humans, and unlike modern chemical food preservatives, bacteriocins have been ingested by people safely for thousands of years in cheese and yogurt.

In addition to expecting safe, fresh food people in the developed world expect to have clean, palatable water running through their taps and into their homes. Although filtration combined with a variety of cleaning agents can eliminate harmful organisms and many contaminants from the public water supply, other compounds that affect the taste (tastants) and smell (odorants) of the water can be very difficult to remove. MIB and geosmin are two carbon-based compounds produced by algae. They act as both tastants and odorants, causing clean water to seem musty and earthy, and are not removed during routine water processing. The most effective way to remove these unpleasant compounds is by passing the water through a filter composed of sand and microorganisms. The microbes capture the MIB and geosmin and use the carbon to build their own bodies.[10] By containing the bacteria and sand behind a filter the water can pass through, leaving behind the unpleasant scent and smell, and can reemerge free of bacteria and safe for consumption.

Replacing Fossil Fuel

Although no one knows precisely what volume of fossil fuel remains beneath the Earth waiting to be discovered, nor the year or day when it will finally run out, we can conclude with certainty that it will run out. Interest in new sustainable fuels has increased slowly but steadily over the years, heightening sharply when gas prices peak. Some of the most popular potential sources are ethanol, biodiesel and hydrogen, all of which can be produced using the power of microorganisms.

Ethanol and biodiesel are both carbon-based, combustible fuels. Most of the ethanol and biodiesel being produced today is derived from plants such as corn, but in order to break the tough, complex tissue of plants into liquid fuel the plants undergo fermentation by microscopic yeasts. A mixed culture of bacteria have been used in trial reactors to produce ethanol and other fuel compounds[11] and as the composition of those cultures improves through research and technology they could provide a cheaper, more efficient method of fuel production. Plants require land, irrigation, harvesting and transport, whereas bacteria can grow indoors in factories with minimal nourishment. Using corn or other food products as sources of fuel could have unpleasant economic ramifications, whereas bacteria pose no such threat.

Biodiesel can be used by the current diesel vehicle fleet and is produced by processing oil with common, readily available chemicals. The production of biodiesel yields fuel plus a glycerol soap appropriate for industrial cleaning. The oil needed can be obtained from restaurants after it's been used in the fryer, or can be produced from plants, animals or other organisms. One such organism that is very promising as a source of the oil for biodiesel production is microalgae. Microalgae is a general term for photosynthetic microbes, and can grow in vats indoors or outside, require minimal care, grow very rapidly and have an inherently higher oil content (in some species) when compared to plant sources.[12] Microalgae require only light, carbon dioxide, water and nutrient salts to grow, and many of the nutrients could be reclaimed from waste. Carbon dioxide is currently all too prevalent in the air, and water and sunlight of the quality required are not difficult to come by. To maximize growth sunlight exposure could be maximized without consuming power by designing growth vessels that take advantage of passive methods of light amplification such as mirrors and by increasing the surface area exposed to light.

Another alternative fuel that has gained some popularity is hydrogen gas (H2), which can be used much like petroleum fuels in that it would be kept at a filling station and pumped into vehicles. It is not, however, a combustible fuel but functions instead somewhat like a battery. The hydrogen passes through a fuel cell within the car, and as it does an electrical charge is created. At the end of the reaction the hydrogen attaches to oxygen and forms water. Cyanobacteria, a type of bacteria and microalgae, produce hydrogen naturally. Some species produce enough hydrogen so as to be viable as a source of fuel[13], and are sustainable, easy to cultivate and relatively easy to bioengineer. No matter which alternative fuel becomes the replacement for fossil fuel microorganisms are an excellent candidate as the source.

Though the process of evolution humans have developed a fear of the unknown, of the unseen and of the unfamiliar, and like all evolutionarily conserved behaviors this fear has helped us to survive. Our fear is compounded by the clever urging of advertisements for sanitation products and by news reports of super bugs that never seem to strike. Pathogenic microbes have indeed posed a grave threat to people since before there was civilization, writing or science. Today, however, that fear of and repulsion toward the invisible world may be holding us back. Although some microbes are dangerous, others can hold that danger back and keep us safe. Microbes can help to clean up our messes and fuel our active lives. Scientific discoveries have revolutionized the way we think about many things, but when our minds lag behind we may overlook opportunities that could revolutionize our world.

[1]   Campbell, N. and Reece, J. Biology 6th edition. San Francisco, PearsonEducation, Inc. 2002.

[2]   Waldman, P. Mercury and Tuna: US Advice Leaves Lots of Questions The Wall Street Journal. August 1, 2005.

[3]   NOAA.Welcome to Nonpoint Source Pollution. NOS Education Discovery Kits. Available at http://oceanservice.noaa.gov/education/kits/pollution/welcome.html. Revised January 24, 2006.

[4]   Dallinger, R. Prosi, F. Segner, H. Back H. Contaminated Food and Uptake of Heavy Metals By Fish: A Review and a Proposal for Future Research Oecologia (1987) 73: 91-98

[5]   Burger, J. and Gochfeld, M. Mercury in Canned Tuna: White Versus Light and Temporal Variation. Environmental Research (2004) 96[3]:239-249

6   Doshi, H. Ray, A. Kothari, I. Bioremediation Potential of Live and Dead *Spirulina*: Spectroscopic, Kinetics and SEM Studies Biotechnology and Bioengineering (2006) 96[6]:1051-1063

7   Deming, J. Deep Ocean Environmental Biotechnology. Current Opinion in Biotechnology (1998) 9:283-287

8   Soomro, A. Masud, T. Anwaar, K. Role of Lactic Acid Bacteria (LAB) in Food Preservation and Human Health – A Review. Pakistan Journal of Nutrition (2002) 1[1]:20-24

9   O'Sullivan, L. Ross, R. Hill, C. Potential of Bacteriocin-producing Lactic Acid Bacteria for Improvements in Food Safety and Quality. Biochimie (2002) 84:593-604

10   Ho, L. Hoefel, D. Bock, F. Saint, C. Newcombe, G. Biodegradation Rates of 2-methylisoborneol (MIB) and Geosmin Through Sand Filters and in Bioreactors Chemosphere. (2007) 66:2210-2218

11   Angenent, L. Energy Biotechnology: Beyond the General Lignocellulose-to-Ethanol Pathway. Current Opinion in Biotechnology (2007) 18:191-192

12   Chisti, Y. Biodiesel from Microalgae. Biotechnology Advances (2007) 25:294-306

13   D. De, D. Chaudhuri, S. Bhattacharya, S. Hydrogen Production by Cyanobacteria. Dutta Microbial Cell Factories (2005) 4:36

Week of
Writing

Introduction

Drexel University's third annual Week of Writing (WoW) was held in May of 2008. WoW is a weeklong celebration of writing with an emphasis on creative writing, sponsored by the Department of English and Philosophy, the College of Arts and Sciences, and Magnificent Minds. This past year's events included panel discussions about writing nonfiction, blogging, and poetry, as well as a raucous open-mic extravaganza. The reading marathon remains the centerpiece of WoW. Faculty and students read their own original creative writing back-to-back, a new reader every few minutes, as the audience comes and goes throughout the days.

Each year, the lead-up to the marathon is the WoW Writing Contest, used to determine which students will be invited to read at the event. In 2008, two new categories—opinion/editorial and humor—joined the mainstay contest categories of fiction, poetry, and creative nonfiction. More than 150 pieces were submitted, the most in the contest's history. The high quality of the submissions made the task of selecting winners in each category quite difficult. The judging panels, made up of faculty and professional writers, finally decided on the best creative writing Drexel students had produced in 2008. Those winning students not only read at the WoW marathon and earned prizes, but also now have their writing published in the inaugural issue of *The 33rd*.

Creative writing is among the most challenging fields. Even experienced authors who have been writing for years often struggle to find just the right word. As author Gene Fowler famously said, "Writing is easy. All you do is stare at a blank sheet of paper until drops of blood form on your forehead." The writers whose work appears in this section have stared at that blank sheet of paper, or that blank computer monitor. Whether or not drops of blood formed on their foreheads, they have struggled for the right words to touch their readers and bring their vision to life. The Week of Writing will continue to celebrate and reward their efforts.

Regina Ram

Front Window

my street has garbage women,
and no, you can't bribe them.

i watched my landlord try,
twenty bucks for the gutted house
stoves and cabinets in the back,
an extra ten if they take the sofa—
like how he usually does with the garbage men
who are accustomed to such tips.

garbage women aren't like that.
the one with the weaved hair
the royal blue jumpsuit under her vest,
gold hoops with her name drawn across them
and acrylic curled fingernails

looks at him and says
You Must Be Joking.
and continues to pick up the bags
and move along before he can say
he really wasn't.

Sarah Munroe

Ferns and Oceans

afternoon reading assignment at our desks: Me:
bending low to hide the tears, holding in the sobs, I am
crying over the death of two dogs: One
dead from heroic wounds, the other from heartbroken loneliness.
ending.

fast forward twelve years: My:
grandmother is dying of a weak
heart and my grandfather is feeling the heartache: She
is forgetting—has sometimes forgotten—him, their children, life, joy.
joyless.

knit together in my mind, those dogs and my grandparents: I:
long for my grandmother to die, to end before her
memory leaves her entirely without the impression of: Him
never to regain them together, a lifetime entirely lost to her.
over.

please, but please, Grandfather: Don't:
quit. "do not go gentle into that good night.
rage, rage against the dying of the light": Poems
stories, intertwined written words, overlapping dogs with living and dying
people.timelessness.

ushering forth the day when as you ask: I:
voice the memorial of her through a song
with meaning woven somehow into your lives, just as: The
x that will not mark the spot where her ashes scatter over Maine's ocean
waters.yesterday.

zip up your coat: heartbreak means more than pneumonia.

Thomas Bennett

Man is Defined in Evens

two by 2

it comes in

3 plus 2

slowly seeping

$4^2 + \ln(e^3)$

rambling, brooding, happy

the first with the second

it doesn't A.D.D. ^

cubed root (27) times $- 3\cos(pi)$

the balance has been skewed to misrepresent my client

$2*(e^2) - 0.778$

ignorance, our plea, in the court of direct euphemism

$e^{(pi*i)} * -(1/4) * 10$

lim (as i approaches infinity) = madness

Mathematically solve the even lines

Matthew Lucas

Pondicherry?

A fragrant fern
that grows among bulrushes
and protects army ants, when resting,
from hard rains. A decadent broth of endives
and chives, reserved for the rich and wastrel.
No, a lesser-known Chinese
philosopher who spoke of moths,

temple bells, and such. A town
in Indiana. Once, the name for rolling
one's tongue, but recently changed,
for obvious reasons. Rich shellac
commonly sopped onto linoleum and other
gorgeous surfaces. No, no,

it denotes a state of discomfort, the things of
nightmares: jock itch, swamp ass.
A skirmish fought for orphan's freedom.
Everyone's favorite butler. Simply,
one beautiful word, a place you have never
journeyed, gladly beyond any experience.

Ali Cahill

Universal Human Language (UHL)

I only did it because I was in love. At first, when he suggested it, I thought it was silly—one language, devoid of puns, irony, imagery; a language used only for communication, for all races to use; a perfectly phonetic language with a one-to-one ratio of audio to written capability; with ways to demonstrate sarcasm, questions, emphasis. One language for all. It would erase Shakespeare—which was fine, I could never be bothered by Shakespeare anyway—and poetry; would eviscerate the beauty of language; would condense and consolidate it; would rid it of its idiosyncrasies. It would be a language designed for optimal communication, a language planned ahead of time, not a language that developed out of need for one.

I knew, full-well, that it would destroy me; as a poet, what else could I love besides language? What could be more beautiful than TS Eliot's indecisions? Or more poignant than Joyce's homesickness? Or more tender than Hesse's search for self of Harry Haller and his battle against suicide? The eternal madness of Cummings? The bourgeois classlessness of Bukowski? I could think of no better way to fill my life than with them—but I was intrigued by the idea of creating a language all my own.

So when he suggested it, I played along. I listened to what he had to say. I laughed at myself—imagine, I thought, the poet, eradicating her only tool of expression. But I thought it was just an idea, not anything that could have actually happened.

First we discussed conjugation. And how there would be none of it. Subjects would always be explicit. We considered *subject-verb-object* structure of the Latin languages versus the free spirited way the Japanese form their sentences, with modifiers that identify the subject, object, adjectives, and the verb always at the end. Although we felt mildly constrained by the forced Latin order, we ultimately decided that it would be best, easiest, simplest.

"Everything must be abstracted as much as possible," he kept insisting. "The perfect language is one where you can communicate effectively in any form—written or verbal." This was where the Japanese influence came in; not with their silly three written languages, but with their phonetic alphabet.

We started simply; dot or no dot. And that led to lines. And that led to characters. Which were sounds. Which formed words, which formed sentences. Which represented, in a very careful way, both what we meant and *how* we meant it.

It started slowly. I never thought it would go anywhere.

But the more we talked about it, the more his eyes lit up with delight at each new idea, each contribution I could provide. I wanted him to be in love with me more than I wanted to write poems about how much I loved him. I wanted to be his partner, to secure my place in his future, and this project seemed to be the perfect way.

The more we worked, though, the more I became obsessed with figuring it all out. When he suggested the noun preceding the adjective, I agreed. An infinitely described object was now possible. We debated, intensely, the need for the period. I finally understood how open the project had become. As the Japanese use ka to distinguish a non-sentence from a sentence (or, a question mark), I considered a noise, also, for the end of a sentence. A pause, a comma, was not enough. It wasn't definitive enough.

"What if I just trailed off in my speaking?" he asked. "What if I just... "

I waited a moment, but he seemed deep in thought.

"Well, then I'll assume you're done talking, and— "

"But I wasn't done speaking," he interrupted me.

"Well then I'll let you finish once I realize you're not done."

"But that throws us off track."

I thought a moment.

"Did you interrupt me on purpose?" I asked.

"Of course," he said. He was all about teaching by example.

Once I realized the religious way I clung to the English language as

I knew it, I did away with capital letters, though I use them now. The silly rules of our language that I had spent time defending, I finally relinquished to the categorization of "useless." What makes a language so difficult to learn is that it is unplanned; it has countless spin-offs, dialects, subtle nuances that defy its own rules. This one wouldn't.

After sentence structure, we covered verb tenses and how to determine them from each other. He was against conjugation, but how else to tell when something happened? Surely we didn't need the 16 verb tenses I had memorized for Italian; but didn't we at least need a past and present tense?

Negating verbs was easy enough to do; we stuck with the Romantic way, putting "no" directly before the verb.

Sentences sounded silly, unromantic, and ridiculous to my ears, but I let it go. It was all merely conceptual, right? I thought.

And then the problem of how to make a noun into an adjective into a verb. Should they all have the same root? And here we came to, what we felt, we were most biased on. All romantic languages have their Latin roots. To try and make each word, "talk" and "talkative," for example, completely different would involve thousands, maybe millions, of unrelated words. Who could ever memorize such a tedious language? It would be as ridiculous as memorizing all 25,000 Kanji symbols. Unnecessary. And our language would be anything but.

Trained as a computer engineer, he wrote out all the technical aspects of the project, all the non-functional requirements, or the "ilities": usability, adaptability, timelessness, learnability. The requirements of every system. "They usually go without saying," he said.

I just tried to keep up. The more I heard about the engineering specs for our language, the more I wanted to finish to project. The deeper and deeper I got in, the less I was able to stop thinking about it at the end of the day.

Once, in the middle of sex, I had the brilliant idea to do away with all sentimentality of the language—"fucking," "making love," "having sex." They would all be one word. There would be no gray area in the actions that were performed. There would be no "like doing," as I was so often predictably saying. And in the midst of this thought, I would scarcely help but run with that line of thought, until the next thing I knew, we were both crouched over the next pad of graph paper we used to plot the whole language, our one long documentation of improvement, and I couldn't remember the word for "orgasm" in either language. Or at all.

I was obsessed with completing the language. We worked on it constantly. I thought about nothing else. I couldn't enjoy anything else.

And then, one day, it was done. It was properly abstracted. It was sensible. All that was left to do was open it to the public as an open-source project and wait for it to take off. Wait for the more liberal countries in the world to adopt it, and our condensed, perfect language would take over.

I wondered if I should try to translate the old works of the poets and writers I had loved. But when I opened up my textbooks and books of poetry, the words didn't make sense to me. I had unlearned the complex and nonsensical language I had spoken. I opened up the *Inferno*, but neither it nor its translation made sense to me. Roethke's words were as strange as ancient hieroglyphics.

I threw the books down. Surely this was a joke. I read some lines aloud, but they had no meaning to me. They were gaudy and thick with description; they were out of order, and they punned on nonsensical rhyme schemes. I picked up a villanelle, but couldn't understand it. I had forgotten my own language—poetry

I brought the empty, nonsensical books to him and showed him their blank pages.

"Why," I asked, "don't I understand these?"

But he only shook his head.

"It's not our language anymore," he said.

Months passed, and our language was a worldwide phenomenon. Within five months, Sweden and Norway were speaking it. Soon after, Canada adopted it. Within a year, all the countries in South America were using UHL. Within ten years, the world had adopted it. I could speak with anyone I wanted to; babies were born thinking that the Chinese and Japanese had always been friends. Disputes that had long gone unresolved were settled in the most polite and diplomatic manner. Wars that would have started were avoided. The world, it seemed, was at peace with itself.

And still, we were not madly in love. I would pick up the old books—collector's items now, rare, not available anywhere to buy—careful not to damage them, not smearing a letter, and I would try to remember what they meant. I would try to resurrect the feeling it gave me to read Keats' "Ode to a Nightingale." I tried to remember the perfect way it slid off my tongue. Hadn't he said something about beauty? Wasn't there something deeper and more meaningful to life than the ability to speak with everyone around you?

The stark, loveless language surrounded and asphyxiated me. I thought I couldn't live without him, but really, I couldn't live without poetry.

I found myself subject to some bit of fame, but intensely unhappy. Unable to express anything in more than a few words, unable to love the language I was speaking, I began to refrain from doing so. The simpleness of our cacophonous, ugly language offended me; its structure and rigidity hurt my tongue; its syllables hurt my mouth to pronounce and my fingers to write. I tried to forget it, but every time I looked at him, I couldn't help but wonder, what verb would I have used to describe our emotions before the language was perfected and condensed like it was now? How could I describe, in what tender language, with what gentle words, how deeply I felt for him? I was left speechless.

I found myself quite out of work at this point, being trained in using words and now boycotting them. I took easily to being mute; he tried to interest me in other projects, but they were of no importance to me. I began to fall out of love.

Elected to the Council of Language, which looked after the language and made sure to keep it straightforward and unified, I soon found myself bored by the endless problems that emerged from the dialects in Africa, and the way Bostonians would mix up the words because of the regionality of their accents.

It bored me. I looked up the word for "suicide" in our new language: "to kill oneself." And I realized that I had already killed myself; I had killed poetry, I had killed the language that I had been in love with; I had killed that which fulfilled me most, and now I was stuck with a loveless, vacant language with no history, no meaning behind it, no reason for existing. No idiosyncrasies, no beauty, no inherited meaning.

I wrote him the only word for "good-bye" that I could—since there was only one. It expressed no grief, no emotion, no meaning at all. It was just a word with some smudges over it, some accents, a few round characters.

And when he picked it up and read it, he didn't understand what had happened. By stripping our language of confusion, of meaning, he had made it impossible for him and I to communicate effectively—or at all.

My death was committed by four hands, but mostly my own two.

Eric Zrinsky

Happy Birthday, Marie Dressler

"Everything was closed at Coney Island," she hummed quietly.

The old window slid open with little resistance. She had raised it countless times since she and Danny moved into the small one-bedroom apartment six months ago. The tiny cement ledge that lay directly beneath had become her favorite part of the property the instant they took up residence on Court Street. Daily, she found a few moments of clarity sitting on her ledge, twenty-seven stories above the street, swinging her legs aimlessly. Climbing through, she swore there was something mournful in the sound the dried paint made as the thin glass scraped upward in the wooden frame.

"Coney Island. Coney Island." The words were bouncing in her mind like billiard balls.

She wanted nothing more than to return to that place. The cross-town bus could get her there, though she'd have to leave right away if she wanted to catch it. Without a doubt, the walk would be more enjoyable anyway.

"Everything is different now," she said out loud and to no one inparticular, but at the same time it made her feel pretty, in a meaningless sort of way.

Danny hardly ever complimented her anymore. She could have been the most beautiful woman in Brooklyn, and Danny would hardly notice her at all. His business was no longer thriving, and of course, there were always more important things to fuss over than the minor formalities of love.

In the street, black Lincolns scuttled like cockroaches with no particular destination, scattering with the flickering indecision of a Boerum Hill traffic light. She saw each of them in slow motion, and when she looked down at her bandaged wrists, the deep red stains seemed at odds with the crisp white edges of the clean linen wrap. They were like the pictures you made in the Spin Art stand at Coney. She and Danny had gone there on their first date, now almost twelve years past, and had pretended to be world renowned artists, instead of a couple of drunken 19-year-olds squeezing bright bottles of cheap paint onto rotating squares of paper.

"No line at the carousel today," she said, the open air doing its best to ignore her completely.

It wouldn't matter how late Danny was to celebrate her birthday. Today was her day, and she would delight in it on her own terms. She could ride that white horse all afternoon and there would be nothing or no one to stop her, the bright tinkling music of the carousel reverberating in her spine like the voice of a mother saying, "Welcome home, dear. You did a good thing today. There's no reason to worry anymore."

For a moment, she imagined herself in Dreamland Park before the Hell's Gate fire: the imitation Swiss landscape, Venetian gondola rides, and the entire village of dwarves sweeping past her with an air of refinement. She would become Marie Dressler: Broadway actress, Vaudevillian, outspoken goddess; and the handsomely mustached, one-armed lion tamer, Captain Bonavita, would take her as his lover. They would entertain throughout the day; she running the popcorn stands, constantly fawned over for her artistry and radiance; he staving back the ferocious Black Prince during the contractual six shows a day. The nights, however, would be theirs. Making love in the shadow of the immeasurable, white, Dreamland Tower, all of the one million electric light bulbs burning only for them.

It had begun to snow all across Brooklyn. She thought about the flakes falling on Stillwell Avenue, of the inevitable accumulation on the floors of the carts hanging motionless on the Wonder Wheel. She felt her unwashed hair blowing like dirty brown drapes in the strong wind as her bare feet scraped over the cold concrete ledge. Somewhere, a fire escape swings dangerously in the wind. The intersection at Court and Livingstone is still busy, miles below, people rushing to and from wherever they will be or wherever they will go. In her head she recited a few lines that she composed earlier in the week while sitting on her ledge.

Life will move forward, time will drift on.

They will forget me.

Concrete will crack.

And weeds will grow in the center of Broadway.

The whole world is swallowed in black.

She smiled at the thought of this, finding comfort in its familiarity. It was something she dreamed about often, an unending night time, packs of dogs wandering the streets, reclaiming what was once theirs.

"What would you think of me now, Danny?"

He always had a nervous way of justifying her problems to the neighbors ("She's had a rough life, you know") or talking too loudly in elevators about the prescriptions she took ("Don't feel bad honey, the Risperdal will help all these delusions go away for good"). She didn't want to be understood, not this time. Fuck what the others thought. She wanted to ride the Cyclone, to grip the cold metal bars and to feel the seatbelt hugging her tightly around her middle. She wanted to feel fast, a timeless ebb in the flow of insignificance. She wanted to be a bird, or better still, a bird's feather fluttering in the breeze of a passing cross-town bus. She was excited now, her chest heaving up and down heavily.

"Happy Birthday, Marie Dressler," she thought, smiling to herself.

The ground shuttered under the impact and traffic screeched to a halt. Somewhere someone hummed, "Everything was closed at Coney Island."

Furrah Qureshi

Jane Brown

We are all confined. We employees are all compromising. We on the second floor are all suffocated. We in the right wing are all bored. We in the file room are all dreamers. Anyone who finds themselves in a lowly job void of creativity possesses the greatest amount of untapped creativity.

It was Tuesday and I was alone and I wished I wasn't and I wished my name was not Jane. The connotation of Jane is "Plain Jane" and I certainly fit it: brown hair, brown eyes, brown clothes, I was Brown, my last name was. I am Jane Brown. Average height, average weight, I was a mix of descent from different European countries that now had no significance in my ethnicity due to the presence of so many of them. I belonged to no one, with no one, and I had no companions. I ate dinner in front of the television and then went to sleep.

I never have dreams. I can't ever harness and channel my originality into a beam of randomness; I can only recall, I can't prove anything. That night all there was were memories. I started off dreaming of making my first batch of muffins at five years old. I poured muffin mix into a bowl, chopped up strawberries, added a pinch of sugar, just a pinch, and then started mixing them with a large wooden spoon, in my car. I was fifteen and driving on the highway, at twenty-five miles an hour, while all the other cars raced by me at what I perceived to have been ninety miles an hour. I drove right to a restaurant where I was to be having my twentieth birthday party. Five of my friends were there, I only had five. I opened up my purse and rolled a pair of dice onto the monopoly board and it landed on—

On Wednesday when I went to work I found my self out of imperative things to do at only ten o'clock. I don't know why my employers expect me to do excessive amounts of busy work. I hate them by the way.

I stared at the clock, 10:05, 10:15, 10:30, 11:06, 11:05—it was terrible. I swiveled a little in my chair, folded and unfolded paper, tried to write my name enough times so that it might actually mean something—it was readful. Then by three o'clock I was fed up, with myself. I grabbed a pile of papers and began to walk around acting as if I was busy. I entered the elevator and the mail guy was there.

"Hey Jane," he said.

I was shocked he knew my name.

"Hi."

"Well I've run out of things to do, have you?" he asked me.

"Yes, at ten," I replied laughing.

"What do you do to slaughter the time away?"

"Everything, well, I think about everything."

"Me too. It's funny though."

"What?"

"I don't see you slaughtering anything." We both laughed.

"If only I could," I said staring away from him at the wall of the elevator.

"Do you want to go watch a movie with me tonight?"

"On Wednesday?"

"Why not, it's the exact middle of the week, the best day."

"Alright."

That Wednesday night we watched *The Matrix*, the next Wednesday *The Shawshank Redemption*, and when we were watching *Jerry Maguire* he leaned in and kissed me.

Over the course of the next few months, he gained my trust. I loved his exoticism. He was a 6'1, wild haired, grey-eyed, slightly crooked nosed man of Slavic descent. He was proof of the existence of something more. We'd give each other rides to work and meet in the evenings to watch movies. After we had sex, which we did a couple of times a week, he'd tell me about absolutely everything. Movies, the past, the future, nature, books, places, we talked about everything except for work. I always got the feeling that he didn't like to be reminded of his monotonous job. So I didn't remind him.

But that's not how it goes with a used-to-be-insecure person, because nobody used to be insecure, you either are or you aren't, and I was. I couldn't rid myself of my non-dreams.

Nights would pass where I spent hours doing my phonics homework from grade school only for it to turn into a basketball as I aimed in gym class when in junior high to inexorably miss. I'd turn around, ball in hand, to a crowd of staring people from anyone who was nobody in my life. Front row center sat my parents with a sorry look on their faces as they squirmed uncomfortably. Second row left sat my teacher from sophomore year in high school pushing her glasses up as she stared at nothing in particular. And then in the very back, the farthest corner from me, somewhere in Siberia, a billion miles a way, a thousand leagues under the sea and a hundred light-years from the stage I was standing. I saw myself.

It had been months into my relationship and I couldn't accept it. The way he looked at me, the way he smiled at me, the way he spoke to me, it was almost admirational— I really just couldn't fathom that anyone would ever feel anything of the sort to me.

So I began to distrust him. I noticed the women of the office that he spoke to, the way their hair bounced when they walked, the way he sometimes looked off into space when I was speaking to him, the way he sometimes would raise his eyebrows in disagreement with me and sort of smirk before he would rebut me, they way he always looked downward before he told me he loved me, the quality of the things he'd buy me, the number of times he rubbed the stubble on his chin while he sat across from me on our lunch break, the way he didn't care if any other men would talk to me, the manner in which he told me jokes, how much he bothered to clean his apartment before I'd get there, and that it was all proof of how crazy I was to notice.

I believe it was a Saturday (but I couldn't prove it) when I realized that there was something not right in our relationship. I felt that he constantly was not as truthful with me as I had always expected a lover should. Yearsof being alone had given time for an idealized notion of love to foster in my head and control my heart—and so I was incapable of continuous jubilance.

But, then a few days later, three, while I was in his apartment brushing my hair he called me into his sitting room.

"What is it?" I inquired, uninterested. He was sitting in a plain white button down shirt with his sleeves rolled up and in jeans. He looked quite nice. He pulled from a bag five envelopes and called me to sit next to him.

"Whose mail is that?" I asked, not recognizing the names.

"Some people from the office."

"Did you forget to give it to them? Are you saving it for tomorrow?"

"No."

"Then why do you have it? Do you know them?"

"No."

I stared at him.

"Every day, I take five envelopes, and I burn them."

"Every day?"

"Well, I take them everyday I go to work, but sometimes I don't burn them until the end of the week."

"How long have you been doing this?"

"Since a little after I got the job."

"... Why?"

"Mm, mmm."

I continued to stare at him.

"Wanna burn one?"

"No" I responded, slightly irritated, turning away from him.

"What?" he exclaimed, suddenly jumping up.

I stood too. "I don't want to burn any fucking envelopes, OK?" I had never used that word before.

"Forget it okay," he said, calming down and turning towards me again. "I don't know why—"

"What, would I not get it?" I asked, tilting my head to the side, my arms folded.

"Sometimes I really don't get you," he said, laughing.

I wanted to tell him there was nothing to get, that I was just a boring fileroom junkie. But I didn't know what to say, I had never possessed a way with words. So I went home.

"I know the mail thing is a little weird, but is it that repulsive?" he asked me on the telephone.

"It's not repulsive."

"I love you... are you okay?"

"I'm not... not okay."

"Don't you love me at all? Why the hell am I the one who always has to say it first?"

"I don't hate you."

"Nobody even notices when their mail is gone."

"Well I never noticed."

"I never stole mail from you."

"...I never got mail," I said, silently sobbing. Tears were pouring unrestrictedly from my face. It was a trained technique, perfected during nights under the covers listening to my parents fight, during all the school functions I never went to, all the dates I declined out of sheer shyness, those times I made myself a neglected dinner late at night, the times at the bathroom sink, at the kitchen table, in front of the fireplace, on the living room couch, by the lamp, in the backyard, and sometimes, in my sleep.

"I'm not understanding what happened. Just tell me."

"It all already happened."

"What?"

"Lots of things, lots of times, lots of years ago."

"Do you want me to come over there?"

"It has nothing to do with you."

"Well... are you at least going to come over and watch a movie with me tonight? It's Wednesday."

I was silent.

"We can watch any movie you want."

"Why are you a mail guy?" I suddenly asked, feeling cold. I could tell my question made him cold; we were both freezing.

"It just... happened."

"That's what I say about my file room job."

"Yeah, I know, we always had a lot in common."

I hung up.

I stopped answering his calls, avoided him in the office, ate lunch alone in my car to stay clear of him, listened through doors before I opened them to be conscious of who was on the other side, walked away from the file room if I heard any sort of wheels that could have possibly been a mail cart, got into the habit of walking into a bathroom to check myself in the mirror every single time I passed one—which averaged to be around fifteen times a day—started to carry a comb in my pocket to be able to fix any flyaway hairs at any time, went on a diet of wheat bread and celery, sniffed my shoulders stealthily to insure that I exuded a scent of strawberry, got into the habit of biting my lips—which caused them to be chapped—so I carried chapstick around, and soon enough my pockets were so full of combs and chapsticks and mirrors that they made my hips look too wide and all the time I hated him more. The first few days he called me excessively, the next few sporadically, then once over the course of the next week, and then none.

One random day that I can not recall the name of, my two bosses were meandering about the file room and chatting. I, of course, eavesdropped.

"Seriously Don, it's time to let him go."

"Yeah, I guess."

"You can get any old mail guy, it's not like it's a job of wits."

They both snickered. Not a laugh, not a smirk, not a chuckle, a snicker.

"Um, Jane?" my boss Don asked me.

"Yes?" I said, as my head shot up quickly, surprised he had addressed me.

"You've been here some time right?"

"Some time."

"Are you familiar with... um... er... what's his name, that mail guy?"

"Uhh, yeah." I said, smiling to ward off any hints in my facial muscles that might reveal just how well I knew him.

"Is he any good here? We're thinking of letting him go."

"...He's no good."

Now that it's all over and the time has passed I desperately wished I had it back, that chance. Just like all the chances I had, the way I could have added sugar to my muffins at five, or speeded on a highway at fifteen or approached the good-looking guy in the restaurant at twenty. It's been so long since those moments that I can't remember if they actually happened or if they were just a dream. I know exactly what I would have said. I would have said, "He's no good, but neither am I, I quit." I'm still sitting here in my apartment at the wise old age of 26 and it's been over three years since that moment.

I always imagine him as a painter or a writer or a comedian something, something free.

But I am no longer who I used to be. No longer do I have dreams that aren't really dreams, or count the minutes that pass as I wish I were someone else with some other name, or do a job that requires no work. Did love and redemption ever truly exist in this world? If so, then there are no other words for what I felt for him. But, Oh God, Oh God, Oh God, Oh God! I was so tired of it all. I was tired enough to relinquish all aspects of my uniqueness and all remnants of good times, and for what? For what have I given up the only person in the world who had made me believe through cinematic mastery, persuaded me with poetic debates and eccentric mail burning, and proved to me that I was in fact a me.

I learned that the past could be shed like some old garment that was hideous and thrown into a pile in the corner of the bedroom. Maybe years later it would be picked up again only to rediscover that it had been repulsive to begin with. I could throw it away forever. And then finally, you can't live life trying to prove others wrong, because you have to prove yourself right.

That's really what I had to say, so I must end this resignation letter here and now before it turns sour, again.

Sincerely,
Jane Brown

P.S. He burned the mail so that he could feel free. I wish I burned mail. But I am no mailman.

Deborah Yarchun

Lingo

The street below the El on Broadway and DeKalb was bizarrely empty despite the fact it was dawn. Stale wisps of KFC and Dunkin Donuts coffee blended together in the wind as Jeremiah rounded the corner. He did his best to practice a tighter stride, shoulders back, head high and all that, but found himself slumping back into a loose shuffle. It was too early in the a.m. to adjust his posture for any personal validations, so he fell back into what had characterized his life through high school—that tough alpha-male, king of the street stride.

He was joined by the crunch of boots against glass shards. That's how he noticed her.

Her white heeled Yeti boots covered half her legs. Black tights, the rest, right up to her short grunge skirt with holes she'd probably paid extra for at some Urban Outfitters. Her blonde pony tail was pulled back tight with streaks of reddish highlights that glinted in the sun as it rose over the El.

Everything about her screamed ironic snobbery right down to the crunch of her boots. She must have just stepped out of Goodbye Blue Monday, a hipster oasis/Internet café/clear attempt to make gritty Bushwick the new hot spot, the new Williamsburg.

As their eyes connected, her Yeti boots halted. She'd stopped dead in her tracks and was staring back at him, hipster in the headlights. It didn't take him a second glance to know what this meant. She was scared of him. She thought he was a thug. She'd already consigned him in her mind. Convicted him. He swiveled forward and continued walking, suddenly conscious of the way his pants sagged off his ass.

The footsteps behind him followed, but in his peripheral vision he caught her eyes darting across the street. She was considering her outs, carefully weighing her options. The closed strip club was on their side, the storefront church on the other. She crossed the street. He followed. She must have felt reassured by the fact that he was in front of her, because she kept walking. That and the fact that she didn't have a choice, he was standing between her and the only entrance to the El on Myrtle. Behind him, he could sense her pace slowing, trying to draw distance between them. He could feel her eyes hawking him and his throat tightening.

His fist clenched, as he suppressed the urge to scream back, "Yo! Yeti bitch! I'm not going to rob you!"

She didn't know, he thought. She couldn't know that today was the bona fide start of his new life. He was going to catch the J to the Ghost line, to the F and then down to Kingsborough Community College where he planned to enroll. For Kingsborough he had sagged an inch less and worn a shirt a size too small to be cool. He'd even worn long sleeves to cover his inked-up arm.

He watched as she walked on edge, as if he was going to suddenly spin around with a Glock and fill her private-schooled brain with holes like the ones that dappled her skirt. She'd marked him.

He jingled the chain that connected one pocket to the other, at first unconsciously. Then, as he thought of the effect it might have on her, intentionally. Leeringly, he clinked it at a steady rhythm. Did she feel threatened? He thrust his fists into his pockets and jangled them around. Maybe he had an itch. Maybe a knife.

She don't know my thoughts. She doesn't know my thoughts, he corrected himself.

Lately he'd been deep in the lingo, teasing out the grammatical differences between the hipsters and the cripsters. He'd concluded that ghetto is a state of mind and that it all comes down to whether "you is" or "you are." With careful practice, his "she don'ts" were becoming "she doesn'ts," his "ax," "ask," his "aights," "all rights." She couldn't have known this, not that she would give a shit.

He paused hoping she'd step past him, but she had stopped too. She also couldn't have known that as part of his personal studies, he'd even been inside Goodbye Blue Monday once. Hipster insignia, amongst baby dolls, strings of lights and vintage stuff crapped up the interior. Enough to make a stoner freak. For all this bitch knew, he could have slammed down a two-buck PBR right next to her.

A group of twelve year-old prosti-tots with skirts shorter than Britney Spears's punctuated his thought. They strolled past them, but barely cut the tension. He wondered if she felt safer, now they weren't totally alone.

The girls' high-pitched squeals echoed down the streets and dissipated as they turned onto Willoughby.

He made another sudden movement towards his pocket and then continued walking. He was beginning to enjoy the hell out of jerking this *bougie cracka ass chick* around. Finally, he reached the stairs to the El, climbed halfway up, stood against the wall and waited. He worried that she might have mace, but kept at it anyway.

From above, he watched her stop at the bottom. Saw her hesitate, almost turn back. Then with a conviction that surprised him, she took a deep breath and strutted up the stairs. He let her pass. But still, the game was too good.

As she reached the top of the steps, he pulled his knife out.

Amber Turner

Crazy

I'm crazy. No, I'm not batshit-crazy like Britney Spears. I haven't shaved my head or attacked someone's car with an umbrella. I'm not scary-crazy like Rosie O'Donnell and Michael Jackson. I don't verbally abuse my co-workers or think I'm still 12. I wasn't even kidnapped by aliens—I'm a lesbian—now I'm straight and cheating on my husband with another man-crazy like Anne Heche—I'm more fun-crazy like Mariah Carey, pre-breakdown, circa Glitter. Or maybe it's post-breakdown, circa now—who can really keep up with all her antics? All I know is that I'm crazy. I make no apologies for it, it's just a part of me like my black hair and brown eyes.

My therapist of three years, John, tried to convince me otherwise. His diagnosis? I'm *severely depressed*. "What's the difference between that and manic depression which is just another word for bipolar?" I asked.

"Well, you'd have to be analyzed by a psychiatrist," he said. "I'm a psychologist so I couldn't completely analyze you to figure out if you meet the criteria in place to qualify as a person with bipolar."

My first thought was, *Well, what the hell am I doing here if he's not qualified to qualify me as being psycho?!* But since I'm not typically the rude type, I kept that question to myself. Instead I asked, "So you can't just give me some pills to help me get out of bed in the morning and be done with it? Prozac or Lithium will do. Maybe some Zoloft—I hear that's good."

He just looked at me and laughed. "I can't prescribe you anything because, again, I'm not certified to do that. And most likely, you won't even need it—pills should be a last resort for you."

We went back and forth for ten minutes, arguing over my eagerness to get out of continuing therapy and opting instead to medicate myself with synthetic hormones, hormones that I didn't even need according to John.

"You're not crazy, dear," he said to me in all earnestness.

"But how do you know that I'm not crazy? You're not qualified to analyze me, remember?"

"You're not crazy," he repeated, same exasperated expression playing across his face.

"But how do you *know*? I could be crazy, everything I *do* is crazy!!"

"What do you do that's crazy, Amber?"

"I disappear on people, sometimes for days at a time; I talk to myself frequently, and I mean, full, drawn-out, animated conversations; I sleep all day if I can, I sit around in the dark and I've created a whole other life for myself in my head. I can't even watch the Discovery Health channel anymore because I become *convinced* that I suffer from whatever ailment they're spotlighting that day. Does that sound normal to you?!"

John smiled. "You're not crazy. Crazy people don't think they're crazy. Genuinely crazy people believe that everything they do is 100% normal. So, you see: if you think you're crazy you're obviously aware of what you're doing and therefore can not be crazy."

Damn. He had a point. Or did he? Is it possible that someone can know when they're about to lose it? Maybe I really *am* crazy, but I haven't progressed deep enough into my neuroses.

Mental illness is usually split into three categories: neurosis, psychosis, and sociopathy. Neurotics tend to be people who have high anxiety, depression and hypochondria, while psychotics suffer delusions of grandeur, hallucinations, incoherence, and mania. The main difference between the two is that neurotics are aware of their situation and actively seek help to rid themselves of their disease while psychotics, like John pointed out, don't think anything is wrong with them. And poor sociopaths don't fit into either category because they're so screwed up—they're generally known as psychopaths, somebody affected with a personality disorder marked by aggressive, violent, antisocial thought and behavior and a lack of remorse or empathy. Now, by my therapist's own admission, I suffer from depression so it's not a stretch to think that I'd be a neurotic, right? I occasionally refer to myself in the third person (psychosis)—"Amber is sad right now," "Amber's about to bust some heads," "Amber is fabulous"—and sure, I sometimes think about pushing my roommate down the steps because she's super annoying; but, who doesn't nowadays? If people didn't think highly of themselves, there would be no professors, no Hollywood movie stars, no pop divas; nobody would run for public office or become Catholic priests. The world would be boring. As for wanting to hit my roommate, I would *think* it, but I wouldn't actually *do* it—I'm not an animal, I have self-control. Plus, I'm too little and too cute to go to jail. Big Bertha would be wearing me around her neck as a scarf.

So if most people do most of the things associated with mental illness, does that mean everyone's crazy? I could philosophize on this for days and I'm aware that there are varying degrees to which most people do the aforementioned things; therefore, most people are only probably slightly neurotic. I don't know—I haven't done the research or a census so I couldn't tell you what the answer really is, but I can say this: I don't care what John says, I am totally cuckoo for Cocoa Puffs.

It makes sense seeing as though my mom's younger brother is schizophrenic. My uncle, like many of the people suffering with this disease, was diagnosed in his late teens and early twenties with bipolar disorder. Because of his hard drug use, alcohol abuse and the mental and physical abuse he suffered as a kid at the hands of my deranged grandfather, his bipolar escalated to paranoid schizophrenia in his thirties. Read the literature on mental illness and you'll find that it's genetic/hereditary. Since both of my grandparents are nutcases, my uncle's certifiable, my mom's oldest brother and my own father display sociopathic tendencies and my mother is a mess, it was only natural that I'd become a wreck, too.

I remember realizing that something was wrong with me when I was about six-years-old. I wasn't like the other kids. I was outgoing, yes; I had friends, but something was still a little off. I was a timid child, afraid of my own shadow, and then suddenly I'd become enraged and would fight with people. It was the strangest thing. Kids get picked on all the time; it's sort of like a right of passage into adulthood, but I just couldn't take it. More often than not, someone would get hit or cursed out (I had quite the mouth on me in the first grade, courtesy of a public school education, thank you very much!) and the attacks would be vicious. I recall calling some kid's mom "a fucking dirty whore" even though I didn't know what that meant and it was an unprovoked outburst, or at least what the kid did to me didn't warrant that kind of language, although I can't remember now, it being so long ago. I also bullied a lot of my so-called "friends" so I doubt they really hung around me because they liked me, more like they were terrified I'd drop kick them in the head or something.

Things went horribly wrong the following year when I was molested. I don't remember the specifics and who the fuck would want to? All I know is that it happened repeatedly by someone I was close to and trusted—it was a nightmare. I never told my mom and she still doesn't know; it would break her heart and she'd just blame herself. But because I couldn't talk about it, I got angry. I got so angry, in fact, that I internalized that anger and began hating myself. I hated everything about me: my hair (I hated the braids my mom would spend hours doing), my face (my nose was too fat and my head too big), my body (I had a fat gut and boys would tease me), everything. I couldn't even look at myself in the mirror without crying. Hell, I *still* can't, and don't even think about trying to take my picture. It's horrible, but I just felt useless. I guess that's around the time I began imagining an alter-ego for myself in my mind.

My alter-ego doesn't have a name exactly. No, as generic as my name is, I can't really envision myself with anything else. I've tried, but the names never stick for long. I was Charisma Bradford, Janelle Chambers, Ava Loren Moore, and countless others that came and went. It was nice being these different people and adopting different personas to go with the name changes. Ironically, my alter ego isn't quite that different from the real me. She's much prettier with skin not riddled from acne scarring, but she's still funny and talented. She's got way more friends than I do, but she's still just as loyal to them as I am to the handful of people I consider friends in real life. She still has the same convictions and beliefs as me, and she still thinks she's a nut; however, where we differ is, this girl doesn't let anything keep her down or have her feeling bad about herself.

She's a famous singer/songwriter/actress/screenwriter/journalist; she's got a super hot musician boyfriend named Will; she has three Oscars, a Tony award, *and* twelve Grammys; and she's insanely rich and happy. This is what I imagine all day, every day. I spend so much time in that world that I get accused of not living in this one. Yet, John thinks I'm normal. I don't know about anyone else, but I don't know one other person who does this. Although, I think I would be awfully intrigued if I did ever meet anyone else who did this. Maybe our alter-egos could become friends and, if it's a male, we could run off and get married in a three-million-dollar ceremony befitting a pop culture icon such as myself—all of this would be in our minds, of course. Poor Will would be drop kicked to the curb, though, and I'd feel bad about that. He's been such a great boyfriend all these years.

And that is why I *have* to be crazy! Who has an imaginary boyfriend that they've planned their life with? Not a normal person. I would've planned my life with my ex, Che, but he doesn't want to be with me because he thinks I'm psycho. That may have something to do with the fact that he's not *actually* my ex, meaning we didn't *actually* date, but we did have sex so I thought that should count and then proceeded to infringe myself upon every aspect of his life. I would call, text, and instant-message him obsessively and then, if he didn't answer in a timely manner, I would resort to berating him about his rude behavior. I wanted him to be my boyfriend so bad that I forced him to swear that he wouldn't sleep with anyone else, and then I wouldn't even bother to have sex with him myself or open up to him emotionally. I think I can count on one hand the amount of times I said anything of substance to him. I wouldn't even really be listening to him when he was talking to me about his life. That is, until I was angry at him for cheating on me when, technically, since we weren't a couple, he should've been free to do what he wanted. I listened to him bitch and moan about his messed-up childhood, things he'd say to me in confidence mind you, and then I'd write a nice little blog on MySpace about it. *That will teach him to disobey me!* I thought.

He was *not* pleased with Amber. In fact, all the little quirky things that initially drew him to me (the speaking in the third person, the ability to just say whatever it is I think with abandon, the overactive imagination), wound up being the exact things that scared him off. Then there was the fact that I kept contacting him after we "broke up" and would curse him even more than I did when we were together—that didn't go over well, either. Our final conversation pretty much summed it up: "Hey, Che—it's Amber. I just wanted to see how you are."

"I'm good."

"Well, that's good I guess. You know you made a huge mistake by walking out on me. You are going to grow old and die alone because you're an asshole." Pause.

"Um, Amber, I have a girlfriend and we're getting married."

"What?! We just stopped talking last week!"

"Yeah, well, I've been talking to her for awhile now and we have a lot in common."

"Like what, you're both whores?"

Laughter. "No, but that's funny."

"How is my pain funny? And what the hell does she have that I don't?"

"Amber, I don't want to talk about this. I'm sorry you're hurt, but let's just leave it as is."

"No! Tell me what I want to know *now!*"

"You really want to know?"

"*Yes!*"

"Okay—you're fuckin' crazy. It's just that simple. My girlfriend may not be as fun as you, but at least she's not an emotional ticking time bomb like you. I can't deal with your craziness anymore—you should really look into getting some medication."

Needless to say, we won't be walking down the aisle in the future.

I remember the last time I saw my uncle, the schizo. It was maybe five years ago. He was in really bad shape mentally. Over his life, he's been committed more times than I can keep track of and this time he decided he was going to leave home for good. He didn't feel like he could offer anybody anything anymore and he was terrified that his wife was trying to kill him. Sadly, he wasn't going to a mental hospital this time; he packed a backpack with as many clothes as he could, put on three layers of clothes, a couple pairs of socks so he wouldn't get cold, and prepared to live on the streets where he was "safe." He hadn't shaved in what looked like years and he kept talking to himself, laughing occasionally and breaking into song about Rapunzel letting down her hair. I looked in his eyes and it was the scariest thing ever—there was nothing there. He was completely gone and at that moment, I knew he was never coming back. I wanted to cry, but I swallowed the lump in my throat and just sat there. I looked at my cousins' faces and all three of them looked so forlorn and lost. Nobody spoke. They were terrified of him. If he talked to them, they wouldn't look him in the face. When he walked by my cousin, Calvin, my cousin practically jumped out of his skin to get as far away from him as he possibly could. My aunt later told us the reason for the kids' fear was because my uncle had threatened to kill them. He said that a man was talking to him from Calvin's stomach, telling him to kill my cousin and his sisters. When my aunt gave my uncle the ultimatum to either go to a mental hospital or get out, he chose the streets. He didn't trust doctors, they were out to get him. So were the CIA and the President.

I cried that night when I was alone. I cried because I remembered the uncle that was funny and vibrant, the one who was clearly on his medication when I was a kid because he was never that far gone—at least, I don't have any recollection of any abnormal behavior. Maybe I just didn't see it then. Maybe the humor and the vibrancy was the mania at work. I cried because my cousins lost their father and the youngest one would never know his dad when he was stable. I cried because I looked at my uncle and I completely understood how he got there. He was always the sensitive one in the family. My mom and her older brother were strong emotionally, but their younger brother would crack under the littlest pressures. My brother is tough; he gets it from my mom. But I was always the one who cried at the drop of a dime. It wasn't hard to hurt me and break me down. I looked at my uncle, who'd been beaten like he was a grown man from the time he was seven-years-old until he left home as a teen, and I saw myself. I was always close to my uncle, being that he's my godfather, and I always felt like we were kindred spirits. So if this could happen to him, what's going to happen to me?

John would say that I'm nowhere near where my uncle is and won't have to worry about that. He'd probably be accurate. I've never been institutionalized and I'm not on medication of any sort. So maybe I'm not crazy after all. Or maybe I'm just crazy enough to be called crazy by everyone who meets me, but I came up one point short on the bipolar test so I'm "normal." Or maybe I've become so desperate for an identity, any identity, that I'll gladly take the crazy label just to fit in somewhere even if it's not the most glamorous place to be. It's a thought, one John would most likely say was correct. But then again, I stopped seeing John so I wouldn't know. Will thinks John's a waste of time and says he loves me just the way I am. And that's fine with me.

Ali Cahill

Re-Writing "The Black Cat"

Recently, Jack and I went to go explore the Edgar Allan Poe House on 7th and Spring Garden. When we got off the El at Spring Garden, the clouds loomed ominously over our heads on the walk to 7th street, almost as if they knew where we were going and were preparing the mood.

As we approached the house, the Raven statue outside seemed to be flapping its dark wings at us in the overcast sky, either welcoming or warning us; I'm not sure which. The big metal door-knock also helped set the mood; Jack picked it up and knocked it once. It let out a loud bang.

Inside, we watched the movie about Poe's life. He was such a successful writer; he had stories published all the time, and poetry, too! I was impressed. His death was very mysterious. I didn't know it was such a mystery, but I surmised that it was a fitting end for a writer whose life focused on the tragic and the gory. I asked Jack what really happened as he usually knows much more about all things literary than I do, but he said he didn't know. I thought to myself that I should write a screenplay about it.

We then got into a discussion with one of the very friendly park rangers who service the house, and he led us immediately into the basement. As "The Black Cat" was published while Poe lived there, we looked around the basement and the park ranger told us about how the description in the story matches nearly identically the basement we were all standing in. It was a little creepy. The rain started to fall in delicate splatters, and the sky was getting darker. It seemed to be a sign. Jack joked about bricking me up inside the false chimney.

The three of us went back upstairs and the ranger gave us a guide for the house and Jack and I walked around. We toured the entire house, which was old and creaky and kind of eerie; we looked in all the closets at the various artifacts, letters, drawings, and pictures that were left to further explain the significance of each room. First, was a very bare kitchen, with a crumbling wall and fireplace. We went upstairs into Poe's room, which was big and had some nice windows that must have provided a stunning view back in the time when Poe lived there. We watched the rain fall.

Up the stairs we went again, to the third floor. They creaked ominously. It wasn't thundering, but it felt like it should be. In Virginia's room, it was dark, and I told Jack not to touch anything or breathe in or he would get tuberculosis. Across the hall in Muddy's room, Jack stopped to admire something in the closet, and I took the liberty of locking him inside it. When I let him out (only a second later), he did not look entertained, but in the dark of the closet, his un-amused face looked even creepier and gorier than it normally does.

We followed the stairs back down and found ourselves outside in the rain, face to face with the Raven. Standing next to the statue, it was much bigger than it looked from the street. I took a picture of it. Jack and I stepped back inside to get out of the rain, and wandered back down into the basement again. I had an idea.

"Jack," I said, "take a picture of me in the little chimney, like you're going to brick me up."

"Don't tempt me," he said.

But I climbed into the false chimney anyway and he shot a picture with his camera phone.

It was, I thought, awfully difficult to smush myself inside the small false chimney. I pulled my legs in and twisted my arms up, trying to look as disfigured as possible.

Done with reenacting "The Black Cat" for our own pleasure, we headed back up the stairs when I realized there was still one more room we had yet to see—the den. This room was definitely my favorite, and Jack and I sat down on the surprisingly comfortable couch and leafed through some of Poe's literary magazines and poetry. I wish they had copies of some of his literary magazines to buy, even if they were reconstructed, because they were really intricate and Gothic-looking, and their design definitely caught my eye. "It would be cool," I mused aloud, "if *Maya* looked like this." Jack quickly said he would construct a similar-looking front cover, and I was glad I let him out of Muddy's closet.

We meandered back into the main room and flipped through the various books of poetry and short stories, T-shirts, and letters written by Poe, but nothing really caught our eye. We thanked the park ranger who had greeted us earlier, and as we opened the door to leave, discovered it was now pouring rain. The walk (or run) back to the El was a fitting end to the Poe visit. On the train platform, I shook the rain out of my hair and shivered. Between the creepy weather, the darkness of the house, and the chimney experience, I was ready to write some moody poetry and contemplate Poe. All in all, I think I have a better understanding of his views on life, and on the time period in general, after sitting by the marble fireplaces and being walled up in the faux-chimney in the basement. And of course, my good friend Jack is my favorite literary companion, with his odd enthusiasm for all things macabre, which is suitable for being locked in a closet; but I'm glad he's not.

Ian Micir

Rebel with an Older, Smarter Sister

Here's every Thursday night of my childhood that I can remember: my dad's friends come over; they shoot pool; they drink cheap beer; they smoke about a half an acre of a tobacco farm. They never leave. (They eventually left of course, but at that age, midnight was still considered late, so I was usually fast asleep by the time the last set of drunkenly uneven footsteps made their way down the driveway.)

They were the coolest guys in the world. I remember my dad would let me hang out with them in the basement if my homework was done. That rule never quite made much sense to me, considering the computer was in the basement, so I was down there regardless. Years later, I realized he was just drunk, but whatever—was young and dumb, and he got away with it. Cheers Pop.

One Thursday night I got slammed with some bullshit project in school that was sure to take me a few hours. In all honesty, I don't remember a damn thing about the project; I just remember I was pissed about having to do it. The only homework assignments that I ever took seriously were English assignments. Scratch that. The only assignments that I ever took seriously were *creative* English assignments. My philosophy at the time was: with all due respect to Hemingway, Shakespeare, and all the other fallen greats, fuck book reports and anything else where you have to base your entire piece on the writing of someone else, rather than creating your own line of thought. I understood that we all had to learn from those who'd done it best, but I never liked the idea of simply regurgitating another's work.

So instead of doing this other assignment, I decided to write a paper on why busywork homework, like said assignment, is complete bullshit. Through a cloud of smoke, loud music, and profanity after each miscue on the pool table, I wrote my piece. I had a knack for persuasive writing, and I drew a lot of parallels to the real world (no, not the TV show for self-loathing drama addicts). My ongoing theme of the paper was that the schooling system was a lie, in that they told us they were preparing their students to enter the real world. In an echo of my favorite Mark Twain quote[1], my argument was that they did the exact opposite.

I wrote that in the real world, you get paid for the extra work you do outside of your scheduled hours. Hell, if the work's hard enough, you might even get overtime. Whereas, in school, you do it for miniscule credit at best, and if you don't do it at all, they chop the legs out from under an easy A.

I don't remember exactly what my comparison was between a kid who can ace a test without doing the homework and Jimi Hendrix, but it was something involving the line, "All the practice in the world won't get one person in a billion to play a guitar like Jimi." Looking back on it, it sounds completely ridiculous (I've since realized that Hendrix didn't fall out of the womb with an extensive knowledge of psychedelic rock), but I swear at the time, I thought it was a great essay that made some pretty valid points.

I was a celebrity for a day. I showed my best friend the paper and he made me print out copies and hand them out to a bunch of people. For the next few hours, I'd catch random high fives in the hallway and pats on the back from people I barely knew. It was great. I was a revolutionary genius.

Above all, there was one person I couldn't wait to tell—my sister, Melanie, who, at the time, was majoring in English at Columbia University. Growing up, I'd hear her reading her class papers to my parents and they were so proud that someone so young was so damn smart. She was, and continues to be, the best writer that I know first-hand. I wanted to be her, and I suppose I still do, from a writing standpoint.

So after school, I walked down to the computer, pulled up the essay, and fired it out in an e-mail that I'd hoped she'd get right away. Three days later, I got my response; and thirty seconds after that, I was embarrassed.

I never knew anybody could be ripped apart in so few words. She gave me a short paragraph about how disrespectful I was to everyone who'd ever bothered to teach me a damn thing. I got that. I understood immediately, and I wished I'd never written a word of it. While I don't remember all of her exact words, I do remember these: "Ian, you're good, but if you don't learn to be more responsible with your writing, it won't take you anywhere."

Responsible. Writing. Two words I'd never thought could co-exist so closely in the same sentence. If some guy had walked up to me the day before and told me I should be more responsible with my writing, I would have looked at all nine of his heads and asked, "What the hell does responsibility have to do with writing?"

Answer: everything and nothing. Writing alone doesn't always require responsibility, but certain times it can. That day, I didn't craft a well-written argument—I was an immature kid that wanted to bitch about having to do homework, and my writing was nothing more than a vehicle for it. Persuading kids to hate homework is no more difficult than luring the sand to the bottom of the hourglass—the work is already done. Hell, Eminem made a multi-platinum career out of the same principle.

In just a few short sentences, my sister ripped me apart, and to this day, it's the most constructive piece of criticism I've ever received. The way she put it, I understood, and I feel like with each passing year since then, I've grown to understand it a little bit more. I thought I was great. But great is not an adjective self-applied, it's an adjective earned.

Only a fool kings himself from his own end of the checkerboard.

1. "I have never let my schooling interfere with my education."

Andrew Fiorentino

The Aisle

It loomed before him, a veritable menagerie of bright colors that filled his vision. Aisle 5, the Hawaiian shirt aisle at Value Land, a blinding array of flowery prints for casual wear. The aisle stretched from one end of the massive store to the other, Hawaiian shirts piled high on both sides. It had, Rick was convinced, something resembling its own gravity. Now and again, out of the corner of his eye, he thought he saw someone fall into the mass of cheap cotton, swallowed whole, never to emerge. This image, he thought, was a function of the fear that this textile behemoth struck into him.

It was the evening of the day before Casual Friday: Semi-Formal Thursday. Since bringing in consultants to help improve the workplace environment, Rick's employer, Gigaspan Inc., had replaced Casual Friday with themed Casual Friday, a change that was naturally the source of much workplace hubbub and, indeed, a certain degree of brouhaha. Tomorrow was Hawaiian Shirt Friday, when the hustle and bustle of the office would, upper management had been led to believe, be replaced by calm and camaraderie. The entire office would be uplifted by the friendly, casual atmosphere lent to Gigaspan by the presence of bright, flowery clothing and the lack of ties. Cohesiveness would be improved, synergy would be synergized, and with some luck there wouldn't be any more sexual harassment lawsuits, though the lawyers weren't holding their breath.

The aisle had one shopper, one employee, and about six billion Hawaiian shirts. Time seemed to slow as he cowered beneath the mountain of shirts, half hiding behind the Value Land employee who had been sucked into helping him. Her name was Gloria. Her name tag read "Cheryl," a clerical error that had not been corrected in the eight years she had been a full-time employee of Value Land. It also said that she was an assistant manager, which she was not, and that she would be happy to be of service to you, which she would not. She kept the name tag because she was required to wear a name tag. She also had spent the past three days restocking the Hawaiian shirt aisle with the newest selection, which was just like every previous selection, but not faded from months bordering on years of bombardment by fluorescent light. This made her an expert on Rick's particular situation.

Rick's particular situation was that, as a quiet, reserved, sexually insecure man who went golfing on Sundays and wore only solids, he owned exactly zero Hawaiian shirts, which was one fewer than he needed, and several more than he wanted. Cheryl, as the unfortunate soul assigned to aisle 5, had helped many a man of business select a casual-but-not-too-casual shirt for many a Casual Friday. She referred to Hawaiian shirts by their true name, Aloha shirts, with the self-importance that had caused her to fail to be promoted to assistant manager for eight years running. She'd gone through the process of trademarking the phrase "Cheryl's shirt suggestions," just in case she wanted to start a fashion consultation business, but the only bit of fashion she knew was Hawaiian shirts. Everyone who came in looking for a Hawaiian shirt took her first suggestion.

"No," said Rick. "Not that one."

Rick stared with some trepidation at the shirt hanging loosely from a bit of metal wire that might, with some imagination, be called a hanger. It was pink. It had hibiscus flowers on it. The flowers were also pink.

"Well, what's wrong with it?"

Rick explained, in his head, that he had formerly been the owner of a pair of pink boxer shorts, which he was sort of but not completely sure his boss had seen on one occasion when they were both using the bathroom. Rick's greatest fear was that his boss had noticed him surreptitiously watching him while they were peeing, and that he had looked over, noticed Rick's pink boxers and hungry stare, and jumped to the conclusion that Rick was a closet homosexual, which was absolutely and unequivocally true.

Cheryl made her next shirt selection with the speed and precision that could only be achieved by someone who had semi-meticulously restocked that very shirt the day before. It was a significantly more heterosexual blue, and instead of flowers it sported much manlier pictures of speedboats and yachts. It was the Gregory Peck of Hawaiian shirts. The one yacht even looked vaguely like a particular boat Rick had been eyeing for some time now. That particular boat, as it happened, was precisely the one owned by a certain Raymond B. Larsen III, President and CEO of Gigaspan. Rick's mind spun with the horror of showing up to work wearing a shirt with a picture of the CEO's boat on it. Ass-kisser, they'd call him. Brown-noser. For the first time, it occurred to him that maybe he should take off work.

As Rick's eyes glazed over with fright, Cheryl began to get the message that it was time to select another shirt. She wordlessly replaced the shirt, breathing an internal sigh of relief as the red faded from her customer's face, and selected another. This one was a particular favorite, the last of its kind. It was festively decorated with two martini glasses, one with a lobster inside it, the other with an unidentifiable lizard that might possibly have been intended to be an alligator. Relative to the rest of the shirts on display, this was a tuxedo. Cheryl unbuttoned it and helped Rick put it on.

It tore slightly in the left armpit, then in the right one.

Upon trying to move his arms, Rick found that they were confined to a position between being up in the air and at his sides, unable to settle on the happy medium of any position resembling normality. He stared at Cheryl helplessly.

"That's the last one we have in stock," Cheryl said helpfully. "It's an extra small. Why don't you look at yourself in the mirror?"

Rick obliged, making the small trek over to the full-length mirror at the end of the monstrously large aisle. Although he had started going to the gym recently, he was still a little flabby, and the tiny shirt highlighted that he had developed a slight case of man boobs. The red in his face made its triumphant return.

"Do you see this?" Rick's voice rang out high-pitched, approaching hysteria. "Do you see how this one makes me look? Do I *look* like an extra small to you?"

Her shirt suggestion rebuffed once more, Cheryl was beginning to become frustrated. Did he even *know* how long she had been in the business of selecting Aloha shirts for the casual gentleman? She had spent very nearly a quarter of her life working at Value Land, serving all sorts of customers, and this one couldn't settle on an Aloha shirt to save his life. Just as a deep hatred began to germinate within Cheryl for her own life and this man who had complicated it so, she was saved by the intercom.

"Cheryl to the register, please, Cheryl to the register."

"I'll see you when you check out!" she said cheerily, and with that she scurried down the length of the aisle, eventually vanishing in the distance before she reached the end, and leaving Rick the lone human being among the countless Hawaiian shirts.

After delicately stripping off the too-small shirt, Rick deposited it on the ground and began pacing up and down the aisle, brooding. Did fate have it in for him? Could he lie to get out of work? Would he ever be happy with himself? Was this aisle the same size as or bigger than the Great Wall of China? Would the next season of Project Runway be as good as the last one? The latter was a comforting, distracting thought, and he wrapped himself in it for a while, closing his eyes and continuing his pacing, mind aflight with the wonderful world of fashion design, with which he was still ill acquainted.

When Rick opened his eyes, he was standing in front of the most beautiful Hawaiian shirt he had ever seen. The shirt, an oasis of blue and green and orange, patterned together in an indescribably wonderful manner, once his eyes fell upon it, would not look away. A single tear came to his eye, so perfect was this shirt. He approached it little by little, praying to whatever god would listen that it was not a mirage. With cinematic slowness, Rick reached out his hand and grabbed the tag. It was a medium. It was his size. His search was finally over after the most unimaginable pain, not only in the store, but also at home for three hours before he'd been able to motivate himself to leave.

Delicately, for fear of damaging it, Rick took hold of the shirt's hanger and tugged. It didn't go. Suddenly alarmed, he pulled harder, but the hanger stubbornly refused to vacate the place where it had comfortably become settled. With shaking hands, Rick reached inside the mass of shirts to remove his chosen article from its hanger, disentangling it from the piece of twisted metal that was so intent on keeping it from him. He pulled again.

The shirt pulled back. Rick let go with a yelp of surprise, and would have stumbled backward and fallen awkwardly if not for the shirt holding on even when he was not. His cries for help echoed through the aisle, but were met with stoic silence. As he was dragged closer, the shirts looming over him, cheerfully menacing, Rick made one final, muffled cry for help, before he was finally swallowed entirely by the roiling mass of Hawaiian shirts.

Casual Friday at Gigaspan was canceled due to a lack of employee interest.

Michelle Pagnani

Getting Out Alive

5:47 a.m. You were supposed to be awake two minutes ago.

6:03 a.m. You have thirty minutes to get to the end of the driveway.

6:14 a.m. Seriously, wake the fuck up. If you're late for school, you'll have detention. You'll have to watch Mrs. Levin's fat jiggle when she laughs with the office secretaries. You'll have to listen to jokes about inadequate husbands and the latest episode of "Sex and the City."

6:23 a.m. Good, you're up. You don't have time for anything but a shower, which means Mickey will tease you during third period. He'll want to know why you don't wear make-up and why your hair's up for the fourth time this week. You'll tell him that his caustic remarks aren't getting him any closer to the inside of your pants.

7:04 a.m. Your stomach bellows in an otherwise silent homeroom. Maybe it's a good idea to eat breakfast.

8:15 a.m. Mr. Gluck stops his lecture to glare at you. You've been whispering impurities again. He wants to send you to the office but you just got the highest grade on his midterm.

8:19 a.m. You tell Vic about your weekend. Mom thought you were snoozing in suburbia when, really, you were getting high at a college party. Guys tried to grope you while your boyfriend was in the bathroom. Around three in the morning, you attempted to calculate the number of days till you would be rid of that gassy slob in study hall.

9:22 a.m. Just so you know, AP exams start in three days.

10:30 a.m. Lunch with the evangelist and the ditzy girl who managed to get into your Honors Physics class. You will talk about God, exams, and how you fucked your boyfriend last weekend... Kidding, you're not that kind of bitch.

11:58 a.m. You skip gym. The class has dwindled since archery started three weeks ago. Coach Avery is too busy flirting with students to remember to take attendance. In about a year, you will turn on Channel 6 and see his face next to a caption that reads: "Local teacher faces charges of child molestation."

12:23 a.m. You find Julie sitting on a tree stump next to the tennis courts. She's sipping a Yuengling and hands you one. There are ten more.

1:39 a.m. Guess what? You skipped more than just gym class. When you try to get a note from the nurse, she will be unsympathetic to your slurred pleas.

2:17 p.m. Sarah gives you a tic-tac.

2:26 p.m. FYI: you should probably avoid that teacher who hates you. The one you've never formally met. Yeah, the one who was offended by your statement in the yearbook. She doesn't think Top Ten students should reference "Another Brick in the Wall" when discussing their achievements.

2:52 p.m. The self-proclaimed hot chick eyes you down in the hallway. She doesn't like that your acne is gone and your boobs are growing.

3:01 p.m. Time for track practice. You're going to hurl.

4:12 p.m. Told you.

5:15 p.m. You realize that your Dad forgot to pick you up. You ask the only available person for a ride. When she drops you off, she casually admits that she thought your house would be bigger.

5:20 p.m. Your uncle is visiting. He wants to tell you that you can't go to UPenn. Your parents don't have the money. Your Dad thought it would be better if you heard this news from someone other than himself.

5:27 p.m. You plot to key your uncle's Porsche.

6:49 p.m. After a therapeutic bubble bath, you debate whether or not to do your homework. You are inevitably seduced by a Calculus textbook.

8:22 p.m. You call your boyfriend. He's really busy. One of the guys is trying to break into Jeff's room using a hanger and a PlayStation controller.

9:47 p.m. You stare at the cap and gown hanging from your desk chair. You think about what you'll be doing in four years, when it's time to graduate all over again.

Michael B. Harris-Peyton

God Pays Taxi Fare

Mikhail pulled the only green cab in all of Manhattan off towards the curb, watching as the normal yellow cab that had previously been occupying that spot pulled itself sluggishly back into the traffic. It was close to five-thirty in the evening, and the traffic was moving just fast enough to remind people of what speed escargot traveled before the French got to them.

It was also raining slightly. Mikhail sighed. The man with his arm out put it down and got in the passenger seat, next to him, with a grunt. Mikhail felt some cold water from the man's briefcase as the man jammed it between the glove compartment and his knees. Mikhail hit the meter with his gearshift hand and then asked:

"Where to?"

"Penn Station."

Figured.

The man shut the door and put his seatbelt on in what could possibly have been the most disjointed way possible. Mikhail subtly dodged the man's left elbow and he shifted back into drive and tried to stick some tiny corner of his cab into the traffic glacier.

Mikhail loved the awkward silences when his passengers were in the passenger side seat. No, really. He did this for his health. It was just so reinforcing to have someone sit two inches away from you and not say anything except, "Penn Station," with a crappy Midwestern accent.

He drove cabs because he hated subways. Those things were just one long, subsurface, aluminum, rattling, urine-smelling awkward silence, being passed from one person to another. It was one big awkward silence—it was just the parties to the silence that changed. Americans.

"You're not from New York?" Mikhail finally said as the cab started to move just fast enough to justify leaving his foot near the gas pedal. His accent was almost gone, which was no doubt comforting to this very stereotypical-looking white man.

"Neither are you… " The man squinted at Mikhail's cabdriver license. "Mikhail Assad."

"Actually, I've lived here for a number of years."

"I was born in America."

"I was talking about New York."

"Isn't Mikhail a Russian name?" the man said, turning to look at him as Mikhail rounded a corner. "You don't look Russian."

Sometimes he wished Penn Station was closer.

"It's also Arabic," Mikhail said shortly.

"Really?" the man asked.

Mikhail really wanted to say, "No—I'm just screwing with you. I'm Russian, a big communist Russian. Oh, and I hate America. Hail Stalin."

"Yes," was what he actually said.

"You're an Arab?"

"I was a Syrian."

"Oh—Syria. Didn't that get invaded?"

"No."

"Oh… oh! Riiiight, yes," the man said, apparently justifying his stupidity to himself. "I remember watching that movie… *Syriana*, was it? That place looks kinda dangerous."

"Syria sucks. Actually, I believe most of the movie took place in Beirut."

"Yeah."

"Which is not in Syria."

"Oh."

"As a matter of fact, I don't think Syria had anything to do with that movie at all. And it kind of gives Syrians a bad name, because some piece of the name of the country is used in a title about corrupt oil royals and nasty American backroom deals."

Mikhail preferred the awkward silence.   •

"You know, I would expect you to have an accent, being from Syria and all."

The image of Mikhail pulling a lever and ejecting this man from his cab on a rocket-powered passenger seat flashed across his mind. He desired to say: "I would expect you to have less of an accent, working on the east coast where they frown on mangling your vowel sounds."

"I've been here since I was fourteen," he said, deciding against alienating a passenger when they were still blocks from his destination. "I don't remember much except the weather."

"Sandy?"

"Humid, actually. Unbearable," Mikhail said, feeling himself move his consciousness away from the passenger and towards the spot of the road in front of the cab.

"You know, if you hadn't said anything, I would never have known that Mikhail wasn't just a Russian name."

Mikhail seriously considered telling this man how, when he had filed for his cab driver credentials, the man behind the glass barrier at the old computer terminal had been a total dunce. He'd explained in his, admittedly, then-accented English repeatedly that when his name was rewritten into English, it was spelled Mikha'il. In the end, he had given up and just resigned himself to a life without an apostrophe.

A cab cut him off, nearly sending him into the cab in the traffic formation next to him. Before he could stop himself, he unleashed a torrent of impolite words, primarily in Syrian Arabic. His passenger was noticeably taken aback.

The white person, "Oh no, an angry Arab!" reaction.

They finished the rest of the ride in idle conversation. The final thing they discussed as the man opened the door was the fact that Mikhail had gone to NYU.

"You're the most well-educated Arab cab driver I've ever met," the man said, handing him cash. Mikhail made change, and put it in the man's hand.

"You're the dumbest American I've ever met."

Click. Door closed. Passenger relationship over.

An old man in a gray coat held his arm straight out, and stood crookedly off of the curb, soaking his right foot in the rainwater.

"It's *hail* a club, buddy, not *heil* a cab. It's a car, not a führer."

Mikhail felt motivated to pick up this man, for some reason.

"Where to?"

"The Starbucks."

"Ah," Mikhail said. The man got in. It was a very unusual destination request.

"Any particular one?"

"I'm fond of the one in Lawrence, Kansas, but since I'm not entirely there, the one in Times Square, please," the man said.

"Morning!" the old man said happily, as he shut the door.

"It's evening, actually," Mikhail said, petulant.

"Not in Fiji—or on the Moon," the man asserted, with the tone of a professor.

"I assume that's true," Mikhail said, passively, as he pulled back into traffic. "So, are you from Kansas?"

"Not particularly."

"America?" Mikhail said, caught very off guard by the preceding comment.

"Define 'from,'" the old man said.

"Eh… " Mikhail hesitated. "Are you all right?"

"All left, too," he answered, looking out the window passively.

"What?"

"All left—left, the hand you don't write with. The direction you should have turned eight seconds ago."

Mikhail cursed, and turned back.

"Sorry," Mikhail said, laughing.

"It's alright. See that guy—he's going to have an aneurism. Well, he won't die for another six days. That's the sort of stuff I know."

"Do you now? That's interesting." Mikhail tuned this guy out; as long as he paid his fare, he didn't care.

"You're not listening."

"Yes, that's very nice."

"You broke your ankle when you were fourteen during a Soccer game; you did it half on purpose, in order to delay your parents departure to this country. It didn't work."

Mikhail almost hurt his neck turning to look at the man.

"I should seem familiar," the man suggested.

"You do, strangely. I can't place it," Mikhail said genuinely.

"I'm God, actually."

"What?"

"I'm God. God? You know, the big old guy in the sky who used to smote things?"

Mikhail opened his mouth to say something, anything, but could only drive.

"You said you were going to Starbucks?"

"Yeah. I hate Starbucks—I also happen to love Starbucks. It can be a very annoying thing, to have every perspective on everything. It can also be very un-annoying."

"I imagine so," Mikhail stammered. "You're confusing the crap out of me."

"Well, the fact is that I don't really have feelings in the same way you do. I also have an odd perspective on time."

"Talk about an existential crisis," Mikhail said.

"Can't have an existential crisis if you don't exist… well, not in any normal sort of way, anyway."

Mikhail had the sudden urge to jump out of his cab.

"I wouldn't recommend that. I kind of want coffee," God said, answering his thought.

"That's a really creepy parlor trick," Mikhail said.

"I'm not really much on parlor tricks. Of course, I don't really have a parlor… "

"You know what?" Mikhail said triumphantly, convinced that he'd determined that this clearly crazy man could not be God. "If you're here, how can you be God? Who's running the show right now?"

"I am."

"But— "

"Everywhere, man, all the time. Also means I'm never quite all in one place, I guess. But then again, the concept of place is really only important to corporeal beings such as yourself," God said. "Speaking of place, we're at it."

"What?"

"We're at the place you were taking me to before I sent you into a psychological crisis. The Starbucks. We're there."

Mikhail realized they were just across from the Starbucks.

"Oh, here's a neat fact: There are a couple of places in the world where a Starbucks is adjacent to or across the way from another Starbucks. If you take a map of the world and connect all these places with a straight line, do you know what you get?"

"Huh? What do you get?"

"A non-uniform polygon with, like... a hundred sides. And a ruined map. I made that particular pattern totally random. It's the only thing in the whole universe I made that way."

"Why are you telling me this?"

"I think it's really cool." God smiled. "Anyway, as soon as I enter the Starbucks, you're going to get rear-ended. You'll be fine, of course. Your girlfriend will call as soon as you get home and tell you about how she's a teaching assistant starting next week, and you'll go out to celebrate. You'll be up late, at her place in Brooklyn and having amazing celebratory... anyway, you know."

"Ah," Mikhail said.

"Stay cool, man," God said, giving the peace sign.

God stepped out of the cab completely, leaving Mikhail staring at the passenger side door. He watched as God weaved his way through the stationary taxis, getting rained on.

Mikhail's attention was then diverted by an odd crunching noise. He glanced in the rearview mirror, at the cab driver behind him.

The jerk had rear-ended him.

Ian Micir

Drop by Drop

Tuesday, October 30th, 2007 4:45 p.m.

I've never seen the Drexel quad look quite like this before. The best hand we're ever dealt is a couple of Jesus freaks handing out free bottles of Dasani water with little stickers on them that read: "Christ on Campus." (Of all waters, they choose Dasani—a product of Coca-Cola, who, up until 1929, put cocaine in their soft drink. Water into wine, soda into narcotics—what's the difference?)

But this crowd isn't here for bottled holy water. No sir, this is Philadelphia. Why, we're just a few blocks and a couple hundred years away from the site where some rebels in wigs signed a paper and claimed an identity for us. This was once the beating heart of a nation, and thank our lucky stars, we've got a pulse once more: "The Debate at Drexel."

But the scene before me isn't the debate; it's just the quad a few hours beforehand. All we've got out here is a few people being interviewed by Chris Matthews—a small event in the big scheme of things. But what a sight to see: cameras everywhere, crowds of people lined up against the fence bordering the MSNBC stage, signs held above heads in a horizon that obscures the sunset. There's even a group of construction workers who came in a pack of twenty or so, probably in an effort to strengthen the concentration on a specific issue concerning the working class. This is America—the democracy where every vote counts, and everybody gives a damn that theirs does. We just got lost for a short while in thinking that a drop of water added to an ocean doesn't make a difference. It does. However slightly, the water rises.

And what a feeling it is to look around and see a few hundred people gathered together for the pre-game show to a political debate. It's the type of enthusiasm that a college lacking a football team seldom sees. Every vote does still count and after a long drought, Philly's political enthusiasm is back with a vengeance.

Tuesday, October 30th, 2007 5:00 p.m.

Five o'clock hits and the crowd erupts for all the wrong reasons. Somebody on the stage points to Chris Matthews to let him know he's live, and ten seconds later, thirty different cell phone conversations start with, "Dude, are you at home? Turn on MSNBC—I'm on TV!"

There are two main cameras on stage—one on Matthews and another on whomever he's interviewing. As the two of them alternate in dialogue, the sections of the crowd directly behind them take turns jumping up and down in an effort to catch the camera's eye.

These people aren't here for politics. In fact, anybody who is interested should be at home, because I'm ten feet from a speaker that's supposedly hooked up to the on-stage microphones, and all I hear is a faint puff whenever somebody pronounces a "B" or a "P."

One lady taps me on the shoulder and hands me a sign that says "Biden" on it. I explain that I'm not voting for him and she tells me, "That's okay, just hold it up."

What? I'm not apologizing for stepping on her foot; I'm saying I'm not voting for him. I want to ask her what "that's okay" is supposed to mean, but she walks away almost immediately, leaving me with only my confusion and her colorful piece of construction paper.

Time passes, the sun dips out of view, and the crowd dissipates until round two of the Matthews interviews, which is set to take place at seven o'clock.

Thursday, November 1st, 2007 3:30 a.m.

What a tease. Everybody was there because of their lust for the camera (except maybe the construction workers, one of whom told me they were only there because some student told them about the free pretzels). I doubt if there was a definitive moment where we lost our grip on it, but somewhere between Charlie Chaplin and Brad Pitt, our culture redefined the American dream as five minutes of false fame in front of a camera. Five minutes of a drunken *Youtube* video; five minutes of spewing profanity, throwing chairs, and flailing punches on *Jerry Springer*; five minutes of jumping up and down in the background of a talk show at Drexel. It no longer matters why we're seen, just *that* we are. We've become a nation of six-year-olds in a 7-11 who want nothing more than to turn around and wave at the security camera so our friends can see us on the monitor behind the counter. And throughout this whole thing, I've learned that if there's one social situation I'm uncomfortable with, it's being part of America's non-stop parade of narcissism.

Let me just clarify that it's not *completely* meaningless for people to show up with signs. While I don't personally consider holding up a paper sign stapled to a yardstick to be synonymous with political activism, I do recognize that it's better than nothing. People were there, for better or for worse. I was just upset that the motive for it all was their obsession with being on TV. If the next Presidency is to be decided by which candidate has the most citizens dedicated to holding up a sign with his or her name on it in the background of a talk show, we should all be prepared to hear the sound of a big loud flush fairly soon.

But somebody's got to win; this is fact. If it's Obama, *South Park* will have a blast when Eric Cartman finds out we have a half-Kenyan President with the middle name Hussein. If it's Hillary, *Family Guy* can do another episode with Bill Clinton parading around the White House naked with a half-empty martini in his hand. If it's somebody else, then we'll get a whole new genre of jokes.

Personally, I don't want a female President; I don't want a black President; I don't want a white President. I want a President—period. One who will live up to the capital "P."

I intend to add my drop to the ocean, and when I do, the moment will come and go in an instant. There will be no visible change in the water level; there will be no dramatic splash to let me know something significant just happened. There will be no reward. But someday, somewhere, some wave might come crashing onto the shore and I'll be left to wonder if that wave started with the ripples from my drop.

I can live with that.

Michael B. Harris-Peyton

Big Fences Make Bad Neighbors

Let's just build a giant fence along the southern border. No! Let's just build two giant fences—in parallel! It's not like that will be horribly expensive. The only real issue we have to worry about is—and what are the odds of this—that an illegal immigrant will think to bring hedge-clippers. But only the terrorists have hedge-clippers anyway.

It will be a sad day in United States history when some politician thinks that we can solve illegal immigration with a fence. It will also be the day when they say the greatest danger to perceived homeland security is a pair of sufficiently sharp cutting shears. Fences will not solve the problem. It might, however, cut through American towns, as the most recent plans for a border fence in Texas, along the Rio Grande, would. The no-man's land between the fences and the border would contain the U.S. side banks of the river, including a number of back yards and houses. Illegal immigration prevention, right in your living room. Literally.

The proposed solution to illegal immigrants simply cutting through or hopping the fence would be: cameras. But you have to pay people to watch cameras, and extra government employees lead to bigger bureaucracies, and larger budgets. The whole plan is a colossal waste of taxpayer funds: funds that Congress could be wasting on its myriad of other insanely foolish ideas, like buying both evolution-based and creationism-based "science" books for our schools, in the interests of acknowledging all perspectives, regardless of how mindlessly ridiculous they are.

Another poorly thought out idea that was proposed as a solution to illegal immigration was so elegantly beautiful in its simplicity that you knew there had to be a catch—the "let's just deport all them pesky illegal immigrants" plan.

Problem number one: there are an estimated 12 million undocumented immigrants in the continental United States.

Problem number two: The Immigrations and Customs Enforcement Agency stated in September that the approximate cost of deporting all these people would exceed 94 billion dollars. And in that figure, they did not completely cover the costs of hunting down and catching all those undocumented immigrants who didn't want to go back. If you can't believe how insane this sounds, a spokesman for the agency laid out how they arrived at that figure for CNN: He said the amount was calculated by multiplying the estimated 12 million people by the average cost of detaining people for a day: $97. That was multiplied by the average length of detention: 32 days. ICE officials also considered transportation costs, which average $1,000 per person. But that amount can vary widely, the spokesman said. Some deportees are simply driven by bus across the border, while others must take charter planes to distant countries, he said. Finally, the department looked at personnel costs, bringing the total to roughly $94 billion.

On top of all this, one has to take into account the effect on the economy if 12 million people suddenly stopped working. The undocumented worker and their production make up a significant part of the economy, which would disappear if, as in the dreams of many politicians in both parties, illegal immigrants just fell off the face of the earth.

But what is to be done about illegal immigration? It is certainly not fair that undocumented immigrant workers do not pay taxes, and it is certainly unfair that they use public services without contributing to it in the same way as citizens do. In order to even suggest a solution to the problem, the sources of the problem must be addressed.

Legal immigration into the United States is difficult, time consuming, and often expensive. The citizenship examinations also, perhaps unfairly, contain technical questions about U.S. law that many American citizens cannot answer—for example, the line of presidential succession. There are few native citizens who can recite the line of succession off the top of their heads beyond the President, Vice President, and Speaker of the House.

In the case of the most prominent source of illegal immigrants to this country—Mexico—it is particularly complicated. Public opinion is often very anti-Mexican-immigrant, and both governments are somewhat awkward in their dealings with one another on the subject of immigration itself.

There is something deeply hypocritical about the hardline position against illegal immigration. There seems to be contextual amnesia going on—an American citizen of the anti-immigrant persuasion can go from openly discussing the foreign origin of their ancestors to talking about how immigrants "come over here and steal our jobs and not speak English."

News flash: your ancestors were probably poor, illiterate immigrants who most of the time didn't speak English either. And they had the advantage of arriving, most likely, in an older America with much looser border controls. If you're that severely anti-immigration, you're not "conservative," and you're definitely not a "real American"—you're xenophobic. You're also a hypocrite. The only people who can even claim to not be descended from immigrants are Native Americans. And from what the history books say, your ancestors weren't very nice to them. The anti-immigration argument is often so flawed that it approaches the irrational.

The fact of the matter is that we should not be looking at these people with hatred and intolerance; we should be making it easier for them to become legitimate citizens, and to contribute wholly to society. The cost of getting rid of them exceeds the cost of keeping them, and honestly, we need them.

America needs all the people it can get. We certainly have the space, and with the declining birthrate, we'll need more immigrants in order to stay on-par with the rising power of countries like India and China. America was built by immigrants, and that singular fact should be the first thought when it comes to dealing with the country's immigration issues.

Eric Zrinsky

"1984" in 2008

I am writing this letter because I have given up. Terrorism has won in the United States. We have lost complete control of our own lives, of our means of travel and transportation, of any feelings of security or normalcy. But I'll let you in on a little secret... it has been over six years since anyone has crashed a plane into one of our buildings. And still, we feel creeping anxiety of the impending terrorist affront on a daily basis

I'm going to take a moment here to clarify for you just what the word terrorism actually means, since our own government seems to have forgotten or severely misconstrued the true definition. Terrorism is the state of fear and submission produced by terrorization, or the use of violence and threats to intimidate or coerce, especially for political purposes. Blowing up buildings and mailing poisonous letters aren't the only way to ensure that an already paranoid country continues live in fear. Sometimes terrorism is subtle, deliberate, and is not always brought to us across deserts or oceans. Sometimes terrorism is internal.

At this juncture, we are afraid of our own shadows. We have signs in our airports requesting that we report any suspicious or unusual behavior to such and such agency of authority; encouragement to join the fight against terrorism. Big Brother will keep us safe, right?

The American government argues that these measures are for our own protection. They use bunk statistics like "there haven't been any terrorist attacks since we have stepped up national security." But then again, how frequently were we being attacked before 9/11? Fortunately for us, building bombings weren't exactly a daily occurrence here in America. With that in mind, how can anyone possibly claim that these stepped up security measures have made us any safer? I could argue that the demise of "Boy Bands" is what has made us safer at the turn of the century in the United States. Hell, there haven't been any building bombings since N'Sync broke up.

The reaction to the guerilla-marketing technique used by "Adult Swim" and parent company Turner Broadcasting System, Inc. in Boston only further proves the incompetence and inadequacy of law enforcement and intelligence agencies in the United States. Protecting this country starts with "informed" law enforcement and government agencies. It starts with being able to tell the difference between an actual threat... and what is basically a child's toy. Check out a picture of these things here: (http://l.yimg.com/www.flickr.com/images/spaceball.gif), and cower, cower in fear.

Perhaps we didn't learn our lessons from the witch hunts of times past. So, here's another little secret I'd like to share with you—the world wasn't any safer after wrongly accused men and women were burned at the stake in Salem, and it isn't any safer now that 18 Light-Brites have been removed from Boston overpasses and buildings.

If a man stands up in a theater to reach into his suit jacket pocket for a pack of gum, and someone, seeing this act panics and screams "Gun!" and the entire theater clears out, who has committed the act of terror, the man reaching for gum in his pocket or the panicked theater patron? Should the gum chewer get 5 years in prison (like the proposed sentences for Peter Berdovsky and Sean Stevens—the infamous Boston terrorists who planted the ads for Turner)? In America, post 9/11, the answer is apparently a resounding YES.

Personal accountability has become a farce. It is much easier to blame someone else than to admit our own shortcomings as a nation. The tragedy of September 11, 2001 could have been prevented if our "intelligence" agencies had done their jobs correctly. If you don't believe that there might have been prior knowledge of these attacks—information that was for the most part ignored—why don't you check out http://www.prisonplanet.com/911.html. I mean, after all, you *do* believe everything you read and hear in media anyway, don't you?

So call me a bleeding-heart liberal. Call me a leftist. Call me a communist for Christ's sake. It doesn't take a political affiliation to realize we are being duped. It's taking a look at eight years worth of bad choices made by a presidential regime more concerned with advancing their own political agendas than with keeping America safe. We are no longer American the diverse, America the brave, or America the beautiful. We are America the scared, America the uninformed, and America the misdirected. Terrorism has won. Call your senator to see how you can do your part spreading the fear.

Furrah Qureshi

A Writer's Right to Write

It was a Wednesday afternoon and I was sprawled in between two different uncomfortable chairs flipping channels until I stopped on Vh1 to watch *America's Most Smartest Model* where two intellectually-crippled male models ran on a treadmill for five minutes straight as I watched for five minutes straight. My friend walked in and asked what I was watching, and only then did I feel shame. And so I asked myself, when and how I had become so inept. For that absurd five minutes of my life was I okay with watching trashy Vh1 shows?

The world is changing at a faster rate then it ever has before. We've swiftly made the switch from an industrial society to an informational one. News can tenderly be received at any moment on websites like CNN.com. Rampant opinions from all walks of life can be expressed in the blogosphere. Words like "blogosphere" no longer are underlined with red squiggles in Microsoft Word documents. Information is proliferating while print media is dying. Flashy images resonating from the television in HD quality are now even becoming a hassle when free streams of the same content plague the internet and are themselves plagued with advertisements and un-blockable pop-ups. Information is shoved into all of our minds at all points of the day. But was it just information that educated us? Wasn't it more about the process? And more so, the quality of the process? Contrary to my most sincere wishes, watching *Law & Order SVU* marathons on TV does not qualify me to be an attorney. Given this concept, news and information shouldn't be accumulated from just any C-Span gorging thirty-something with a blog.

Looking up The Treaty of Paris on Wikipedia because it is too bothersome to ask your professor in class is a great marvel of the 2000s. I am happy to live in a time when we can do that. But writing your twelve-page term paper, a biographical essay on Millard Philmore, based on the commercialized information *solely* accumulated from Google isn't right. When the information is dumbed down, does that mean we, the one's processing it, are too?

Print media, mostly newspapers, are on their deathbeds. But the necessity of these structures relies on their prestige. Credible newspapers like the *New York Times* or the *Wall Street Journal* require a standard of integrity and insist their journalists be educated, well-researched and great at what they do. They do provide the information slower than their nanosecond counterparts on the internet, but the information is revealed with quality and merit. When you read a newspaper article, generally, you are reading good writing. The process in which you are acquiring knowledge is what will turn you into a knowledgeable person.

Books, something alien to most outside of English classes, are again a necessity. Seeing a movie is an easy gratification process. The details and beauty of verbal style are often (not always) excluded from cinema. When everyone realized it was so much easier to watch a movie then read a book, print media had its first near-death experience. If print media has survived the fight against shiny thirty-minute newscasts with Tom Brokaw, I hope it can stand up to shinier thirty-second podcasts with Brian Williams.

I write all this not as a neo-luddite, but as one concerned with the quality of information and the quality of writing in our society. As my own run in with *America's Most Smartest Model* showed me, it really is easy to lose yourself in the ease. And it really is complicated to be a complex person.

I fear for the value of writing skills. Studio executives have decided to circumvent the rights of writers and instead overpopulate television with short-lived reality TV ventures. Putting "Deal or No Deal" on three times a week is nauseating. Reducing the "Conan O'Brian Show" to office antics and Leno to interviews with third- rate celebrities makes a sordid hell for insomniacs. I fear tomorrow I may tune in to FOX to see the latest reality venture of strippers playing Hungry Hungry Hippos, hosted by that guy from *Tron*. Studios are so bent on degrading writers that they would rather let thousands of electricians, set managers, prop distributors and yes, writers, go unpaid and unemployed instead of acknowledging the necessity of writing.

The first day of the writer's strike, Fox played my all-time favorite episode of *The Simpsons*. It was the one where Moe's birthday solitude catapults his sad and typically pathetic snippets written on Post-It notes into stylish poetry (with the help of Lisa of course). The episode is saturated with witty social commentary and jabbing remarks. Classic lines like "The happiest people in the world, writers," and that magnificent scene where Lisa feeds bread crumbs to grad students from a park bench, who are being starved and whipped by their professor, exemplify the beauty of modern satire. Writing an episode mocking writing is genius. And while shows like The Simpsons push boundaries and pose questions as well as entertain, they do not provide the complex process of education that books provide. Good books don't give you answers, they ask you questions. I support and love modern marvels like TVs and iPods, but I do not let that interfere with my unquenchable quest for self-intellectualization.

I read.

JenkinsgroupInc.com unfortunately solidified my fears and justified my rants with their statistics. It turns out that print media is quite unpopular. One third of high school graduates never read another book for the rest of their lives. Scary? Well 42% of college graduates don't read any books after graduating. Scarier? 88% of U.S. families did not buy or read a book in the last year. And the scariest statistic for me and my career is that 70 % of books that are published do not make a profit.

And so, when we talk about the relevance of print media, ask yourself if you are reading this article on recycled paper, or *The Triangle's* website.

Faculty
Writing

Introduction

Writers render their perceptions from far off places and times; rarely do they live close to us, and rarer still do we know them or have the opportunity to know them, if only because they have died. They're almost always strangers with disembodied voices to whom we have no easy access. This can be a source of frustration to anyone who has wanted to ask a writer to elaborate on a particular point or to share their experiences with the nuts and bolts, from conception to execution, of a written subject.

In the following section, examples of the work by Drexel faculty have been included in *The 33rd* as representations of fine writing. The authors are alive and kicking and on campus; some may be your teachers now or in the future. You can see from the pieces that the subjects range from the various aspects of the "environmental movement" to the pleasures of cooking, and you can assume that each subject presented particular challenges that the authors had to grapple with in the same way that all writers must, including, of course, those in a composition class.

Stacey Ake

Ain't No Such Thing as Ethics Nohow

"If Expediency and Righteousness are not father and son they are the most harmonious brothers that ever were seen." Ambrose Bierce, *Epigrams*, 1911

As an occasional teacher of ethics, frequently in its stranger avatars such as professional ethics and medical ethics, I am regularly faced with the task of sharing my own personal "ethical views" with my students. And—alas!—my views often seem to be rather disturbing, to some folk at least.

To put it bluntly, I simply do not believe in the existence of ethics. In fact, as I tell my somewhat astonished undergraduate audience, Stacey's First Law of Ethics is: There are no such things as ethics (where ethics is defined as a variety of positions or perspectives, equally legitimate, from which an issue may be observed; for example, one's own "code of ethics"). Moreover, an obvious corollary is: There is no such thing as ethics (where ethics is a realm or discipline akin to music or literature, for instance, in which debates about various codes of ethics might take place).

As I see it, ethics, as it stands now in the United States, is merely a glorified "CYA policy." This, I tell my students, is Stacey's First Law of Ethical Reality: Ethics is/are a CYA (cover your hindermost parts) policy, used to create a lovely buffer between whatever questionable action took place and the ever-vigilant lawyers who are trying to sue your hospital or workplace or person.

However, for no particularly logical or understandable reason, when such a CYA policy is articulated using the thoughts of obscure (and, fortunately, dead) German or Anglo-American philosophers, it is viewed as somehow meaningful. But it is not. It is merely the hindsight justification of a pragmatic decision based (most often) on economics. Was the tube pulled on the coma patient in the interests of the patient, the hospital, or the insurance company? Well, when the family sues or a newspaper inquires, out comes the "ethics committee" to perform a song-and-dance or write an insightful whitepaper, about the ethical correctness of the hospital's decision. In other words, "ethics" as it is used and discussed today is simply high falutin' PR, most closely resembling the flowers your significant other brings you just after (or before) they cheat on you.

This leads me directly to Stacey's First Law of Ethical Analysis: Follow the Money. Of course, this notion is not original to me. It was, according to both Woodward and Bernstein, the repeated suggestion of one "Deep Throat," during a perilous Nixonian escapade that would turn out to be an uncanny foreshadowing of almost all subsequent Republican political and fiscal behavior: Watergate. But in his observation of the monetary aspect of "ethical" decision-making, Deep Throat was both particularly apt and astute. For when, in any culture, success has become the only measure of value, and money (cash) the only coin of said success, there is no other option but to follow the money, for that is the only thing that is real, in any strong sense, to the folks involved in any transaction, whether that transaction be business, interpersonal, private, or public.

The truth of this was brought home to me upon reading an old *Newsweek* article, "Who has the right to die?" about the Schiavo case in Florida (see the November 3, 2003 issue). For those unaware of the particulars in this case, it happened that in 1990, Terri Schiavo, then 26, collapsed due to heart failure brought on by a potassium imbalance and, although resuscitated, eventually went into "a persistent vegetative state" from which she had not recovered. In the fall of 2002, her parents, Bob and Mary Schindler, along with Florida governor Jeb Bush, prevented her husband, Michael Schiavo, from removing her feeding tube and thus "allowing" Terri to die. With the Religious Right behind the parents and the ACLU behind the husband, the United States (or, at least, some small part of it) once again descended into the binary hell of black 'n' white thinking that has so indelibly pock-marked American public discourse of recent history.

Think abortion, and you'll see what I mean.

So, what I say is, follow the money.

In 1992, Michael Schiavo won a malpractice suit against Terri's gynecologist for not detecting the potassium imbalance that led to her heart attack. Along with the proceeds from another malpractice suit, Terri (or, more pointedly, her guardian) received $700,000, which was placed in a trust fund for her care, while her husband received his own recompense of $300,000. And the trust fund guardian? Her husband Michael. But Michael was now convinced of the futility of rehabilitating his wife, so he wished to discontinue any life-supporting efforts. Terri Schiavo's parents (remember the Schindlers?) attempted to terminate Michael's guardianship but to no avail. And thus, the games began.

The battle between parents and husband over the fate of Terri Schiavo (and her trust fund) had, by 2002, gone on for more than 10 years, but nowhere in this macabre story was anyone really talking about the ethics of the "right to die" or the "right to life," despite all the public rhetoric and exhortation. The only person whose life or death hung in the balance—Terri Schiavo—was in no position to exercise any of her rights, actual or implicit. So, what was the Schiavo case furor really about?

Money. Plain and simple.

No, not the money involved in the Schiavo case itself, but the money to be saved by, say, the insurance industry in not having to fund a problem started by technology. Cases like Karen Ann Quinlan's, Nancy Cruzan's, and others are not really medical or even ethical cases per se. They are cases of technology run amuck, of people (usually parents) demanding those very miracles that science (especially medicine) has advertised itself as possessing. And because technology keeps alive those who would have normally died within a matter of days or weeks because of their injuries, parents and loved ones hold out as long as possible for the expected miracle. But such miracles are expensive, and the only fairy godmother (read: underwriter) of these medical miracles is the insurance industry, and it can ill afford to fund everyone's medical fantasies. Now, the logical move in such a case would be to disabuse people of their fantasies, as when a parent, who cannot afford some particular childhood fantasy, say an expensive toy, works to convince the child that such-and-such a toy is "not all it's cracked up to be." Convince the child to change his or her desires, and the need to worry about financing the bike, the computer, the in-line skates, or whatever, immediately disappears.

And that "argument against fantasy" is just what we are being sold in this article.

We have long been sold a bill of goods concerning those fundamental rights "to life, liberty, and the pursuit of happiness" in which life (and liberty) are not worthwhile without the ever-elusive happiness. In its original formation, courtesy of John Locke, the rights were "life, liberty, and estate (or property)," and today, we view happiness as some kind of property or commodity. Thus, we speak of the quality of life—is it a happy one? a "fulfilling"one?—and not of life itself. Moreover, we have been brainwashed to the point of not even noting that it is the right to the *pursuit* of happiness, and not happiness itself, that we are somehow guaranteed. For this reason, to protect our "property"—i.e., happiness as commodity—we have, as a culture, stopped taking risks. This would include the risk of paying for, or making sacrifices for, our own rights and even our own happiness. This avoidance of risk limits a person's adventurousness in how they might go about pursuing happiness. And, in lieu of said pursuit, we sit at home and wait for happiness to come to us with as little exertion as it took to get those two other unalienable rights: life and liberty.

Given this, and the fact that we live in a culture where the idea of "happiness" is almost perfectly annealed to the possession of money, we see why money and not any other human value plays such a large role in cases like Terri Schiavo's. It's not as if anyone involved in this mess actually cares about the well-being of Terri herself.

Let me put this in another way. What would happen if the Schiavo-Schindler family were told that they had to take their wife-daughter home and care for her themselves like thousands of families before them and like many millions of families in the rest of the world care for their own sick? What if the technology, and the ease and easiness of "care" it provides, were removed? For, in the Schiavo case, technology has proven to be just another way of turning money into trouble. What if they were asked not merely to care about, but to care for, Terri? What if the debate were about the nature of their humanity, their human dignity, and not their daughter's? What if this ruckus had really been a matter not of money, but of the responsibility to care for Terri Schiavo? For instance, if, as her parents contend, Terri had flickers of consciousness, wouldn't these flickers be more likely to be fanned to a flame if her mother and father fed her regularly, whispering quiet and gentle words of encouragement, rather than letting their daughter be fed to the accompaniment of the gurgling of her feeding tube?

But that is much too much responsibility, one might say, too much *personal* responsibility to ask of her parents. And that is, in fact, my point. Technology, and our dependence upon it and those who are expert in it, has led to our believing in a too solid, too definitive line between life and death. It has left no place for dying. Moreover, we now see death as we see life, as an individual phenomenon and not as a group activity that must somehow have quality (and perhaps even happiness?). Furthermore, such an unexamined dependence on the experts of technology-driven decision-making has taken from us, we the people, our liberty, our freedom, to act independently in the external world. By becoming dependent, we have reneged upon the most fundamental right of a human being: to be held personally responsible for his or her own actions. Without this, no declaration of independence is possible for any human being.

What if the Schindlers had cared enough about their daughter to let her die in their arms, as humanly and unconsciously as she had come into their world, rather than let her eviscerated existence stand as a symbol of their love and care, an expensive gift that they were unable to pay for themselves? Terri didn't benefit from the life support, but somebody did.

What if everyone had agreed and said, "We don't want the actual work of caring for Terri Schiavo, but we would like the money?"

In conclusion, I leave you with my one maxim of Ethical Training and Education: Make a Decision. Make any decision, but do it on your own. Doing this will not teach you anything about ethics per se, but it will teach you a great deal about being human, and who it is you really are when it is your own ass that you need to cover. And, sometimes, that in itself is education enough.

Ron Bishop
The Evergreen Hedge in My Front Yard

No red Corvette for me—my midlife crisis has consisted thus far of tracking down old friends and acquaintances, primarily to make sure that they're still alive.

So it was in the fall of 2005, when after months of emails to old friends, countless visits to the message board at the website that publicizes goings on in my hometown (Maplewood, New Jersey, a suburb of New York City), and more than a few poorly organized web searches, I found Bobby Zipse.

Now a John Deere sales manager living in Canada with his wife and five kids, Bobby was, during the 1970s at least, the person in the world I most admired, mainly because he taught me how to play, or to improve my lackluster performance in, a laundry list of sports.

We started with football when I was 10 or 11 (and he was 13 or 14), worked our way through various track and field events (the evergreen hedge in our front yard never grew higher than four feet after I knocked off its crown using it for a practice hurdle), and ended up, right before I went away to college in 1979, with lacrosse. For the record, I still can throw a tight spiral 50 yards—exactly once without crumbling to the ground in pain.

If Bobby was outside on our tree-lined suburban street, playing a sport with his friends, he would almost always let my friends and me join in. What appeared to be his democratic nature would on many occasions lead nearly everyone in our neighborhood to coalesce for a massive, sprawling game of baseball, touch football, or lacrosse.

There was an implied, but tactfully administered, pecking order—he and his friends were more skilled than we were; they would at times make that point abundantly clear by keeping the ball away from us with consummate skill and checking or tackling us with extra gusto. But if we hung in there, and tried to improve, they eventually would compliment us.

Professional sports never had a better ambassador, or a better salesperson. My burgeoning interest in sports, stoked by Bobby, repeatedly led me to ask my parents to help me buy, or buy for me outright after my nagging became intolerable, what I needed to play. Mitts, soccer balls, lacrosse sticks, my first pair of Nikes—Bobby had a tangible impact on the fiscal health of the area's sporting goods stores, the biggest of which at the time was the now defunct Herman's World of Sporting Goods. Armed with our new equipment and propelled by Bobby's instruction, we spent most summers, weekends, and after school afternoons playing pick-up games—some that resembled actual sports, and others whose rules were completely made up.

Over the Hump

My friends and I had grown tired of using our sneakers, stones, and pieces of brick to simulate the width of a net for our pick up hockey games, which usually took place somewhere on the street outside my house. The curbs were not high enough to stop even a low shot, and the fact that our street had a hump in it to promote drainage added to our problem; when we became skilled enough to get some real power behind our shots, the humped street acted like a golf tee, which posed a grave danger to nearby windows and the people behind them.

The "hump" also added a few degrees of difficulty to stick handling and passing the ball. Passes had to be fast and straight, or the curb would pull them astray. Stick handling moves had to be short and crisp, and they had to be made at the top of the hump—roughly a foot of space—or gravity would take its toll and pull the ball toward the curb.

I had discovered hockey in the winter of 1975. I was a newly minted Buffalo Sabres fan, thanks to the exploits of the famed "French Connection" line. I tried to replicate the play of Gilbert Perrault, Rick Martin, and Rene Robert. Soon, my friends—perhaps because hockey involved controlled violence meted out with sticks—took up the game. With only five or six players, we would rotate on offense and defense—two forwards against one defenseman and one "steady" goalie—"steady" because it was a real pain in the neck to take off our makeshift goalie equipment—my old catcher's shin guards and chest protector—to get in some time at another position.

The lack of a decent net frustrated my friends and me—now teammates on the so-called "Maplewood Lightning"—for some time. Several store-bought nets collapsed, thanks to the frightening speed and intermittent accuracy of our shots—or our rough and sometimes clumsy play (it all depends on who is telling the story). Finally, one winter in the mid-1970s, my friends and I appropriated enough wood, mainly from my family's garage, to fashion a fairly sturdy frame. Because we didn't know how to fashion sound wood joints, it wobbled quite a bit. We ended up creating a play where one of our offensive players would sneak behind the net and pull or push one of its corners. The goalie usually could not cover the added space.

Finding something to use for the net itself was a larger challenge. We first nailed old bed sheets and later a plastic tarp to the frame, but we tore them both easily with our shots—a boost to our egos, but ultimately quite frustrating. We eventually found what we thought was the perfect material: two pieces of sheet metal, each about 3 by 9. Using a pair of tin snips lifted from the toolbox of our goalie's dad, we trimmed the excess length, and figured we could overlap the pieces on the frame. We never really knew where the metal came from, although the sexy, macho-wannabe narrative that emerged within our group revolved around a late-night theft from our high school's metal shop.

The metal gave the net needed stability, and made it impervious to our hardest shots—even those taken by Russell, our best player. The sound made by the hockey ball or puck hitting metal was a short clap of thunder. We liked that—the louder, the better. What we didn't like was our discovery that the net we were so proud of now weighed in the neighborhood of 100 pounds. This was great when we blasting shots at our steady goalie, or shoving each other into the net (the crashes resonated beautifully through the neighborhood), but it became a bit of an issue when neighbors chased us from in front of their homes (an exodus whose timing corresponded to how tired my dad was of fixing windows), or when we went "on the road" to the tennis courts at a nearby park. Still, 387 goals in a partially imaginary 65-game season is nothing to sneeze at.

Testing Their Mettle

I revisited the exploits of the Maplewood Lightning, and my other pick-up game experiences, after I met my wife in 1994. Her oldest sister and her husband have two children: a boy, Brian, and a girl, Colleen, who were then six and four, respectively. They are talented, smart, funny, loving, wonderful kids (now young adults) whose daily schedules would test the mettle (and possibly inspire the envy) of a *Fortune* 500 CEO.

I had the chance to look at their schedules—closer to spreadsheets, actually—and wondered if they ever had any time to get a bunch of friends together to organize a game of something. Too much is going on in their lives, I thought, although I harbor no disrespect for the choices they or their parents make. I also noticed that they also live quite a distance from many of their closest friends. They seemed to barely know the other kids their age who lived in this affluent suburb of Philadelphia. I realized how lucky I was that we could grab the net, which was stored in my garage, and play without any parental involvement whatsoever, until our goalie's father, a Methodist minister, bellowed for him to come home). I also realized that I was lucky to have lived fairly close to most of my closest friends.

I wondered if they had the energy or the inclination to play pick-up games. I had played basketball, hockey, and baseball with them during family parties, but did these unstructured games continue? I also wondered if they might just be tired, given their other activities. This is not a rare set of circumstances for children from middle-class or affluent families, those that can afford to expose their children to a *variety* of activities. The key word there, though, is variety. Having our children do so many things in an organized fashion seems to take the fun, or at least the catalyst, out of unorganized play—just getting friends together to play around. In pick-up games, there is often no goal, no outcome, no achievement to be had, nothing to add to your resume that will get you into Penn or Harvard. It's just playing around for no reason, other than to play.

But again, this is *not* an indictment of busy parents, or overachieving, overscheduled children, overcompensating parents, or suburban sprawl. I don't want to cause Baby Boomer parents to bore their children with endless "You kids are so lucky; you have no idea how rough I had it when I was a kid" stories or lead to the publication of a "Just Play" version of those ridiculous motivational posters (the word "Persistence" appearing under a setting sun springs to mind) sold in mall kiosks and advertised in in-flight magazines. I simply think we need to explore the cultural importance of pick-up games in order to develop a sense of what made them such valuable experiences, and to gently encourage our kids to take some lessons from these experiences and apply them to their lives. Pick-up games have been pushed aside by our achievement-obsessed culture, but they have not disappeared. Still, how pick-up games are conducted and the meaning they have in the lives of those who played has changed significantly. This change can teach us about slowing down and about the value of imagination.

Many of the parents who push their children came of age in the supposedly hedonistic "if it feels good, do it" 1960s and 1970s—the age, if you believe the ads thematically anchored in these decades, where nothing happened except Woodstock, hippies whirling frantically in the mud, smoking pot in VW vans, and listening to "Going Up the Country," "Gimme Some Lovin'" or the soundtrack to *Saturday Night Fever*—only those songs. While I certainly qualify as a romantic for that era, I wonder if these Baby Boomer parents aren't overcompensating just a little, demanding that their children not repeat what they now believe to be, thanks at least in part to the rise to prominence—and endless bellicosity—of conservative pundits like Ann Coulter and Bill O'Reilly, their dalliance with aimless relativism.

Our parents yelled at us to find something to do, but they more often than not let us do the finding. My friends and I used to receive only mild rebukes from our folks for "hanging out." Eventually, we'd do something—maybe not something structured or productive—but something. Not all of our activities provided opportunities for learning. But today, it seems as though kids won't choose to have an experience unless they can wring from it every drop of information or preparation for the next task. There simply isn't any time for just "hanging out."

The Ringleader

Until he went away to college, Bobby was our ringleader for these activities—our negotiator with angry neighbors whose hedges had just been compromised by bodies lunging awkwardly for fly balls or their early evening post-dinner calm shattered by our raucous play. He was our agent, our lawyer, our teacher.

I can't be sure if he truly loved having to hang around with younger kids, or if he ever became frustrated at having to repeatedly teach us the finer points of play. He never expected anything in return, and seemed to derive a great deal of satisfaction from seeing one of us properly execute a pitching motion, cradle a lacrosse ball, or punt with ample hang time.

And, even though we all dreamed—OK, I still dream—about playing a sport professionally, there was a sense of realism in the group that, barring a miracle more stupendous than the U.S. hockey team's win over the Russians during the 1980 Winter Olympics, loving a sport was as far as we would go.

We learned how to play from each other. We'd try something new. We sucked. We probably could have benefited from taking part in an organized league, or trying out for a school team, but we improved nonetheless. We broke windows, crashed into each other, never kept score, hit cars, improved our physical condition, got faster, stronger, hit and threw further—all on our own.

In my case, I still love most of the sports we played—and my brother, whom I had to literally drag outside to play with us, now reports that he is a diehard New York Mets fan. Go figure. We had no goals, and our ambitions, such as they were, were in other areas. We argued, fought, checked illegally, and sometimes threw at each other's heads. We had fun—and we didn't have fun.

We had also formed a community of sorts—we didn't know it, of course. It was largely temporary—there were lasting friendships that existed apart from the games. Taking part in our ad hoc community required little emotional investment.

Just "Jamming"

Our exploits on Kensington Terrace are an extended example of what scholar Eric Eisenberg would call "jamming," or "personally involving, minimally disclosive exchanges between individuals." We didn't play baseball, pepper our goalie with ten-foot slap shots and dodge the "hump" as part of a broader strategy to get to know each other.

Conversations that took place during our games were limited to school, baseball players and other athletes we liked, girls we didn't have the nerve to talk to, and the creation of the games themselves—along with a liberal sprinkling of profanity. We didn't share a lot about ourselves our hopes, our dreams, our relationships with our parents—with one another.

For all of the time we spent together, I knew only a little about Bobby Zipse. Likewise, he probably knew very little about me. I knew that he was the first adolescent person on our block to own a mini-bike (which he let me ride by myself without any cajoling), that he had three sisters (the oldest a nurse) and a brother, a pilot who flew for United Airlines, and that his mother put up the same lights, in the same configuration, around their front door every Christmas, but that was about it.

We were not close—but it didn't matter when he was teaching me, or one of my friends, how to flick a wrist shot, or when he was slapping a tag on me during a rousing game of "running bases." When we played on the street, my close friends were often there (including one who most of my friends and students refuse to believe is named Joe Kuhl), but we wanted to play, not reflect or share ideas about the state of our 1970s world.

Eisenberg argues that despite this lack of closeness, these experiences are significant, especially today, when we seem to be interacting less frequently with folks with whom we are not intimately connected, and more frequently, but with less depth, with the people to whom technology so readily connects us.

If the mass media are any guide, we think we are intimate with many people. We have become quite skilled—and quite ready—to reveal, to share. We reflect at the drop of a hat—to each other, to our therapists, to Dr. Phil and Oprah. This is all well and good, but Eisenberg reminds us that encounters with people we are not close to can also play a significant role in shaping the self.

Our tendency to shy away from contact with casual acquaintances is caused partially by our belief that these interactions are "phony, staged, and unfulfilling in comparison with 'deeper' relationships," according to Eisenberg.

As a result, we spend more time judging each other on the basis of "the desirability of their personalities or motives" than on the "results of their actions." Think about our criteria for electing a President, or even a state senator: we prefer good-looking people who entertain us, and who don't bore us with reams of information about major issues.

The Privatization of Meaning

Much of this occurs, Eisenberg contends, thanks to what we will for the moment call the "privatization of meaning." The individual experiences people, places, and events, and then constructs and nurtures meaning about them. You develop and "own" the meaning you hold, say, for your grandmother, or your first kiss. Another group of scholars, including the celebrated theorist and writer Mikhail Bakhtin, argues that we actually "rent" meaning, which gives it more of a community flavor.

You, or a friend, might choose to share stories about your grandmothers, and then make a connection through the similarities (and differences) in your experiences. The social aspects of communication are more important than what you intended when you send a letter or an IM to someone. Knowledge, claims scholar Kenneth Gergen, is not "something people possess in their heads, but rather, something people do together (author's emphasis)." Thus, it is more illustrative to explore the meanings that emerge from interaction rather than those that reside solely in the head of an individual.

Even with the immense popularity of websites like Myspace.com, and in the face of the fear-mongering coming from our elected leaders, we still feel that we truly need to get to know someone before we can move down the road to a more intimate connection, or to the formation of a community. Ironically, we spend so much time talking about ourselves that we damage our ability to, in the words of John Lennon, come together. We get so caught up in self-revelation that we forget why we've come together in the first place, as Richard Sennett might argue.

Instead of exploring the origin of our feelings, Sennett contends, we spend too much time explaining our feelings to other people. Our capacity for public expression actually suffers as we continue on our "search for a selfhood." We have, Eisenberg argues, lost our "appreciation for the emotional rewards of public life." We are left isolated and unable to interact productively. As a result, we embrace group situations where "homogeneity of values" is a good thing—where dissenting ideas are squelched, and where differences in personality are submerged.

Pick-up games provided us with the chance to balance "autonomy and interdependence," as Eisenberg writes. Too much interdependence can stifle the creativity of a group's members, while too much autonomy can lead to anarchy, or, at the very least, seemingly endless personality-driven battles, and to the group accomplishing little.

Led by Bobby, we experienced what has been called "a sense of mutual presence." We didn't always like the people we played with out on Kensington Terrace; our games saw their share of what sportscasters call "chin music" and mini-brawls. We fought, got over it, and continued to play. We were, to borrow Eisenberg's word, "compatible." That was enough. No exaggerated, fawning over involvement in each other's business for us.

We agreed to comply with some arcane rules (a fly ball that dropped untouched on to the manhole cover at the intersection of Kensington Terrace and Lincoln Place was automatically a home run), even if we believed that the author of those rules was out to lunch.

We had no goals, other than to play without getting injured and to avoid damaging property. Values were not freely expressed, and did not evolve all that much. Little time was spent discussing fair play. And although I was convinced at age 14 that I might have a small amount of real talent for baseball, I did not have, to use a term popular with politicians, an agenda.

It was enough to just play. We came together around the games. My closest friends—Joe Kuhl and Chris Young—were rarely involved in these games. And only Bobby had extensive experience in organized sports. Yet when the games took place, we forgot our individual trajectories. As Eisenberg notes, "this perception of unity facilitates the smooth coordination of action." So while I harbored my Major League delusions, my younger brother was trying to figure out how to hit the most cars on the block with a single hit. But largely thanks to Bobby, we played on.

The Hopeless Romantic

It's pretty obvious that I hold positive romanticized memories about my pick-up game experiences. There are days, especially as life in an academic department becomes more complex, where all I want to do is grab the gloves and baseball that I always keep in the back of my car and beg someone to play catch. It is my hope on those days that a few tosses will transport me back to the tree-lined street on which I grew up, and wash all of my troubles away.

But not all of my pick-up game experiences were positive or enlightening. For starters, I knocked out one of my brother's upper front teeth when he was about six years old during a game of catch in front of our house. His "adult" teeth never came in completely straight, a development for which I still feel responsible. And in my futile effort to someday join the New York Mets pitching staff and, during the winter, the defense corps of the Buffalo Sabres, I broke every window on two sides of our garage. My dad eventually gave up making me pay out of my allowance—earned largely from working for him—to have them fixed.

And not every game on Kensington Terrace ended with us basking in adolescent reverie, either. Our hockey fights were real, as were our dalliances with "chin music" during baseball season. We suffered more swollen lips than you would see at a Steven Tyler look-alike contest. Many games of "running bases" deteriorated into rugby scrums on our front yard. We uttered more profane words than non-profane words on any given day, and our cultural and ethnic sensitivity often left quite a bit to be desired. But I would still, any day of the week, trade a two-hour committee meeting for the chance to play an extended game of catch. I'd have to first consult with my deteriorating body, of course.

One last story before we conclude: my son is six years old. He suffers from cystic fibrosis, and has significant developmental delays, including low muscle tone (hypotonia). He hasn't yet learned to walk on his own, although he deftly pilots his walker through the halls of his school and the more cramped confines of our first floor, and communicates using a limited range of signs, including his favorite, "all done," (think of an abbreviated "safe" call by an umpire), usually deployed when he's had enough to eat.

I would be lying if I said I never thought about all of the typical, and even atypical, "father and son" activities we aren't able to participate in because of his disabilities. In my selfish moments, I feel cheated. He and I will likely never fan out in the back yard for a game of catch. I may never be able to replay the climactic scene in *Field of Dreams*, where Kevin Costner (as Ray Kinsella) reconnects with the spirit of his father by playing catch on the baseball diamond constructed in his Iowa cornfield.

Since I have only modest success at putting aside my needs and wants, it took me a while to give catch a try with my son. Then, about a year and a half ago, I started gently nudging him to hold a tennis ball, then a street hockey ball, and, eventually, a baseball. At first, his hypotonia prevented him from holding even the lightest of the balls in his small hand. He held them tentatively. He struggled bravely to raise them above his head. He was at first able only to drop the ball into my first baseman's mitt.

I have no idea why, other than the increased strength in his hands, that he persisted; not once have I seen the "all done" sign. But one morning during the early weeks of the 2006 baseball season, I stood next to the wheelchair, ready to receive the ball. But Neil reared back and threw the ball; it deflected off of my stomach and plopped into the glove. My only words during the next five minutes were, "Way to go, buddy!"

Today, I stand ten or fifteen feet from the wheelchair. His throws typically bounce a couple of times, but they reach me. I walk back, congratulate him on every throw, kiss his head, and place the ball back in his hand. Now and then, he reaches me on the fly. Now and then, he throws the ball into my toolbox, a nearby empty joint compound bucket, the wheelbarrow, or the peppermint plant directly outside the entrance to the garage—and then laughs heartily at the sounds he makes.

If I never play catch with anyone else, I'm happy.

I'm not sure that he gains anything from playing catch. It may have helped to strengthen his arms and hands, but that's not the point. He likes it. I like it. We do it together, then move on with our days. We may play the next day, or I might let him help me sweep the magnolia leaves from in front of the garage. No drive to achieve. No attempt to keep score. It makes him laugh, and almost always makes me cry.

So do me a favor: pass the joy of play on to your kids; don't keep it to yourselves. It may take some effort, since the narrative we tell each other about the wonders of organized activities is so entrenched. Don't make play an organized affair designed to help them achieve. Cancel the play dates, keep them home from camp—and whatever you do, don't ever write the words "play time" on your calendar or Blackberry.

Let them play—no, really, just let them play. The way we did, thanks to Bobby Zipse. The way they want to.

Author's note: this essay is based on excerpts from When Play Was Play: Why Pick-Up Games Still Matter, *to be published in late 2008 by State University of New York Press.*

References

Bahktin, M., Holquist, M., Liapunov, V. & Brostrom, K. (1982). *The dialogic imagination:* Four Essays. Austin, TX: University of Texas Press.

Eisenberg, E.M. (1990). "Jamming: Transcendence through organizing." *Communication Research,* 17, 139-164

Sennett, R. (1974). *The fall of public man.* New York: Norton.

Robert Brulle

The U.S. Environmental Movement

Abstract

The U.S. environmental movement is perhaps the largest, most long lived, and complex social movement in the U.S. To understand this movement from a sociological viewpoint requires an analysis of the different belief systems or "discursive frames" that define the different communities that make up this movement. This paper starts with a description of these discursive frames. Using this perspective, it then describes the historical development of the different communities, and their relative levels of economic resource mobilization.

The U.S. environmental movement is perhaps the single largest social movement in the United States. With over 6,500 national and 20,000 local environmental organizations, along with an estimated 20-30 million members, this movement dwarfs other modern social movements such as the civil rights or peace movements. It is also the longest running social movement. The first local environmental organizations were founded before the Civil War and several still existing national environmental organizations, such as the Sierra Club, the National Audubon Society, and American Forests, were founded in the late 19th century.

The question facing social scientists is how can we understand and examine this enormously complex social movement? There are three commonly used approaches. First, sociologists examine the belief systems that define the various components of this social movement, which is termed Discourse Analysis. Secondly, the development of the social movement over time is examined using Historical Analysis. Finally, the techniques used to garner financial resources for the organization is examined through the perspective of Resource Mobilization Analysis. By combining all three of these perspectives, one can gain a more complete picture of the environmental movement.

Discourse Analysis of the U.S. Environmental Movement

The first approach is to view this movement as the group of distinct communities, each based on a particular world view. For example, if you were asked to describe organized religion in the U.S., you could list all of the various denominations, such as Catholics, Jews, Episcopalians,

Baptists, etc. When you describe religion using these terms, what you are saying is that there are a number of different religious communities, each based on a particular set of beliefs.

This approach can be applied to describing the U.S. environmental movement. Just like organized religion, the environmental movement is made up of a number of different communities, each based on a particular world view. Sociologists label these different world views as "discursive frames." A discursive frame is the set of cultural viewpoints that informs the practices of a community of social movement organizations. Each discursive frame provides a cultural viewpoint from which the environmental organization acts. This discursive frame defines the goals and purposes of the organization, and provides guidance for the actions of the organization.

For example the Wilderness Society belongs to the discursive community defined by the discourse of Preservation. This discursive frame focuses on the preservation of intact ecological systems and protection of biodiversity. Oriented by this viewpoint, the Wilderness Society seeks to create and maintain wilderness areas, and to ensure the long-term ecological diversity in these areas. Conversely, the Center for Health, Environment and Justice is informed by the discursive frame of Environmental Health. It seeks to protect the health of urban area residents by eliminating toxic chemicals from their environment. So while these two organizations both have an environmental focus, their discursive frames are distinct.

When you look at the U.S. environmental movement from this perspective, it is clear that it is comprised of several distinct communities, each based on a unique discursive frame. Thus to understand this movement, it is important to recognize its multiple foci based on unique discursive frames. There are eleven major discursive frames that define the environmental movement in the U.S. Thus to understand the environmental movement, you must be familiar with each one.

Wildlife Management

The oldest and first manifestation of concern over the natural environment appeared in the U.S. over the issue of hunting. Around the middle of the 19th century, wealthy Americans became concerned about the depletion of wildlife for hunting. These sportsmen organized the first environmental organizations. These organizations lobbied for the creation of bag limits on both game animals and fish. This movement expanded into a national movement toward the end of the 19th century with the appearance of organizations such as the Boone and Crockett Club, and the National Audubon Society.

In the early 1930s, this movement underwent a profound shift. Up until this time, the only strategy followed was to control the demand on fish and game animals through limiting the number of animals that could be taken, or by limiting the hunting season to a specific time period. However, due to the loss of habitat, this strategy was unable to ensure that a sufficient number of game animals was available. Thus a new strategy of wildlife management was created. This strategy focused on both reducing demand, and also in increasing the supply. To increase the supply of game animals, wildlife refuges were established. This strategy of managing both the supply and demand of game animals has worked successfully since its development. This approach defines a major environmental discourse in the U.S. Its key components are:

• The scientific management of ecosystems can ensure stable populations of wildlife.

• This wildlife population can be seen as a crop from which excess populations can be sustainably harvested in accordance with the ecological limitations of a given area. This excess wildlife population thus can be utilized for human recreation in sport hunting.

• The scientific management of ecosystems can ensure stable populations of wildlife.

The discourse of Wildlife Management defines both a unique viewpoint, and the practices of a distinct community of organizations. This community is centered on wildlife conservation issues, and they define their objective as conserving or rationally developing our wildlife resources to provide for human recreation needs. They use words such as "maximizing the supply of game" or "conserve our wildlife resources." Some major organizations in this discursive community are Trout Unlimited, Ducks Unlimited, and the National Wildlife Federation.

Conservation

Perhaps the most influential early discursive frames in the U.S. environmental movement was developed by the Conservation Movement. Around the turn of the 19th and 20th century, there was a great deal of concern regarding the over-exploitation of natural resources by market forces. This concern led to the creation of the Conservation Movement. These organizations, such as the American Forestry Association (founded in 1875), advocated government control to ensure that these resources would continue to provide an adequate supply for the economy. This philosophy was put into practice during the administration of Theodore Roosevelt in the creation of the National Forests. Over the time period from 1900 to around 1960, this perspective dominated American environmental policy.

From the viewpoint of the discourse of Conservation, nature is a resource to be used by society to meet human needs. This forms the basis for collective action to ensure that natural resources are used by applying the criteria of rationality and efficiency to achieve the maximum utility to society. Key components of this perspective are:

• Physical and biological nature is nothing more than a collection of parts that function like a machine.

• Humans need to use the natural resources provided by nature to maintain society.

• Nature can be managed by humans through the application of technical knowledge used by competent professionals.

• The proper management philosophy for natural resources is to realize the greatest good for the greatest number of people over the longest period of time.

Organizations based on this discourse define their objective as conserving or rationally developing our natural resources to meet long term human needs. They use words such as "ensure wise use of natural resources" or "bring about efficient conservation and development." Some organizations in this discursive community are the Society of American Foresters, American Forests, and Scenic America.

Preservation

The third environmental discourse to emerge in the U.S. during the 19th century was Preservation. As economic development expanded across the U.S., there was the growth of concern regarding the disappearance of "wild" lands. In 1890, a dramatic proclamation was issued by the U.S. census bureau. The census reported that it could no longer define a frontier line. For a country that had previously thought of the west as an inexhaustible source of natural resources and land, this was a profound psychological shock. This meant that the U.S. was running out of natural resources and wild areas.

This led to a concern over the loss of wilderness and the animals that occupied those areas. Based in this concern, a number of organizations arose, such as the Sierra Club (founded in 1892). These organizations advocated for the preservation of wilderness as both a natural and spiritual resource. This discourse took the form of Preservation. It defines a spiritual and psychological relationship between humans and the natural environment. In this discourse, nature in the form of wilderness, untouched by human activity, has intrinsic value. Nature also serves as a site for self renewal through the experience of its aesthetic beauty. This translates into a concern over the preservation of scenic areas, wilderness, and wildlife. Key components of this perspective are:

- Natural systems are self-creating evolutionary wholes that cannot be reduced to the sum of their parts. Hence nature is not a machine, but an intact organism.

- Human actions can impair the ability of natural systems to maintain themselves or to evolve further

- Wilderness & wildlife are important components in supporting both the physical and spiritual life of humans.

- Human values go beyond those measured by the national income accounts to include the preservation of wild lands and life.

- Continued existence of wilderness and wildlife is critical to the spiritual well being of humanity.

- Protection of wilderness areas and wildlife for the current and future generations is an essential environmental task.

Several key features identify organizations based on this discourse. First, they define their objective as preserving wilderness in a pristine state, untouched by humans. This includes leaving all of the plants and wildlife that inhabit that area to develop in a "natural" manner, i.e. unaffected by human influences. They use words such as "preserve and protect" or "ensure the continued existence of wilderness areas." Some Preservation organizations focus only on a specific species or geographic region. This is reflected in the name of the organization. Some examples of these types of organizations are the Sierra Club, the Wilderness Society, and the Nature Conservancy.

Reform Environmentalism

The most dominant discourse of the present day is Reform Environmentalism. Thisdiscourse is, in fact, so dominant, that it is generally used to refer to the multiple discourses that make up the current environmental movements. However, this was not always the case. Up until around 1966, environmentalists were commonly referred to as Conservationists. This all changed in the mid 1960s. In an enormous expansion of the environmental movement, reform environmentalism rose to its current position of dominance in under a decade.

Concerns about pollution have been around since the mid 1800s. The development of industrialization brought the burning of coal, the concentration of factories, and human crowding in urban areas. This created environmental problems in the industrial cities in the U.S., and included crowded tenement districts, air and water pollution, garbage disposal problems, and occupational hazards in the rapidly expanding factories. The brunt of these environmental problems was borne by the working class and the poor. As Brian Obach shows in his essay, this environmental pollution had adverse impacts on worker's health and economic opportunities.

The concerns over urban environmental pollution first manifested themselves in the Sanitary Movement. The Sanitary Movement arose after the Civil War to address community health problems. Its aim was to improve urban living conditions, and dealt with problems such as sanitary water supplies, sewage systems, garbage, and air pollution. This was followed by concern over the excess of refuse and garbage in urban areas. Several protests occurred and a number of civic organizations were founded in the 1890s to demand urban cleanliness. This movement became known as the Municipal Housekeeping Movement. This movement primarily took the form of antilittering campaigns, education about sanitary procedures, city cleanup days, and advocating effective sanitation ordinances. Finally, around 1900, labor unions began pressing demands to address the exceptional levels of exposure to environmental pollution in urban factories.

However, these issues were not a major focus of the leading discursive frames of the early environmental movement in the form of wildlife management, preservation, or conservation. Following a number of highly publicized environmental pollution incidents, and spurred on by the publication of Rachel Carson's book Silent Spring, pollution concerns rose dramatically among the American public. This gave rise to a new discursive community oriented around a concern that links human health and survival to environmental conditions. In this discourse, nature has a delicate balance, and humans are part of it. This perspective emphasizes that nature is an ecological system, that is, a web of interdependent relationships. Humanity is part of this ecological system. Hence, human health is vulnerable to disturbances in the ecosystem. This animates action to identify and eliminate the physical causes of environmental degradation. Key components of this perspective are:

- Natural systems are the basis of all organic existence, including humans.

- Humankind is an element within natural ecosystems, and hence human survival is linked to ecosystem survival.

- Ethical human actions (actions which promote the good life for humankind) necessarily promote action toward all life on earth in an ecologically responsible manner.

- Proper use of natural sciences can guide the relationship between humanity and its natural environment.

Organizations based in this discourse identify their organization's purpose as protecting the earth's ecosystem and human health. The purpose of these organizations tends to use phrases along the following lines: "to protect and enhance human welfare and combat environmental deterioration" or "this organization is dedicated to improving environmental quality and public health." Some of the well known organizations in this discursive community include Greenpeace, Environmental Defense, and the Natural Resources Defense Council.

Deep Ecology

Following the rise of Reform Environmentalism in the 1960s and 1970s, there was increasing disillusion with the results that the existing environmental movement was able to realize. One area of concern was the increasing exploitation of the few remaining natural areas in the U.S. These concerns gave rise to the formation of the Deep Ecology movement in the early 1980s. Although part of the environmental movement, it is much more radical in its belief that the requirements to maintain intact natural systems should take precedence over human needs. At the core of this discursive frame is the belief in the intrinsic value of all nature that will ground a respectful way of living in and with the natural, non-human world. In this discursive frame, nature is seen as a value in its own right, independent of human existence. Humanity is only one species among many, and has no right to dominate the earth and all of the other living organisms. This creates an ethic of radical wilderness advocacy. Unlike Preservation, which seeks to keep what remains, Deep Ecology seeks the restoration of fully functioning ecosystems, in which the evolution of life, unaffected by human actions, can continue. It also advocates the inherent rights of all nonhuman beings to exist in their natural state. In this sense, Deep Ecology makes a moral argument for the preservation of the natural environment. Key components of this discourse are:

- The richness and diversity of all life on earth has intrinsic value.

- Humankind's relations to the natural world presently endanger the richness and diversity of life.

- Human life is privileged only to the extent of satisfying vital needs.

- Maintenance of the diversity of life on earth mandates a decrease in the human impacts on the natural environment and substantial increases in the wilderness areas of the globe.

- Changes (consistent with cultural diversity) affecting basic economic, technological, and cultural aspects of society are therefore necessary.

The organizations based in Deep Ecology generally define their objectives as acting to preserve the rights of all nonhuman beings to a natural existence, unaffected by human intervention. These organizations define their aims using words such as "defending the intrinsic rights of species to life" or "placing ecological considerations first in any decision making process." Some of the well known organizations in this discursive community include Earth First! and the Sea Shepherd Conservation Society.

Environmental Justice

A second component of the U.S. environmental movement that arose in the early 1980s was the Environmental Justice Movement. Like Deep Ecologists, there was a deep sense of disappointment over the results of the 1960s and 1970s environmental movement. However, the concern of this community was not on wilderness. Rather, it was on the unequal burden of pollution that was placed on poor and minority communities. Thus they were concerned with exposures to persistent toxic pollution, in the form of local toxic waste dumps, high levels of air pollution, or unhealthy and polluted living conditions. From these concerns, a unique community arose that focused on urban environmental issues in systematically disadvantaged areas.

The discursive frame of environmental justice accepted the link between human survival and ecosystem survival as defined by Reform Environmentalism. However, instead of focusing on the physical causes of environmental degradation, this frame sees environmental problems as creations of human social order. Hence the solution of environmental problems lies in social change. Key components of this viewpoint are:

- Domination of humans by other humans leads to domination of nature.

- The economic system & nation-state are the core structures of society that create ecological problems.

- Commoditization & market imperatives force consumption to continually increase in the developed economy.

- Environmental destruction in low income/racially distinct communities, or Third

- World countries originates in the exploitation of the people who live in these areas by the dominant social institutions.

- Resolution of environmental problems requires fundamental social change based on empowerment of local communities.

Thus Environmental Justice organizations focus on the social creation and resolution of environmental problems. While these groups focus on a large number of issues, they all seek to protect local communities from the adverse effects of environmental degradation. Additionally, regardless of their specific focus, groups based in the discourse of environmental justice define their objective as changing the social order in some manner to solve environmental problems. The means to carry out this goal include holding government and corporations accountable through democratic processes or by bringing legal suits to end toxic waste dumping. Some organizations with this orientation describe the purpose of their organization in terms such as "Create economic democracy through localized decision-making," "develop grass roots capabilities to involve local citizens in resolution of their community environmental problems," or "abolish environmental racism," Some of the leading environmental justice organizations include the West Harlem Environmental Action Coalition, the Southwest Network for Environmental and Economic Justice and the Indigenous Environmental Network.

Environmental Health

A discursive community closely associated with the environmental justice community is the environmental health movement. While the environment has always played a key role in community health, the relationship between environmental pollution and specific illnesses is still not widely acknowledged. However, in a number of diverse locations, individuals noticed a strong relationship between environmental pollution and their health. Some of the key examples was the extremely high rate of breast cancer among women on Long Island, and the increasing rates of asthma among children exposed to automobile exhausts.

From this concern, a movement took shape in the late 1980s that focused on the relationship between environmental pollution and human health. The unique discourses of this movement defined the perspective of Environmental Health. Key components of this viewpoint are:

• Human health is the outcome of interactions with physical, chemical, biological and social factors in the natural environment, especially toxic substances and pollution.

• To ensure community health requires a livable and healthy community, with adequate social services and elimination of exposures to toxic or polluting substances.

• The precautionary principle (no technology or material can be used unless it is proven environmentally harmless) should guide industrial development.

The organizations in this discursive community seek to reduce the use of toxic materials and to ensure a safe and clean environment for all peoples. Organizations in this movement describe their purposes such as: "Preventing exposure to toxic materials that cause breast cancer," "creating safe schools to protect our children's health" or "ensuring that medical waste from hospitals is disposed of in an environmentally responsible way." Some examples of actions taken by these types of organizations include ensuring that all toxic materials are removed from schools to ensure that children are not exposed to them and ensuring the safe disposal of industrial wastes. Some of the leading environmental organizations in this discursive community include the Center for Health, Justice, and the Environment, and the 1 in 9 Breast Cancer Action Coaliltion.

Ecofeminism

The fourth environmental discourse to develop in the 1980s was Ecofeminism. This discursive community grew out of the feminist movement. Thus it links the development of a patriarchal society and the domination of women by men, to the domination of nature by humanity. Specifically, Ecofeminism defines the problem of ecological degradation as originating in the treatment of nature as an object to be possessed and dominated, instead of a partner to be cooperated with. This cultural treatment of nature is tied to the development of a patriarchal society and the domination of women by men. Just as man dominates women, humanity dominates nature. Thus the resolution of our ecological problems thus entails a shift from a manipulative and controlling culture toward both women and nature to a culture of cooperation. Key components of this discourse are:

• Earth is home for all life and should be revered and nurtured.

• Ecosystem abuse is rooted in androcentric concepts, values, and institutions.

• Relations of complementarily rather than superiority between culture/nature, human/nonhuman, and male/female are desirable.

• The many problems of human relations and relations between the human and nonhuman worlds, will not be resolved until androcentric institutions, values, and ideology are eradicated.

There are very few ecofeminist organizations in existence. Those that do exist focus on empowering women to function as decision makers. Some examples of the purposes of ecofeminist organizations include: "Representing the viewpoints of all women in international affairs" or "facilitating the development of women in leadership roles in the environmental movement." In addition, they seek to correct the perspective in economic development programs that fail to recognize the role of women and the household economy in the overall system of economic production. The largest and most well known ecofeminist organization in the U.S. is the Women's Environment and Development Organization.

Ecospiritualism

In 1967, a landmark essay, by Lynn White, titled "The Historical Roots of Our Ecologic Crisis" appeared in *Science Magazine*. In this essay, White argued that the western biblical tradition, on which both the Jewish and Christian faiths are based, was the root of the environmental crisis. Since the bible created a separation of man from nature, man was seen as master of and apart from, the rest of creation. This image, White argued, created a wholly anthropocentric view of nature, in which man was commanded to subdue the earth. So the exploitation of nature for man's needs was natural and appropriate. The remedy for our ecological crisis was clear. He argued that if the biblical belief system created a disregard for the natural environment, and led to our ecologic crisis, we need to develop a new religious viewpoint that would accommodate man to live in harmony with nature.

This viewpoint posed a major problem for western religious theologians. The ecological crisis created doubt of the Christian idea that a providential God was providing for humanity. Following this essay, a number of different religious thinkers developed unique religious perspectives that integrate concern over the natural environment into religious belief systems. Out of these writings, a unique discourse of Ecospiritualism emerged. Key components of this discourse are:

• Nature is endowed with spiritual value.

• Humanity, as part of nature, has a moral obligation to preserve it intact.

• Religious beliefs need to be developed that embody this ethic.

• These beliefs can then inform actions to create an ecologically sustainable society.

This new viewpoint spread through the U.S. religious community, and by 1995, virtually all of the major churches in the U.S. issued proclamations on environmental degradation. Additionally, in 1993, the National Religious Partnership was formed. This organization is composed of the United National Council of Churches, the U.S. Catholic Conference, Consultation on the Environment and Jewish Life, and the Evangelical Environmental Network. This action united the major Protestant, Catholic, Jewish, and Evangelical communities into one organization focused on developing and implementing religious approaches to combat environmental degradation. Recently, this viewpoint has gained increasing support in large evangelical churches. So while this discursive community is rapidly expanding, it has a unique structure. Its organizations are not single focus social movement organizations. Rather, they involve religious organizations that are expanding their role into environmental affairs. It is important to realize that there is no absolute line that defines the environmental movement. Rather, it is a gradient, moving from organizations that have an exclusive focus on environmental issues to those that deal with environmental issues as part of a group of associated issues. The final two discursive frames that are being examined in this paper fall into this category.

Animal Rights

The first related discursive frame is animal rights. Concern about the treatment of animals dates from 1866 in the United States, when the American Society for the Prevention of Cruelty to Animals (ASPCA) was founded. Although the primary focus of this movement has always been on domestic animals and pets, it has also been a significant actor regarding the treatment and preservation of wildlife. For example, Henry Bergh, who founded the ASPCA, was a key force in trying to stop the indiscriminant slaughter of Bison in the 1870s. This concern over animals has developed into a well defined discursive community. In this discursive frame, all species are seen to have intrinsic rights to realize their own evolved characteristics, and to live an independent life free from human direction or intervention. Key components of this discourse are:

- All of creation is endowed with an ability to define itself and evolve.

- Life thus has a right to be left to develop according to its own character.

- Humanity has no right to infringe on these rights of animals.

The organizations in this discursive community usually focus on both the protection of domestic and wild animals. There are a large number of organizations that focus on the rehabilitation and release of injured or sick wildlife. Some of the better known animal rights organizations in addition to the ASPCA include the Free Willy Keiko Foundation and People for the Ethical Treatment of Animals (PETA).

Anti-Globalization/Greens

The second discursive frame related to the U.S. environmental movement is the Anti- Globalization/Greens frame. This frame, which arose in the 1990s, focuses on the rise of a global economy and the impacts of this process for both the quality of life and its impacts on the environment. Specifically, it sees the process of economic globalization and the weakening of national labor and environmental standards as encouraging a "race to the bottom" as nations lower these standards to attract business investments. Key components of this discursive frame are:

• All humans and their communities deserve to live in an equitable, just and environmentally sustainable world.

• Global abuses—such as ecological destruction, poverty, war and oppression—are linked to global capitalism and the political and economic forces that have allowed the development of social inequality and injustices.

• The coercive powers of international financial institutions need to be eliminated so that national governments are accountable to the democratic will of their populations.

This community of organizations is still developing. The first large scale collective action of this community in the U.S. was the series of demonstrations in conjunction with the meeting of the World Trade Organization in Seattle in 1999. This community is loosely organized in the U.S. Network for Global Economic Justice, a coalition of over 200 social movement organizations. Some of the better known organizations in this community include the Ruckus Society and the Pesticide Action Network of North America.

Distribution of Organizations by Discursive Frame

The number of organizations in each discursive frame is shown in Figure one.

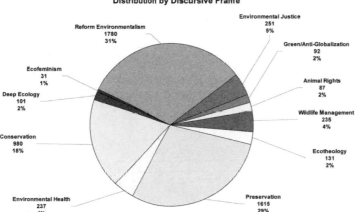

U.S. National and Regional Environmental Organizations Distribution by Discursive Frame

Figure 1

As this graph shows, the largest number of organizations are found in the long established discursive frames of Reform Environmentalism, Preservation, and Conservation. Together, these three discursive frames represent 78% of the environmental movement. All of the other discursive frames represent 5% or less of the total organizations. Thus, although a great deal of attention is given to the newer discursive frames in the academic literature, the environmental movement continues to be concentrated in these more conventional and long lived discursive frames.

Historical Development of the U.S. Environmental Movement

The second approach to understanding the U.S. environmental movement is to examine its historical development over time. The current environmental movement is the result of the cumulative historical development of the different discursive communities over the past 150 years. This growth in organizations is shown in Figure 2. To simplify this presentation, the number of discourses illustrated has been reduced. First, due to the relatively small number of organizations with the discourse of Wildlife Management and its close ideological similarity with Conservation, these two discursive frames have been combined.

Secondly, due to their small numbers, organizations with the discursive frames of Animal Rights, Deep Ecology, Ecofeminism, Ecospiritualism, Environmental Health, Environmental Justice, and Anti-Globalization/Green have been combined into one category, labeled here as "Alternative Discourses." As this graph illustrates, there was a substantial increase in the levels of organizational foundings starting in the mid-1950s up until around 1967. This was followed by explosive growth starting in the time period 1968 - 1970 and again in the 1988 - 1990 time frame.

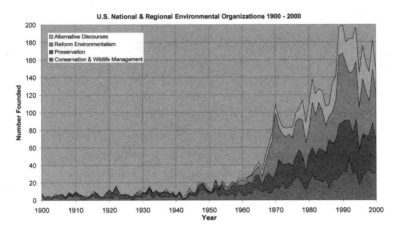

Figure 2

To further examine this growth by different discursive frames, the relative growth rates of the different communities are shown in Figure 3. This graph clearly shows that the discursive frames of Preservation and Conservation/Wildlife Management were dominant up until the end of the 1930s. In the 1940s, there was a significant rise in the number of alternative discursive organizations. This was due primarily to the increase of environmental health organizations founded during World War II. Additionally, the founding of Preservation organizations dramatically declined in the 1940s. However, in the 1950s, Preservation foundings increased rapidly and Conservation/Wildlife Management foundings started a long slow decline. Additionally, Reform Environmental organizational foundings started a long and steady increase, which culminated in an explosive rate of growth in 1970. Additionally, as more alternative discursive frames were developed in the 1970s and 1980s, there was a slow but steady growth in these organizations in the time period from 1960 on.

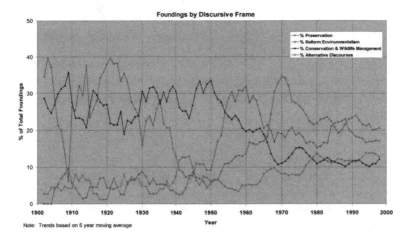

Figure 3

What this graph shows is that there are unique developmental dynamics to each discursive community. It is the cumulative impact of these different developmental dynamics that have lead to the highly differentiated environmental movement we encounter today.

Economic Resource Mobilization

The third approach focuses on the economic resources that each discursive community has available to promote its particular environmental agenda. The mobilization of economic resources is an extremely important determinant regarding the effectiveness of a discursive community to realize its goals. Every year, all nonprofit organizations are required to inform the U.S. Internal Revenue Service of their annual income and expenses. Based on this information filed with the IRS in 2003, Table 1 shows the total income of these different discursive communities.

Table 2: Income Distribution - Top 50 U.S. Environmental Organizations, 2003

Organization	Income	% of Income
NATURE CONSERVANCY	972368622	18.85
WILDLIFE CONSERVATION SOCIETY	347533674	6.74
SIERRA CLUB FOUNDATION, THE	241236005	4.68
CONSERVATION INTERNATIONAL FOUNDATION	229267098	4.44
POPULATION COUNCIL	197888299	3.84
WORLD WILDLIFE FUND	175582103	3.40
NATIONAL AUDUBON SOCIETY	172642826	3.35
TRUST FOR PUBLIC LAND	153915522	2.98
NATIONAL WILDLIFE FEDERATION	132004722	2.56
SIERRA CLUB	88203029	1.71
TIDES CENTER	69567396	1.35
AMERICAN LAND CONSERVANCY	68110320	1.32
FRESH AIR FUND	65459125	1.27
CHESAPEAKE BAY FOUNDATION	61007116	1.18
CONSERVATION FUND	60133583	1.17
ROCKY MOUNTAIN ELK FOUNDATION	55418970	1.07
ENVIRONMENTAL DEFENSE	51657887	1.00
NATURAL RESOURCES DEFENSE COUNCIL	50063972	0.97
WORLD RESOURCES INSTITUTE	48241872	0.93
BRANDYWINE CONSERVANCY	39007586	0.76
EARTHJUSTICE	34266715	0.66
OCEAN CONSERVANCY	31981555	0.62
DUCKS UNLIMITED	31475354	0.61
INSTITUTE OF ECOSYSTEM STUDIES	30206097	0.59
ASSOCIATION OF VILLAGE COUNCIL PRESIDENTS	29865852	0.58
PHEASANTS FOREVER	27824126	0.54
YOSEMITE FOUNDATION	25967512	0.50
WILDERNESS SOCIETY, THE (TWS)	23180201	0.45
NATIONAL PARKS CONSERVATION ASSOCIATION	22147238	0.43
DEFENDERS OF WILDLIFE	21779921	0.42
NATIONAL ARBOR DAY FOUNDATION	21337542	0.41
AFRICAN WILDLIFE FOUNDATION	18861831	0.37
STUDENT CONSERVATION ASSOCIATION	18714956	0.36
WATER ENVIRONMENT FEDERATION	18687081	0.36
PEOPLE FOR THE ETHICAL TREATMENT OF ANIMALS	18652096	0.36
WETLANDS AMERICA TRUST	17171656	0.33
ANTI-CRUELTY SOCIETY	16932539	0.33
INTERNATIONAL FUND FOR ANIMAL WELFARE	16634365	0.32
ENERGY FEDERATION INC INCORPORATED	15537392	0.30
ENVIRONMENTAL CAREERS ORGANIZATION	15468856	0.30
SAVE THE REDWOODS LEAGUE	14546107	0.28
AMERICAN FOREST FOUNDATION	14351443	0.28
COASTAL CONSERVATION ASSOCIATION	14265263	0.28
CENTER FOR INTERNATIONAL FORESTRY RESEARCH	12466225	0.24
ASPEN CENTER FOR ENVIRONMENTAL STUDIES	12402810	0.24
WATER ENVIRONMENT RESEARCH FOUNDATION	12042492	0.23
NATIONAL SAVE THE SEA TURTLE FOUNDATION	11349324	0.22
MANOMET CENTER FOR CONSERVATION SCIENCES	11212735	0.22
GREENPEACE FOUNDATION	10986369	0.21
NATIONAL ENVIRONMENTAL TRUST	10715102	0.21

As this table shows, fully 50% of the funding of the environmental movement is under the control of the organizations with a Preservationist frame. This is followed by the other three mainstream discursive frames of Reform Environmentalism, Wildlife Management and Conservation, who range between 20.4% to 12.2% of the total income. The alternative discourses have very low levels of economic resources. Even if they are all combined, they total less than 5% of the total income distribution.

This economic distribution is mirrored in the income ranking of individual organizations. Table 2 shows the total and percent income distribution for the wealthiest 50 U.S. environmental organizations. Income among environmental organizations is highly skewed to a few extremely wealthy organizations. The Nature Conservancy, a large land trust organization, receives nearly 19% of the total environmental movement's income.

Table 1 - Income Distribution by Discursive Frame - 2003

Frame	N	% of N	Total Income	% of Total	Mean	Median
Animal Rights	35	2.5%	95,542,298	1.9%	2,729,780	420,819
Conservation	223	16.0%	627,813,084	12.2%	2,815,305	345,421
Deep Ecology	34	2.4%	17,763,087	.3%	522,444	270,092
Ecofeminism	4	0.3%	2,027,480	>.1%	506,870	115,100
Ecospiritualism	12	0.9%	8,776,361	.2	731,363	149,452
Environmental Health	33	2.4%	36,683,659	.7%	1,111,626	503,346
Environmental Justice	38	2.7%	57,301,562	1.1%	1,507,936	385,728
Green/Anti-Globalization	9	0.6%	8,844,870	.2%	982,763	571,318
Preservation	536	38.6%	2,590,627,143	50.3%	4,833,260	296,873
Reform Environmentalism	404	29.1%	1,048,293,688	20.4%	2,594,786	395,409
Wildlife Management	62	4.5%	656,084,214	12.7%	10,582,003	310,477
Total	1,390	100.0%	5,149,757,446	100.0%	3,704,861	348,058

It is important to note that this list only shows the top 50 organizations. There are another 1,339 organizations that are not shown in this table. Between them, they divide the remaining 25.2% of total income. Thus the vast majority of environmental organizations have very limited economic resources available to them. Thus it is no surprise that the ones that mostly appear in the press and before Congress are those organizations with sufficient funding to build and maintain a strong staff and organizational structure. Accordingly, one of the key areas of focus in current research into the environmental movement, then, is why these funding differentials exist.

Conclusion

The U.S. environmental movement is not a monolithic structure. Rather it is composed of a number of different discursive communities. Each of these communities has its own specific issue focus. Additionally, they developed under different historical and political circumstances and have widely varying levels of economic resources. To understand this highly complex social movement requires that we use the full range of social movement perspectives.

One certainty is that this is not a static movement. Over the past century, it has developed several new discursive frames, and will most likely continue to do so in the future. There are several areas of potential development. For example, there has always been an uneasy alliance between trade unions and the environmental movement. Will they be able to develop a united political program? Additionally, the rise of environmental justice and the greens as significant actors in the movement has shaken to more established environmental organizations.

How will these newer approaches work out within the overall environmental movement? Finally, the discursive frames that were once dominant have been replaced by other approaches. What discursive frames will become dominant in the future? How this movement will evolve in the future is an open question. However, as it has in the past, it will continue to be a major player in the politics of the United States.

Suggested Readings

Bernstein, S. 2001. *The Compromise of Liberal Environmentalism.* Columbia University Press: New York

Brulle, Robert J. 2000, *Agency, Democracy, and Nature: The U.S. Environmental Movement from a Critical Theory Perspective*, MIT Press: Cambridge
Buell, F. 2004. *From Apocalypse to Way of Life.* London: Routledge

Bullard, Robert D., 1990, *Dumping in Dixie: Race, Class and Environmental Quality*, Boulder, CO: Westview Press

Dowie, M. 1996. *Losing Ground: American Environmentalism at the Close of the Twentieth Century* MIT

Fox, Stephen, 1981, *The American Conservation Movement: John Muir and His Legacy*, University of Wisconsin Press: Madison

Hays, Samuel P., 1972, *Conservation and the Gospel of Efficiency: The Progressive Conservation Movement*, 1890-1920, New York: Athenaeum

Hays, Samuel P., 1987, *Beauty, Health , and Permanence: Environmental Politics in the United States*, 1955-1988, New York: Cambridge University Press

Nash, R., 1967, *Wilderness and the American Mind, New Haven:* Yale University Press

Oelschlaeger, Max, 1991, *The Idea of Wilderness: From Prehistory to the Age of Ecology*, New Haven, Yale University Press

Paula Marantz Cohen

Fred Astaire and the Art of Fun

An Oxford conference allows scholars, performers and fans to share their passion

Fred Astaire, who was born in 1899 in Omaha, Nebraska, began performing on the vaudeville circuit with his sister Adele. She was six; he was four and a half. Twenty years later, they were Broadway stars in such shows as George and Ira Gershwin's Lady Be Good. This show and two others went on to even greater acclaim in London, where Adele met and married a British aristocrat, leaving Fred to forge a career on his own. Quickly, he made his way to Hollywood, where his "charm", as David O. Selznick would say, was "so tremendous" that it overcame the famously dismissive studio assessment: "can't act, can't sing, balding, can dance a little". Over the next twenty five years, he would exert almost complete artistic control over some thirty films. George Balanchine and Mikhail Baryshnikov called him one of the greatest dancers in history, while Gershwin and Irving Berlin preferred him over all other vocalists. Astaire made art which, in the words of his character in The Barkleys of Broadway (1949), seemed to be "fun set to music".

Film scholars, English professors, dance and music historians, performers and plain enthusiasts gathered at Oriel College, Oxford, last month to pay homage to this achievement with semiotic analysis and singalongs. The Fred Astaire Conference was conceived by Kathleen Riley, a post-doctoral Fellow at Corpus Christi College, and her American collaborator Chris Bamberger rather in the way that young people in old Hollywood musicals decide to "put on a show". That it was put on at Oxford had its rationale in Astaire's life-long affection for England, where he had so much early success and where he recorded some of his last, most personal albums. In some of his better films—Top Hat, The Gay Divorcee, Damsel in Distress, and Royal Wedding—Astaire sings and dances his way through ballrooms and drawing rooms, with English characters and manners as foils to his freewheeling American spirit. Indeed, Astaire as "the American", the New Man of the post-First World War era, was a subject addressed by a number of participants at the conference: fashion writer G. Bruce Boyer, for example, spoke to this point in his paper on sartorial style, noting how Astaire's soft-collared shirts and comfortable sports jackets came to replace the high starched collars and constricting suits of his Europeanized counterparts. Astaire's wardrobe, like his blithe personality, graceful movement, and natural vocal style, represented a New World of playful ease against an Old World of entrenched formality.

One of the highlights of the conference was the presence of Astaire's daughter, Ava Astaire McKenzie, who bears a striking resemblance to her father and was game to answer questions dear to fans' hearts: "Is it true that Fred woke you up for school by dancing around the room?" "Only a few steps." "Did Fred ever watch his old movies with you?" "Not really. He didn't like to look back." Also present to give insight into Astaire's character and creative process was the veteran British record producer Ken Barnes, who worked with Johnny Mercer, Bing Crosby and Frank Sinatra, as well as Astaire. Barnes recalled how he had persuaded Crosby and Astaire to duet on an album in the 1970s, telling each that the other had signed before either had, and how he had cajoled Astaire, by now retired from dance, to record a few tap steps for one of the tracks by demonstrating what a facsimile of tap dancing would sound like. "Nothing sounds like feet but feet", Astaire protested, and proceeded to do the steps himself.

John Mueller, a professor of Political Science and the author of Astaire Dancing (1985), an authoritative work on Astaire's musicals, focused on Astaire's drive for continual innovation and perfection in his routines, showing clips in which he performs a "wraparound" movement—a series of steps in which he encircles his partner with one arm, then unwraps her and returns to their initial position. The move, Mueller pointed out, was originally described in Vernon and Irene Castle's dance manual, but Astaire improved and then elaborated on it each time he used it. The idea of variations on a form was taken up by Todd Decker, a professor of Musicology, who discussed Astaire's use of jazz motifs borrowed from African-American musicians such as Fats Waller and Lionel Hampton. Astaire was the only film dancer who danced to the Blues, and his deep understanding of jazz became apparent when Decker compared his dance routines with Hampton's recordings. Refuting the conventional wisdom that Astaire's musicals are cinematically undistinguished (a myth based perhaps on his famous remark: "either the camera dances or I do"), the film and television historian Patricia Tobias demonstrated Astaire's technical astuteness, showing how he made sure that camera tracking always complemented bodily movement and kept the dancing figure within the central third of the frame; editing was done with such subtlety as to be practically invisible. The dance historian Beth Genné used video clips to show how Balanchine had incorporated Astaire's fluidity and posture into his repertory for the New York City Ballet (in one, the former Balanchine prima ballerina Maria Tallchief was seen telling two young dancers to "make it more Astaire").

A number of revelations, large and small, were offered: of Astaire's Jewish ancestry and of a rare clip of Astaire dancing on stage in The Gay Divorce (permitting comparison with the same number in the subsequent movie with Ginger Rogers). It was also revealed that Astaire could be difficult to dance with—at her debutante ball, Mrs McKenzie said, she and her father had been the only couple moving in the wrong direction. A Fred and Ginger panel examined that famous partnership in detail, John Mueller asserting that Ginger Rogers was among the best actresses of her time, a statement he backed up with clips showing her reactions as Astaire sang—what better test of acting talent than to react convincingly while someone croons to you? A lively discussion evolved around the subject of Rogers's dresses, traditionally maligned for being "in the way": a view that is now undergoing revision. Even the famous feather-shedding confection for "Cheek to Cheek" in Top Hat (a dress parodied by Judy Garland and Astaire in Easter Parade) found apologists. It was agreed that Rogers's dresses were often a "third partner" in the dance; her ability to "control" them, a notable feat. Finally put to rest was any suggestion that the two stars disliked each other. According to Mrs McKenzie, her father never said an unkind word about Rogers—but then, he seems never to have said an unkind word about anyone.

A feature of the conference was the continual stream of testimonials on how Astaire had, to borrow from the Gershwin song, "changed my life". (Many had first seen Astaire in Top Hat on television when they were twelve or thirteen, holding tape recorders up to the TV to capture the songs—a confession that could only be made in the company of fellow enthusiasts.) It concluded with tributes by professional performers and a presentation by the celebrated Gershwin expert and concert pianist Jack Gibbons, featuring bravura renderings of the Gershwin numbers from Astaire's movies, transcribed by Gibbons directly from the films. He interspersed these with a demonstration of Astaire's extraordinary piano-playing technique in the Harlem Stride Piano style, and recounted anecdotes about Astaire's friendship with Gershwin. It was no wonder the two men had an affinity for each other; they had a similar sense of rhythm and musical taste as well as a shared drive to challenge themselves and others. Gershwin's songs were preternaturally difficult to dance to, and Astaire was probably the only performer who could properly dance to them.

If there had been any doubt as to Astaire's genius, or the cultural influence he exerted on the twentieth century, it was put to rest by the end of the conference. For many there, Fred Astaire had long been a solitary passion, so that this marked a rare opportunity for shared appreciation. The end might have brought its melancholy as the participants dispersed, but the spirit of Fred Astaire had been present, Ariel-like, infusing the proceedings with his magic.

Ingrid G. Daemmrich

Tickling the Senses: Game-Playing in Hypertext Literature

This paper proposes that in order to function as a humorous medium, hypertext literature must show that it can play seductive games with the imagination as well as the senses.

As he awakens from his charmed dream, in which he has become an ass, Bottom in Shakespeare's *A Midsummer Night's Dream* muses: "man is but a patched fool, if he will offer to say what methought I had. The eye of man hath not heard, the ear of man hath not seen, man's hand is not able to taste, his tongue to conceive, nor his heart to report, what my dream was" (4.1.211-14). Since the invention of the printing press over 500 years ago, dramatists, poets, and fiction writers have filled in all the "nots" in Bottom's observation by appealing to our imagination. We laugh and cry, hear and see, taste and touch by reading their printed words. They invite us into what Neal Norrick has aptly called the "play frame" that entertains us by conjuring sensory images in our minds.

But what if we could take a more interactive role by selecting and manipulating literature's play frames? The Internet offers such an opportunity in the form of digital or electronic literature. George Landow defines this new literary expression in Hypertext 2.0 as "text composed of blocks of words or images linked electronically by multiple paths, chains, or traits in an open-ended, perpetually unfinished textuality described by the terms *link, node, network, web,* and *path*" (3). By integrating hypertext links with colorful designs, animation, and sound, and making it all accessible on the World Wide Web, digital literature could become, according to Janet Murray, "the brink of a historic convergence" between authors and technology. This convergence promises, according to Katherine Hayles, "nothing less than a radical transformation of writing and reading, writer and reader" (24). Are Murray, Hayles, and other proponents of digital literature right? To test their view, I have chosen three games commonly played by literature both to entertain audiences and to promote itself: literary jokes, tricks, and comic skirmishes; ironic paradoxes that play multiple viewpoints against each other; and parodic games that deconstruct and reconstruct texts into what Norrick terms "intertextual jokes." I will illustrate each with a print and a digital work in order to pose the question: Do digital literature's manipulability and multimedia approach add to traditional literature's humor and entertainment value? Or do they distract from them?

Literary games, tricks, and comic skirmishes

In Part 2, Chapter 14 of his masterpiece *Don Quixote of La Mancha*, Miguel de Cervantes plays a double game of disguise and make-believe not only with his characters but also with his readers. We join in his squire Sancho Panza's shock and surprise when "a nose of huge size, hooked in the middle, all covered with warts, and of a mulberry color like an eggplant" appears just as Don Quixote is about to assault his adversary, the Knight of the Woods. While it frightens Sancho out of his wits, it immediately inspires Don Quixote to imagine that it is some "monster or else... a human being of some new species..." Only after he has felled his unknown opponent and is about to finish him off is the double mystery solved. Raising the unknown knight's visor, Don Quixote discovers "the very face, the very figure, the very image of [his friend] Sanson Carrasco." His words to Sancho, "Come...behold what you have to see but not to believe...learn what wizards and enchanters are able to accomplish" amusingly jar with Sancho's discovery that the huge nose has magically metamorphosed into "a clownish nose of varnished pasteboard" tucked into his old neighbor Tomé Cecial's pocket (623). For Sancho, the mystery is solved: the huge nose is his neighbor's mischievous joke. But for Don Quixote, and by extension, us readers, the mischievous tricks of the wizards and enchanters will continue to shape the humor of the novel. Each new encounter serves up new tricks and interactions between Cervantes' memorable characters.

Now, what if instead of watching the story play out, we could make up some of those tricks and interactions ourselves? Readers of hypertext literature can do just that, because cyber-literature gives them the tools and directions and invites them to craft their own entertainment. The site of the entertainment shifts radically from inside the imagination to outside on the computer screen. It presents a multiplicity of hyperlinks, each leading to a multimedia environment that engages all the senses. We are constantly invited to select among a host of possible paths, all designed by the artist to entertain readers and to play games with us. In "Fibonacci's Daughter" by the well-established artist M.D. Coverley, the central focus is the spiral, and the central motto, "Life spirals in." So, readers can select characters, plot, and reading sequence, but the constant presence of a brilliantly colored rotating spiral indicates that all reader-determined choices will "spiral in," that is, magically connect. Still, we have choices. Do we enjoy playing mathematical or verbal games? Tricky mathematical equations and enigmatic proverbs abound to play bewildering games with us. Do we want to get to know the character behind the enigmatic proverbs? We can choose to read Annabelle

Thompson's autobiography. It traces her development from the child of gamblers to her predilection for number games that playfully connect her with the thirteenth-century Italian mathematician Fibonacci. These games lead to her activities as petty criminal and owner of the exotic Bet Your Life shop in a deserted wing of the Huntington Mall and end in her puzzling disappearance. Or do we prefer the more active game of solving a double murder? We then select the five parts of a "Feature Article from the Orange County Ledger-Times." In a series of interviews by an unnamed reporter, they ostensibly trace the mysterious connection between Annabelle's "reverse insurance" business of insuring teenagers against the risks in their love relationships with the deaths of two popular football heroes from a nearby high school. As we attempt to solve this murder, we are repeatedly enticed into choosing hyperlinks that bring up the computer-generated mathematical formulas Annabelle uses to calculate her charges to her clients, or to other characters and their stories, or to the career of the reporter writing the feature article. We could ignore these hyperlinks, as well as the distracting background wallpaper pattern and Muzak. But do we? Or don't their colorfulness and intrusiveness trick us into temporarily abandoning our hunt? So, though we can choose the path we want to take through the tale, Coverley's spiral draws us into her game, much as Don Quixote's vision of the nose as the work of enchanters entices us to play his game.

Still, the nexus of the game is located in very different spaces. Whereas Don Quixote's adventures take place in the intersection between the authoritative printed text and the reader's imagination, Coverley's hypertext presents the unstable, variable, not even retraceable environment of successively competing links. Because readers construct the text by selecting which links to follow, the entertainment becomes dependent on actions rather than the imagination. If, as Peter Brooks observes, the entertainment of fiction builds on the desire to "seduce and subjugate the listener," what happens when listeners become partners in the seduction and subjugation?

Ironic paradoxes that play multiple viewpoints against each other

Emily Dickinson often used her poetry as a private game board to try out how multiple perspectives could be played out with and against each other. An example is Poem 177:

As if some little Arctic flower,
Upon the polar hem,
Went wandering down the latitudes,

Until it puzzled came
To continents of summer,
To firmaments of sun,
To strange, bright crowds of flowers,
And birds of foreign tongue!
I say, as if this little flower
To Eden wandered in—
What then? Why, nothing,
Only, your inference therefrom!

    The first words, "As if," immediately transport us into a play frame, where it's possible to conceive of an Arctic flower "wandering" to a tropical land. Playing on our conventional identification of the tropics as paradise, the poet imagines that it would have "To Eden wandered in." A lovely image, but where does it lead? Instead of answering the question, the poet throws it like a ball back to her imaginary reader, by curtly stating, "Why, nothing,/Only, your inference therefrom!" Her toss back to the reader transfers the authority to solve the puzzle from the poet to the reader. Those who, like Dickinson herself, enjoy illogical puzzles will laugh at her cleverness.

    Instead of presenting a verbal game dressed in conventional verse, Deena Larsen's poem "Stained Word Window" provides a number of colorful blocks engraved with single words and arranged in a pattern recalling the game of hopscotch. Readers are invited to hop into the game by running the cursor over the blocks. This action generates a series of puzzling poems from Larsen's invisible store. We choose. Will it be YOUR? Then a poem appears:

Lives are composed of silence—
Delicate movements in an alien world
As you pick over the gravel stones
Searching for something we cannot see

Or OUR? Another enigmatic verse appears:

The pronoun keeps shifting,
Like leaves under the waves—
Breathing simultaneously until
The current lifts under us
Separating the pale fronds of we into
you.
me.

The poems feature enigmatic word plays that rival Dickinson's intricate verbal games. The difference lies in the timing. Whereas Dickinson's puzzles are permanently printed on a page and can be read repeatedly, Larsen's appear and disappear so quickly that our eyes momentarily glimpse a word or two, only to be replaced by others the instant our hand moves the cursor over the next block. The mental verbal game becomes an intriguing hand-and-eye play. Both the text and the imaginary connections that it evokes become dependent on the actions of a complex coordination between our hands and our eyes. Does this physiological shift from eye-text to hand-eye-text engage or disengage the imagination? The answer to this question will determine the future of hypertext literature.

Parodic games that deconstruct and reconstruct texts into intertextual jokes

Of all its diversions, literature's favorite game is playing with itself by creating a text that parodies previous texts by echoing, exaggerating, distorting, inverting, or ridiculing them. At times, the previous text is visible; at others, there is, as Jacques Derrida points out, only a trace left. Because parody is, according to Michele Hannoosh, literature in the making, it is a way for literature to promote itself. An outstanding example is Lewis Carroll's famous nonsense poem, "Jabberwocky" which he incorporated in "Through the Looking-Glass" and "What Alice Found There:"

> 'Twas brillig and the slithy troves
> Did gyre and gimble in the wabe;
> All mumsy were the borogroves,
> And the mome raths outgrabe.

> "Beware the Jabberwock, my son!
> The jaws that bite, the claws that catch!
> Beware the Jubjub bird, and shun
> The frumious Bandersnatch!"

> He took his vorpal sword in hand;
> Long time the manxome foe he sought—
> So rested he by the Tumtum tree,
> And stood awhile in thought.

> And, as in uffish thought he stood,
> The Jabberwock, with eyes of flame,
> Came whiffling through the tulgey wood,
> And burbled as it came!

One, two! And through and through
The vorpal blade went snicker-snack!
He left it dead, and with its head
He went galumphing back.

"And hast thou slain the Jabberwock?
Come to my arms, my beamish boy!
O frabjous day! Callooh, Callay!"
He chortled in his joy.

'Twas brillig, and the slithy toves
Did gyre and gimble in the wabe:
All mimsy were the borogoves,
And the mome raths outgrabe.

The poem's phonetic and syntactical patterns disclose that it is a parody of the traditional English ballad. It has the typical alternating rime pattern of the ballad. And it sings the tale of a youthful hero who rescues his community by slaying a threatening monster, thereby reestablishing its peace and order. But it also features a superscript (to borrow Raskin's term) that transforms the serious ballad plot into an amusing one by recounting the tale with ridiculous nonsense words. The phonetics of such word combinations as "gyre and gimble," "wabe and outgrabe," "waffling and burbling," "snicker-snack," and "Callooh, Callay" are designed to make us laugh. Serious scholars have traced their possible meanings, and Humpty Dumpty later on in *Through the Looking Glass* gives his own absurd definitions to Alice. But readers are most likely to agree with Alice: "Somehow it seems to fill my head with ideas—only I don't know what they are!" Our double response of laughter at the odd-sounding words and perplexity about their possible meanings make this parody of a ballad a complex entertainment.

In transposing "Jabberwocky" from the printed page onto the computer screen, Canadian mathematician and digital poet Neil Hennessy shifts the focus of its entertainment from a mental into a visual-mental experience. Instead of a poem arranged into stanzas of four lines, he presents readers with individually colored letters that build words. Hennessy describes the process:

> When a letter comes into contact with another letter or group of letters, a calculation occurs to determine whether they bond according to the likelihood that they would appear contiguously in the English lexicon. Clusters of letters accumulate to form

words, which results in a dynamic nonsense word sound poem floating around on the screen with each iteration of the generator...JABBER realizes a linguistic chemistry with letters as atoms and words as molecules.

In creating his parody of Carroll's nonsense poem, Hennessy continues its game of making fun of an earlier text by both imitating and distorting it (in this case, reducing it). But unlike Carroll's poem, Hennessy's has no beginning or end. We can join or leave the game at any moment without missing a significant move. The words just keep sliding by until we decide that we have had enough.

Conclusion:

One way that literature promotes itself as entertainment is to seduce readers into playing its games. Ongoing games are best, because they keep readers engaged. Armed with such seductive tricks as color-coded hyperlinks, manipulability, and immersive multimedia effects, digital literature would seem to have great advantages over conventional texts in attracting and holding readers. As Michael Giesecke asserts, the plain appearance of typographically fixed text cannot compete with the colorful entertainment offered by the Internet. But hypertext also changes the reader's role from enjoying the complex maneuvers of a textual game to actively participating in what Robert Elliott terms "the perilously intricate dance [the author] has set in motion." If the intricate dance consists in clicking successive hyperlinks and being immersed in the resulting multimedia, what happens to Elliott's definition of the reader's role: "to follow the complex maneuvers as closely as possible, recreating them in his mind as he is flung widely about..."? Two answers are possible. The simple answer is that the process of recreating a work shifts from the imagination to the interface between computer screen and user. The complex answer is that cyber-literature offers readers the opportunity not just to recreate but to create a story or poem in conjunction with the artist on a space that increasingly is the preferred venue for amusement. So, while the youthful humor of digital literature may not approach the sophisticated entertainment of traditional texts, its presence on the ubiquitous Internet assures literature a place in the public forum.

Works Cited

Brooks, Peter. *Reading for the Plot: Design and Intention in Narrative*. New York: Knopf, 1984.

Carroll, Lewis. *Through the Looking-Glass and What Alice Found There*. New York and Boston: T.Y. Crowell, 1893.

Cervantes, Miguel de. *The Ingenious Knight Don Quixote de la Mancha*. Trans.

Alexander James Duffield. London: C. Kegan Paul, 1881. Coverley, M.D. *Fibonacci's Daugher*. 2002. http://califia.us/Fibonacci/choice.htm.

Derrida, Jacques. *Of Grammatology*. Trans. Gayatri Chakrovorty Spivak. Baltimore: Johns Hopkins UP, 1976.

Dickinson, Emily. *The Poems of Emily Dickinson*. Reading Edition. Ed. R.W. Franklin. Cambridge: The Belknap Press of Harvard UP, 1999.

Elliott, Robert. "Swift's Satire: Rules of the Game." ELH 41 (1974): 413-428.

Giesecke, Michael. "Literature as Product and Medium of Ecological "Communication". Configurations 10 (2002): 11-35.

Hayles, N. Katharine. The Transformation of Narrative and the Materiality of Hypertext." *Narrative 9* (2001): 21-39.

Hennessy, Neil. "Jabberwoky: The Jabberwocky Machine." 2001. http://www.epc.buffalo.edu/authors/hennessey/.

Hannoosh, Michele. "The Reflexive Function of Parody." *Comparative Literature 41* (1989): 113/127.

Landow, George. *Hypertext 2.0*. Baltimore: Johns Hopkins Press, 1997.

Larsen, Deena. "Stained Word Window." 1999. www.wordcircuits.com/gallery/stained.

Murray, Janet. *Hamlet on the Holodeck: the Future of Narrative in Cyberspace*. Cambridge: MIT Press, 1997.

Norrick, Neal. Intertextuality in Humor. *Humor: International Journal of Humor Research* 2.2 (1989): 117-139.

Raskin, Victor. Semantic Mechanisms of Humor. Dordrecht: D. Reidel, 1985.

Albert DiBartolomeo

Hell on Earth

When a kidney stone taught me the meaning of agony, I also learned the limits of my own weak self.

I've often wondered how I would withstand great pain. I mean the pain of the body, that which registers on the nerves, not that of loss or deprivation that ravishes our emotional life. When the pain came, would I behave with some amount of stoicism and even grim humor, like the protagonists in Hemingway novels whom I so admired? Or would I moan and howl in sounds far beyond intelligible human speech? Last year I found out when a kidney stone made its slow passage through my right ureter. You may not know what ureters are—certainly you wouldn't be too aware that you possessed them until a bit of solid matter larger than the ureter's diameter left your kidney for the journey to the outside world.

This journey can begin suddenly, with paralyzing force. "Like being hit with a two-by-four," one friend told me. "Like being shot with an arrow," said another. But no simile can adequately describe pain, or pleasure for that matter; it must be experienced. We can know the concrete causes of pain, like pressure, too much heat, the splitting of the flesh, but the resultant pain is an abstraction, and like all abstractions it lies beyond the precise grasp of language. We simply don't have the words. We can have trouble, then, describing our own pain and another's pain, even when it manifests itself in grimacing, say, or writhing. Ultimately it remains metaphysical—something to doubt.

My kidney stone "attack" tugged me from an uneasy sleep at 3:07 a.m. The pain was then only a few degrees beyond uncomfortable, and I thought for some hopeful minutes that I might have a strange muscle cramp or that my innards were protesting against the odd-tasting tofu burger I had risked for dinner. I tried to ignore it. I tried to force my thoughts elsewhere. But the pain was insistent. I massaged my side and twisted this way and that, but no amount of repositioning or rubbing relieved the hot spike tunneling through my abdomen.

The pain ascended through the long hours of the early morning toward a level that dwarfed all the other pains I had known before, including an abscessed tooth and torn ankle ligaments. It nearly equaled the spectacular sensation of bringing a hammer down upon my thumb, but that was brief in comparison, a few minutes of localized agony that then settled into a bearable throbbing. The pain in my side was not just severe but unrelenting, a continuous deep gnawing coupled with cold sweats, nausea and other blades of pain that radiated throughout the confused coils of my digestion, causing more mischief there.

I paced the length of the house, took a hot bath, tried some yoga and breathing exercises taken from a dusty New Age book I had once purchased as a cure for all my ills. I pulled my hair, pressed my temples, bit my fist. Before all emotions left me, I cursed with a flamboyance that, were I loud enough, would surely have caused the houseplants to wilt. At one point, I curled up on the floor like the insensate fetus I wished then to be. But no measure I took lessened the pain.

When the sun fully rose, I was still in pain, and still grinding my teeth against it some hours later in the emergency room of a local hospital. A nurse inserted a shunt into the back of my hand and hooked me up to an I.V. meant to flush the stone from my plumbing. It would be an additional hour of pain before I received a mainline of blessed Toradol. In twenty minutes, the pain began to retreat. In half an hour, I was smiling, joking with the nurse and listening to the prosaic conversations of the staff, even as other emergency cases groaned and yelped in the curtained spaces about me. But I smiled and joked because of relief, not elation. In fact, while I was still in the E.R., a peculiar despair began to creep over me.

I was still despondent when I underwent a CT scan two days later because the "calculus" was taking its time to leave my body. I had to wait an hour before the procedure, and I spent the time shivering in the thin hospital robe, my socks and loafers, looking as far from chic as a person can get. Another man waited with me. He kept his face in one battered magazine after the other. We did not speak. He seemed to want to be invisible, and so did I. There was a subtext to this business and it was a dark one.

While waiting, I thought back to the attack and how my desire for the pain to end quickly became a need exclusive of all other considerations. Family, job, achievements, passions and the like all lost their significance. The pain became more than a steel box that separated me from anything but itself, more than a wedge that drove itself between my mind and body, making me more fully, if not totally, the latter. What great pain does, I learned that long night, is obliterate memory, in fact, "all psychological content, painful, pleasurable and neutral," as philosopher Elaine Scarry writes in *The Body in Pain*. When that occurs, we are no more than flesh, bone and blood. We lose our character, who we are. This is the true nature of the joy we feel at pain's cessation—the recovery of our humanity.

Eventually, I was put into the interesting machine and it did its work. Later, still in my airy gown, I was encouraged to see the images assembled on a white screen in a darkened room. It appeared as though I had been sliced repeatedly like a large bolt of prosciutto, and I was reminded of an earlier time.

After fracturing my jaw in my early 20s while playing football, I acquired the X-ray prints of my skull from the oral surgeon. After my mouth had been wired shut and I began to dine on various purees, I'd place the X-rays against the windowpane. With equal measures of revulsion and fascination, I'd gaze upon the pencil-line break in my jawbone, my teeth with their bits of metal, the shadow of my brain.

I felt as though I were looking at my own corpse, my flesh sloughed away by time. This is what would be in my coffin some years later, I thought. The processes that went through my mind at the moment—That's me?—were managed by the very thing I was looking at, a picture of my gray skull's contents set starkly against a blue sky. This was unsettling, but I did not fully realize why until the internist showed me the CT scan images of my torso many years later, when I was much closer to the end of my average life span.

"There are your kidneys," he said, pointing at an image with a pen. "The right one's a little backed up from the stone, which you can see here." He pointed to a white dot near my bladder where the ureter emptied. "It's hung up. If it doesn't move within a few days, we'll have to do something mechanical."

I only nodded. I was not thinking of the "something mechanical," nor of the pain to come should the stone dislodge itself and travel. The pain had been only one component of the despair that followed my kidney-stone attack. The other, and perhaps more disturbing, revealed itself in that darkened room where I was made to confront the notion that we're all just a bunch of parts and slippery workings that are prone to failure like any other mechanism, and with pain usually added. I was also thinking of my own father's kidneys, which were destroyed by twenty years of diabetes and so killed him.

I was thinking, too, of my stepfather, who had died of cancer several years ago after a kidney stone sent him to the hospital—where the routine X-ray, which I saw too, revealed the "well-defined mass" hovering in his ghostly lung. I had been with him in the emergency room while the kidney stone did its work and, over the next four months, while pain and his terminal illness and ultimately the morphine emptied him of himself. Even love, given or received, could not slice through the narcotic haze of pain or the staggering awareness of our own hopelessly mechanistic mortality. This will crush even the most positive of temperaments, the fiercest of wills.

Diagnostic images of my organs glowed on the walls. I got out of the viewing room and the hospital as fast as I could.

Three days later, the stone moved. I had been waiting for it. I had told myself that that tiny rock would not do to me what it had done earlier, that I would keep the upper hand and, in so doing, keep my conscience from seeping away. But before the pain medication kicked in, the pain scattered my mind, and all things but the pain became mere suggestions of themselves. The pain reduced me to a single inflamed nerve and little more. After it was gone, my self returned but an eerie feeling stayed with me. Our psychology, our spirituality, the value systems by which we live are only possible in the absence of ill health or pain. Our essence disappears into great pain, revealing all that we hold dear to be the most fragile of luxuries.

Leonard Finegold

Is Magnet Therapy a Billion-Dollar Boondoggle?

This saga starts with the publication of an editorial on this topic in the *British Medical Journal* (2006 332:4) by physician Bruce Flamm and me (a biophysicist). It is estimated that, world-wide, large sums of money are spent on healing by permanent magnets. These are conventional magnets, of the same type that one uses to attach notes to a refrigerator or steel filing cabinet. (Pulsed magnetic fields are a different item, and are currently being investigated for therapy.) You are invited to enter "magnet healing" into a Web browser, and spend a while in amused bewilderment, for such magnets are advertised to cure almost all the ills and pains that affect woman- and man-kind, including carcinoma. Magnets are advertised for healing by prominent athletes and are allowed to be sold without restrictions, so it is understandable that the person-in-the-street considers them a valuable therapy, with no side *effects*.

We surveyed the published literature and critically examined the best publications. Within the confines of a BMJ editorial, we could discuss only a few publications. By the standards of modern evidence-based medicine, we concluded that not only was there no physics evidence that magnet therapy was effective, but also that it was highly probable that magnet therapy is simply of no benefit. We suggested to physicians that if patients insist on using magnets, then the patients should be advised to use the cheapest magnets (such as those on refrigerators), for we could confidently say that the cheapest would be just as effective as the most expensive, and also that the cheapest would relieve any pain in the wallet.

Now, our publications are typically read by the handful of colleagues in the field, our mothers, and that's about all. To my surprise, were interviewed by many reporters for radio and press, and the article was even covered by the Arabic network Aljazeera (I read the English version). I was leery of reporters, yet can report that practically all reported our article fairly (and Aljazeera added a charming picture of a magnetic bracelet). The article was one of the most accessed of BMJ articles for the month (little does BMJ know that it was our mothers who were repeatedly looking at it). BMJ commendably publishes "Rapid Comments" on papers, which are easily read on line. You may enjoy reading our responses to some of the most rabid of these.

Then, when the shouting and the tumult had died, lo and behold we were mentioned on the front page of the *UK Sunday Times* (26 February, same year) since the National Health Service has now added magnets to prescription items. Pleasingly, NHS gets them at half price. (It appears that one of our rabid responders is connected with the company that sells these items.) It also appears that one Cherie Blair, an eminent lawyer (and a close relative of the UK Prime Minister), believes in them. (It is stated that a member of royalty wears copper bracelets, for they are magnetic. As a physicist, I am most perturbed by this, for copper is simply not magnetic, and so the said member should immediately exchange the copper bracelet for a refrigerator magnet.)

You, Dear Reader, can help me in my bemused bewilderment, by explaining to me (L@Drexel.edu) why able people—who would never fall for a dubious financial scheme—nevertheless fondly wear magnets. An acquaintance told me that she knew I did not believe in them, that she would continue to wear the expensive shoe inserts sent by her sister, but could not wear them in dress shoes since they were too thick. I suggested that she use thin refrigerator magnets. She was delighted to report later that the thin magnets worked just as well. So perhaps I did some good after all.

Coda: There is a spark of hope. The UK has a governmental Office of Fair Trading. Bless them, they stopped one Magna Jewelry from misleading claims that magnetic jewelry relieves back pain. Naughtily, one wonders if the Office will now pursue the makers of the NIH prescription items mentioned above. And then shall we have the spectacle of one arm of the government educating another?

Valerie Fox

It Seemed Like a Good Idea at the Time

The long weekend,
the chocolate-coated, frozen banana on a stick.

Some appointments can only happen if
you use a pencil and they can be dangerous.

Let's take our paper dresses out of storage.
Andy Warhol might rise again

in triplicate. I vow solemnly not to sell
or scratch your high school bootlegs.

In those days, all I allowed myself was to bark
and then I found myself on this bare beach

of bones, three or four weeks
lost, it was the beginning

and I told God, if you don't strike me dead
by Thursday next week I will not change.

Scott Gabriel Knowles

Voting Philadelphia

A startling racket rides up behind me as I stand with my coffee and my map at 13th and Walnut Streets, a sound like the amplified garble of a rock singer heard from the back row. Then it swooshes by, a white car with three twenty-somethings inside, the one in the backseat on a microphone with a bullhorn pointed out the window. Doppler effect in effect.

> We will
> We will
> Barack you
>
> We will . . .
> We will . . .
> *BARACK YOU!*

It was primary day in Philadelphia.

In a city made famous for brotherly love, but known for too long as a divided metropolis, an election provides a rare opportunity to walk up to strangers in any neighborhood and start asking personal questions. Neighbors reconnect after a long winter, hoopla is encouraged, young and old, black and white stand in the same lines, argue and joke, and ultimately push VOTE on the same machines across all four corners of the city.

My goal was to assemble a few representative voices from the crowd on a day when the nation was again keeping its eye on Philadelphia. The pundits were predicting a big day for Obama in the city, but the pundits are addicted to rounded numbers, to ten-second truth dispensing. I was out for some stories.

I had started my day early at the Palumbo Recreation Center in Bella Vista, weaving through the leafleteering brigade outside before handing my voter registration card to my neighbor. An older woman with thick glasses whom I see every time I vote was seated next to two more of my neighbors, a retired postman known on the block as "Mr. Al" and his sister-in-law Josie. You may vote behind the curtain at Palumbo, but that's the only anonymity you will get.

Vote duly recorded (I trust) I headed out for the day, my camera-toting brother—let's call him "The Planner"—at the wheel of a sporty red Philly Car Share ride.

First Stop, Ziehler Playground, Olney, 10:15 a.m.

Teenagers play lacrosse on a lush, green field as Nashanda Westbrooks lingers just inside the sign-cluttered chain link of the rec center. Trim duplexes with small yards form a protective buffer zone in every direction.

A man with thick arms is sitting back on two legs of a metal chair across from her, asking-telling me, "You see any Hillary signs in these yards around here?" I hadn't. "That's right." This was Obama country, Nashanda agrees.

What are the issues that the candidates need to address in Olney, a neighborhood in far north central Philadelphia? Nashanda is pretty young, but she likes her neighborhood and has strong opinions about it. "It's quiet, to me," she says, "compared to North Philly." She doesn't see many problems with Olney, none she can point to right off. The Planner snaps pictures of signs taped to chain link. It was a lull in the middle of a busy day, and we slip away, the chair-leaner still leaning.

Second Stop, Pelbano Recreation Center, Rhawnhurst, 11:00

The boys of Derkas Auto Body are rallying against the squad from the 24th District on the softball field at Pelbano Recreation Center in northeast Philly. A sign on the fence thanks International Brotherhood of Electrical Workers President John Dougherty—who just happens to also be a candidate that day—for his generosity to the community. Hillary signs form a visual escort from the parking lot to the polling place entrance. A white-haired man in a bunny-white sweatsuit and headphones walks briskly past.

With her League of Women Voters voting guide in one hand, and her cane in the other, red-haired Rhawnhurst resident Ileen Green explains to me about her favorite candidate. "He's for change... but, who isn't?" Hillary, on the other hand, is very specific in what she will do as Ileen sees it, especially on health care. Taking 30 pills a day, insulin, and having to visit three doctors a week, health care is very understandably Ileen's number one issue. She is not an old woman, but illness has made her cautious, and this clearly informs her politics.

The Planner walks in close, asks if Ileen will pose for a shot; she pauses, thinks on it, and agrees. "I'm afraid of McCain getting in," she tells me, "I oppose this war." In the end, though, Ileen thinks the party will unite behind the nominee. She doesn't think Philadelphia issues have been addressed much in the primary race, and she would love to see a debate about them, particularly crime.

Ileen Green encourages me to hit the website for the League of Women Voters, then heads on through the crowd of voters, many much older than her, streaming in to vote. The Planner is thinking about getting some pictures of the softball players as we head back to the car—but one look from the side of beef at first base stops him cold. "We'll remember them," he says.

Third Stop, Kendrick Recreation Center, Roxborough, Noon

"Mike Livingston is my man!"

Tom Obst has stationed himself right in the middle of the steps. He stands up to talk to me, occasionally stopping to shake hands or hug and kiss his friends coming out of what is, apparently, the de facto Republican door of the Kendrick Recreation Center in the old working class neighborhood of Roxborough, out in the northwest section of the city.

He makes a lewd joke about Hillary and takes a scolding from a female friend passing by.

Livingston is challenging incumbent Chaka Fattah for the 2nd Congressional District seat, and Obst is talking him up big, along with all the other candidates on the Republican slate. Like a poker dealer he flings cards with his preferred candidates listed on it to passersby.

With close-cropped beard and a bit quieter than his buddy, Jeff Jones stands a few steps down and slips in and out of the conversation. Both of them work for the Philadelphia Parking Authority, though Obst ribs his friend that he is a good guy while Jones is the bad guy. Jones writes tickets, apparently, while Obst works out at the airport. They are both in their late 30s or early 40s, and their allegiance to the GOP makes them minority voters here in Roxborough, though you couldn't tell it from their enthusiasm.

The Republicans helped me when I needed it and the Democrats didn't, so I switched parties," Obst tells me.

I leave it at that.

Both of these guys tell me they like their former councilman and now Mayor Michael Nutter, a reminder of Nutter's popularity across racial and party lines, and the degree to which Philadelphia voters don't easily fall into the simple caricatures that the national media (and the Governor) have created for white voters in the state.

Still, they like McCain for President.

"If Obama doesn't win, a lot of Democrats will go for McCain," says Obst. He and Jones are breaking it down for me. Health care won't change no matter who is elected. Fuel prices and crime, these are the issues that Philadelphians care about. They want to see some money go for public transportation—a view that unites Republicans and Democrats in the city.

"Why kill your wallet when you can take the bus!" Jeff Jones has just coined a slogan that SEPTA would no doubt pay him for handsomely.

Can Livingston beat Chaka Fattah? Obst doesn't miss a beat.

"Do you want to go to Atlantic City and make a bet?" I'm not sure which way he means the crack, so I leave it alone. The Planner swoops in for a candid, but Obst isn't much in the mood. He's more about words than images.

I decide to head to the south entrance to find some Democrats to talk to, and leave Roxborough's Republican gatekeepers on the steps.

"Let's go Republicans!" Obst yells, as I walk through the building and out the other side to speak with Pete Johnston, a center city attorney handing out Obama information, wearing an Obama cap, an Obama button, and able to talk "deep Obama" with me for 15 minutes.

Jobs, social security, and crime top Johnston's list of key issues. "I like his vision, energy, and excitement... he can unite the country." How can Obama help Philly, though? If the national economy is stronger, perhaps if the war ends, then that frees up more money for domestic issues, for urban issues. This is core to Obama's current stump speech—connecting the vast expense of the war to the yawning needs of domestic programs like education and housing.

Johnston was at the massive rally Obama held last week on Independence Mall. He was part of that history, a landmark political moment in an American political landmark.

"A lot depends on tonight," he tells me as I turn to go, "it could be over soon."

We sit in traffic, the red car is uneasy, there's no reason to slow down, but slowed we are. I take the chance to ask The Planner if much can be learned by talking to strangers about politics.

"You mean, are we wasting our time today?" he asks.

"Yes," I reply, "That's what I mean."

I know better, but I am trying to wind him up. It works, and he preaches a sermon of fire and brimstone—his candidate will reveal truth and the nation will be redeemed. The Planner is the type of guy who will try to negotiate votes for his candidate while riding the trolley on the way home from work. He will cut deals, trade campaign buttons, make promises, get wild in the eye. He will drive to Iowa, to New Hampshire—he'll send you speeches at 3:00 a.m. and pump his fist when the right numbers drop in the hopper.

"The best part about this, though..." he pauses, "is that I feel part of *this* city. I am getting it, now, finally, I think."

As he talks I realize I'm pretty much the same. In this age of insta-politics, unmoored from a place and floating through the ether, we are both searching for some soil in which to root our votes.

From the outside you start, but you work towards the core. That's the way it is for us roaming Americans, far from our ancestral political homes, the Planner and I, our home place being one where people might say "Osama" instead of Obama, or tell more than one lewd joke about Hillary. Today we collect stories about politics and the urban character, but ours is also one to be collected.

Fourth Stop, South Philadelphia, 2:00 p.m.

Kurt Fredericksdorf, a brother in the International Brotherhood of Electrical Workers Local #98 is helping an elderly couple across the street. With one hand he is stopping traffic; with the other he is pointing the couple towards the polling place. Kurt is real South Philly, not some bragging, cheese-steak-eating cliché, but the real deal, a blue-collar son of the neighborhood who loves it here, and is making his stand. He has 1500 fellow IBEW members living in the neighborhood and the strength of these numbers ripples through him.

The son of a policeman, and with three brothers on the police force, the city's unions are in his blood. He's out for Johnny Doc today, standing in front of an "Italians for Dougherty" sign, an "Irish for Dougherty" sign, and wearing his own Dougherty t-shirt. Johnny Doc has the biggest operation in town today; you would think he's running for President with the street corner visibility he has. A minivan festooned with Jonny Doc signs pulls up and drops off stacks of t-shirts. A passing woman takes one; it's unclear if she's going to vote or just needs a nightshirt. Kurt is pretty sure that a lot of Republicans are switching parties to vote for Dougherty today.

Kurt wants to see some help for Philadelphia from the national level politicians, on fuel prices, on guns, on economic development. He wants the war to come to an end. He doesn't understand the people he knows who voted for Bush and yet still complain about the state of the nation.

Mostly, though, he's about excitement, not political punditry. "Philly's awesome," he tells me. Kurt is thirty; he is part of the new generation of Philadelphians choosing to stay rather than decamp for the suburbs. "We have Penn, we have the airport, we have the waterfront. This is a slice of heaven!" Two blocks from the legendary Melrose Diner, Kurt Fredericksdorf is making the best case for Philly I've heard in a long time.

Fifth Stop, Kingsessing Recreation Center, 2:45 p.m.

"You can be President too!"

The polling place is pretty empty, but the playground is jammed full of kids just out from school. Dozens of games of pick-up basketball are underway.

"Obama, he can do it!" From a minivan parked just outside the playground gate comes the booming voice of yet another roaming Obama-mobile. Inside, Harrison Ray, Valerie Hayden, and Dianna Matthews (on the mic) idle for a few minutes and tell me about their candidate.

"He wants to help with the genocide in Darfur. He can help on health care, on the economy." In Philly they think Obama will help get the guns off the street. And, maybe, they hope, he will promote economic and education policies that will help to rebuild the African-American families of the city.

They like Hillary, but they like Barack better. They don't mind that Mayor Nutter supports Hillary, but they think Governor Rendell's comments about racism in Pennsylvania crossed the line. They wish Nutter had called him on it.

And just as we are really getting into it, as I'm hearing about how unity between the races is possible, is probable with Obama at the reins, they have to go—it's time to pick up some old folks and get them to the polls. A man is crossing the street in front of the van.

"You, there, in the orange jacket, did you vote? Don't forget to vote!"

Sixth Stop, University of Pennsylvania, 4:00 p.m.

The Planner roams the room looking for candid shots and I stake out the voting booth exit.

Victoria Perez, economics and political-science double-major, plans to go into health care policy research when she graduates. She volunteers in South Philly with Latino immigrants.

If the demographers are correct—and on this they have been right this time around—Ms. Perez represents in her gender, her ethnicity, and her top voting issue that she is a natural for Hillary. And though it takes us a few minutes of conversation before she confirms this for me, I have found the ultimate Hillary Clinton voter.

She saw Chelsea Clinton when she came to campus. Apparently it was sparsely attended. Victoria is not the type of person that you would imagine waving a sign or screaming her head off, for Hillary, or for Obama. She defies the stereotypes that the media have created for college voters—she's focused on issues. She didn't like it that the Penn Democrats endorsed Obama. She tells me that she and her roommates support Clinton, but "still the arguments can get pretty heated at times."

Victoria is from Connecticut, but she registered and voted in Pennsylvania in 2004, in the hopes that she could do her part to swing the state to the Democrats. I note this strategic thinking, but then she finishes with a surprise: Victoria Perez might support McCain over Obama if Clinton doesn't get the nomination.

Final Stop, Dark Horse Tavern, 8:00 p.m.

"Can we turn the TV station to politics?"

The bartender views us with one-part incomprehension and one part disgust. Maybe upstairs, he ventures, but not in his little nook of the bar. The Flyers game is on. "Our game is on too," I venture. He looks at me sideways.

After some fancy arguing upstairs, we manage to get a room with a big-screen tuned to MSNBC. Munching and drinking, the returns roll in. The Planner and I are new to the city, but every time Tim Russert or Chuck Todd starts circling counties and vote totals on the screen we feel a little bit of pride. Philadelphia has turned out in a big way today.

Obama has in fact crushed Clinton in Philly, but not done very well in most other parts of the state. Overall, he has closed a 25 point deficit to 9, a loss he will note from Indiana, where he is speaking tonight.

Hillary is still in PA, in fact she's at a hotel on Broad Street, living it up. Terry McAuliffe tells the MSNBC reporter that Obama "can't win the big states," and for this reason the superdelegates will soon come home to Hillary.

Someone will be interviewing voters in Indianapolis next week, and in Charlotte, North Carolina, and in Louisville, Bozeman, and San Juan. Cities—the microcosms of states, of the nation—will tell the tales of the hopes, frustrations, and realities of this election year. In cities (this city) the nation was founded, its aspirations voiced, its fractures exposed. In cities the issues of crime, education, war, and economy stand out in darkest contrast from the backdrop of a too-gray and apathetic suburbia, of a muted rural America. Cities have been, and remain, the political conscience of the land. The Planner and I order another round.

One of the servers pokes his head in every few minutes to monitor the results, but never says anything. Did he vote? Where does he live? I get ready to interrogate him, but he slips away.

Two guys walk in to throw darts. They are baffled that we aren't watching the game. They leave, muttering.

A man with his wife sticks his head in.

"What's the score?"

"We're watching politics," the planner says, inviting him inside.

"*Politics*! Meh." And with a wave of his hand he brings our election day odyssey to a close. Not everyone gets into the drama and the passion of primary day, especially when the Flyers are playing well. I long for the bullhorn. I want to tell the guy...

"You could be President too!"

Miriam N. Kotzin

RECLAIMING THE DEAD

My father stumbled into death.
We'd turned away a moment,
then a call.
The next spring my mother and I
planted violets that never grew back.
The cemetery has rules, no flowers,
we learned as we stooped
planting around his footstone anyway.

All winter the earth, unyielding,
refused everything.
Now the ground gives under-foot
as I cross the field,
wary as a trespasser.

My mother telephoned her death;
when she died I was on my way.
It rained through the night
after I bought her coffin.
It was ritually correct, the pine
box, pegged. New to my hands,
her rings cut my fingers
as I carried her there, daughter, pall-
bearer, talking to her steadily
since her death. The gravediggers let go.
I heard the splash. I saw her float.
A pump a purposeful machinery
worked until she was settled.

I make my way to the woods,
to the path down to the swollen cedar stream,
loops of brambles,
greening, have caught the hang
of spring.

Usha Menon

The Lure of Radical Islam: Muslims and the Modern World

The United States confronted the death and devastation that results from Islamic terrorism for the first time in the homeland on September 11, 2001. However, such terrorism and the terrible cost it exacts in terms of life and property have been a part of everyday life for many decades in other parts of the world, most particularly Israel and India. In this essay, I explore the reasons why hundreds of young Muslim men resort to violence in the name of religion to achieve political ends.

Terrorism is violence deliberately perpetrated on ordinary people in order to strike terror in their hearts. Terrorism's goal is almost always political. From the late 20th century onward, terrorism has been inspired, most often, by religious extremism. There are, of course, all kinds of religious extremisms: Christian, Muslim, Jewish, Hindu, Sikh, Buddhist. However, I think I can safely claim that only Muslim religious extremism (the "radical Islam" of this essay's title) is global in its scope, targeting Jews, Hindus and Christians in locations across the world.

When the United States was attacked on 9/11, the question on everyone's mind was: "Why us?" And the answers that were initially forthcoming were rather simplistic: "The U.S. stands for freedom and these people are against freedom" and/or "The U.S. is immensely wealthy and powerful and these people envy us." But there are millions of oppressed and impoverished people in the world who do not turn planes into bombs. And the 19 hijackers who did turn planes into bombs were neither poor nor oppressed. They were, however, willing to both kill and die for what they believed in.

So what are the reasons for such terrorism?

In the Islamic world, the answer is relatively simple. Not just Osama bin Laden but millions of ordinary Muslims believe it is religion, the latest chapter in the struggle between Islam and the rest of the world, a struggle that is fourteen centuries old. And this understanding has been the success of radical Islam. Radical Islam has succeeded in persuading millions of Muslims that the miserable conditions that prevail in a large part of the Islamic world is the result of trying to ape the West and that the only way to recapture past glory is through returning to the True Path that Allah prescribed for his followers. According to this perspective, modernization is Westernization or "Westoxification," as many anti-Western Muslim intellectuals prefer to call it. Far from being an isolated fringe, terrorists and suicide-bombers are in the vanguard of this movement to radicalize Islam, sharing their ideology with many millions of their fellow-Muslims1.

In the non-Islamic world, however, the most common reasons are thought to be a combination of some or all of the following: (1) that Islam is a violent and intolerant religion, (2) that people in the Islamic world are burdened by an almost unbearable sense of sorrow and humiliation, (3) that there is an absence of democracy in much of the Islamic world, (4) that oil is the bane of democracy and (5) that the modernizing elite in the Islamic world has been singularly unsuccessful in bringing others within the fold of modernity.

The Nature of Islam

Any debate about the violent and intolerant nature of Islam is not, I think, a particularly fruitful exercise. First, I agree with Scott Appleby when he suggests that the sacred or the holy has the potential for great harm as well as great good: "Neither 'good' nor 'evil' per se, the sacred manifests itself as the ultimate reality...Within its realm power is undifferentiated, neither creative nor destructive in itself, but capable both of generating and extinguishing life" (2000: 28). Thus, Islam is not unique among the major religions of the world in sanctioning violence against the non-believer among its followers. Perhaps a monotheistic faith lends itself more readily to such violence but, again, Islam is not unique in this, certainly not historically, and perhaps not even today.

Second, any discussion about the nature of "true" Islam, whether it is inherently a peaceful religious tradition that has been "hijacked" by a violent and marginal few to serve their own limited and selfish ends or not, would prove to be ultimately futile. It would require searching through the Qu'ran for quotations that are either in favor of or against violence, but the Qu'ran is a text, very like the Bible, that is full of inconsistencies and contradictions. There are likely to be as many verses praising tolerance of the non-believer as there are exhorting violence toward them and therefore, there is little to be gained by such a search, however well-intentioned.

Islam may or may not be a violent and intolerant but secularism certainly finds no place in it. Islam has had its schisms but has never had to contend with the kind of bitter religious conflicts that devastated

Christian Europe in the 16th and 17th centuries and finally drove Christianity to devise a solution that required the separation of Church from State. Thus, in Islam, religious institutions are not marginalized and there is no question about privatizing religious beliefs. Islam, quite simply, permeates every aspect of a person's life.

Islam sees itself very clearly as the culmination of a process of religious evolution that began with Judaism and was followed by Christianity. Devout Muslims believe Islam is the final and perfect expression of Ultimate Truth: Judaism and Christianity are but false and incomplete faiths. This self-understanding is distinctive about Islam. It engenders among its followers a certain sense of superiority, a sense of the rightness of their beliefs, which clearly encourages a degree of intolerance to develop against non-believers.

The Islamic World and its Sense of Loss, Humiliation and Rage

Many, both within and outside the Islamic world, have commented on the deep sense of loss and grief that pervades it. The Islamic world remembers vividly the many centuries when Muslims were the undisputed rulers of the world. Within a couple of hundred years of the Prophet's death, Islam had spread from the Bay of Biscay in southwestern Europe to the frontiers of China, and from the Aral Sea in the north to the Upper Nile in the south. In its heyday, the Islamic world covered more area than the Roman Empire ever did; and, it included within its borders cities that were acknowledged centers of learning where philosophy, mathematics, astronomy, medicine, art and architecture achieved levels of development and elaboration never seen before.

But, as Bernard Lewis (2002) points out, for the last 300 years, the Islamic world has suffered a decline. Its area of influence has shrunk, both politically and culturally and it has increasingly been "on the defensive" (ibid: 195) in its relations with the Christian West. Lewis describes this waning influence and its accompanying humiliations as occurring at three levels: the geopolitical, the societal and the familial. European advances, including that of Russia, reduced the areas under Islamic domination. The dismantling of the caliphate by the European powers in 1924 symbolized this decline most powerfully. Next, "insidious, alien ideas" (Sivan, 1985: 2) like secularism and nationalism have infiltrated Islamic societies and the authority of Islam is continually being challenged. Secularism marginalizes Islam, making it irrelevant in most spheres of human activity, and nationalism, whether Arab or Iranian, weakens Islamic solidarity and, for all practical purposes, replaces it. And, finally, ideas even more subversive than secularism and nationalism, those of gender equality and children's rights, have also breached the boundaries of these societies, challenging and disrupting traditional lines of authority within families.

Thomas Friedman, the Pulitzer prize-winning journalist has repeatedly remarked that humiliation is perhaps the most under-rated emotion in international relations, and perhaps it is. Its relevance in explaining Islamic terrorism is that, among Muslims, the sense of being humiliated transforms itself into a seething rage that then turns to religious extremism in search of a solution. Such an explanation is certainly persuasive but world history is replete with accounts of the humiliations suffered by various peoples and nations, the difference, however, is that the response to such humiliations has rarely been resorting to terrorism. After all, the Islamic world's experience of European colonialism is hardly unique. China and India, each with its own memories of past glory and greatness, were subjected to humiliations as European colonial empires expanded, but there is no Chinese or Hindu terrorism against the West. Similarly, after the Second World War, both Germany and Japan were humiliatingly defeated and Japan, in particular, suffered the lengthy presence of an occupying army and the radical restructuring of its polity, but, again, there is no German or Japanese terrorism against the victors of World War II

The Absence of Democracy in the Islamic World

Many familiar with the autocratic and repressive regimes of the Islamic world explain Islamic terrorism as the only viable outlet available to a people who are denied the more standard forms of political expression that democracy affords[2]. But that still begs the question: Why have democratic ideas not taken root in the Islamic world? Is Islam inherently inhospitable to such ideas?

Karen Armstrong, the well-known authority on Islam, doesn't think so. She says that there is nothing fundamentally incompatible between Islamic thought and democratic ideals. Thus, the idea of a representative segment of the community of believers (*ummah*) conferring (*shurah*) and endorsing laws through consensus (*ijmah*) is not alien to Islamic thought. Devout Muslims are likely to have trouble with the way democracy is defined in the West, a democratic government derives its legitimacy because it is of the people, by the people and for the people. In Islamic thought, God gives legitimacy to the State and granting that power to mere human beings is tantamount to idolatry. But this is not an insurmountable obstacle. As Armstrong herself points out, it is possible to have governments that represent the people without necessarily conforming in every tiny detail to the Western ideal.

The problem, according to her, is not so much in conceptualizing such a form of government but in the practical experience that many Islamic societies have had with democracy. Colonial and neo-colonial interference have often disrespected and disregarded the will of the people. Iran's experience is fairly typical. After the Constitutional Revolution of 1906, the Iranian people established their Majlis or Assembly but with Russian help; the Shah shut it down because he found it inconvenient. In the 1920s, the British, eager to establish a protectorate in Iran, helped the Shah time and again to rig elections. And later still, with American support, the Shah's son and successor, sought to forcibly modernize his country by cracking down on his people, denying then basic human rights and in the process making a mockery of the privileges that democracy supposedly brings with it. Similarly, in Egypt, the popular Wadf party won all seventeen general elections held during 1923 and 1952 but were allowed to form a government only five times. Either the British or King Farouk insisted that the elected government step down and they did.

But are colonialism and neo-colonialism solely to blame? Egypt's more recent history has not been that different from its colonial one. Even a charismatic, modernizing leader like Nasser who believed in Western ideas like secularism, nationalism and socialism, couldn't travel the path to democracy in its entirety. He stifled dissent and instituted one-party rule. And the current President of Egypt, Hosni Mubarak, carries on the Nasserist tradition.

Pakistan's experience is equally telling. Mohammed Ali Jinnah, the founder of Pakistan, demanded from the retreating colonial power, the British, a homeland for the Muslims of the Indian subcontinent and Pakistan was created. The new nation began its life in 1947 as a parliamentary democracy but it did not survive as such for very long. Within a decade or so, acute political instability had created conditions ripe for a military coup and for the last 55 years, Pakistan has been ruled more often by a military dictatorship than a democratically elected government. But the charge that neo-colonialism jeopardized Pakistan's fledgling democracy cannot be made very convincingly simply because there is the competing example of India, a nation with the same colonial legacy, subject to similar neo-colonial pressures, riven by all kinds of cultural, linguistic and religious divisions that nevertheless survives to this day as a functioning, however imperfectly, democracy.

Is Oil the Bane of Democracy?

Those who see the absence of democracy in the Islamic world as responsible for its dysfunctions point to oil as the primary reason for this state of affairs. Initially, however, people in the Islamic world saw oil and the wealth it produced as the solution to all their economic problems. Where state-sponsored socialism had failed the Islamic world miserably, it was thought that oil would redeem it through economic development. But that has hardly happened. Instead of oil leading to more prosperity or greater distributive justice, it has created a new superficially Westernized elite of gulf Arabs who have earned only the contempt of their fellow citizens. And oil certainly does not lead to greater political participation. Governments in the gulf can afford to ignore with impunity the needs and the wishes of their people simply because of their enormous oil revenues. As Fareed Zakaria says so succinctly, "It was the inverse slogan of the American revolution—no taxation, but no representation either" (2002: 246).

This is a powerful explanation for the absence of democracy in the Islamic world but it still doesn't explain the absence of democracy in those countries, Egypt and Pakistan come immediately to mind, that do not possess this natural resource. Despite Armstrong's contentions about the compatibility between Islam and democratic ideas, there does seem to be a dynamic inherent in Islamic societies that incline them to autocratic rather than democratic rule.

The Modernizing Elite in the Islamic World

Many Muslim and non-Muslim observers believe that the elite has not played its expected role in modernizing Islamic societies. When the Islamic world first encountered the power of Western civilization in the late 17th and 18th centuries, it responded initially with respect and admiration. Early Muslim reformers eagerly sought to emulate the powerful West but their enthusiasm was overshadowed by their relative ignorance about economic methods and political institutions honed in the West (Lewis, 2002). They understood neither the complexity of the concepts they were trying to transplant nor the contexts in which these worked and so failed in their attempts.

Zakaria, for his part, sees the failure of these elites a little differently. He agrees with Lewis that they are "superficially Western" (2002: 242) but he sees their failure as more willful than mere ignorance. They are quick to import Cadillacs and Rolexes but unwilling to do anything more. To them "importing the inner stuffings of modern society—a free market, political parties, accountability and the rule of law—is difficult and dangerous" (ibid: 246). To make matters worse, they suffer from a false sense of superiority. Thus, an elderly Arab intellectual reacted sharply to Zakaria's praise of the progress made by East Asian countries saying, "They have simply aped the West...That may be all right for fishing villages. But we are the heirs to one of the great civilizations of the world. We cannot become the slums of the West" (2002: 243-44).

Furthermore, the elites are easily intimidated. They will do almost anything to avoid debunking fanaticism: they don't want to be called "bad" Muslims. Islam is an egalitarian faith in which no one can question anyone else's religious credentials. The religious extremists, however, have no such qualms and don't hesitate to castigate those they disapprove of as "bad" Muslims.

When the elite does take its responsibility to effect modernization seriously, it has only provoked a religious backlash. Whether Turkey or Iran under the Shahs or Egypt the modernizing elite is often militantly anti-Islamic. They have closed down *madrassas* (Islamic religious schools); forbidden people from going on religious pilgrimages, including the Hajj; insisted that everyone adopt modern Western dress and that women give up wearing the veil; and appropriated the endowments of the *ulama*. Such coercion, of course, never works. Far from disappearing, Islam only goes underground and the extremists are handed a potent weapon with which to mobilize the people.

Conclusion: The Lure of Radical Islam

But what is the appeal of radical Islam? The answer to that question has two parts.

The first has to do with Islam's self-perception. To Muslims, it is unnatural and blasphemous that Islam does not rule the world. Instead, Christianity appears to. And as far as Judaism is concerned, Israel is a hated enemy that has decisively defeated them in war and has wrested from the desert a high-technology economy and a modern society. Not only is Islam not pre-eminent in the world today but for many Muslims "Western-style economic methods brought poverty, Western-style political institutions brought tyranny, even Western Style warfare brought defeat" (Lewis, 2002: 207). So in addition to sorrow, humiliation and rage, these Muslims feel confused. They believe, quite sincerely, that there must be something dreadfully wrong with the modern world. They search for an answer and their search takes them to radical Islam. This ideology holds out hope. It says that any compromise with modernity is doomed and that the only way to recapture the glory and greatness of Islam's past is to reject it entirely and return to the True Path that Allah had prescribed for his people. And it makes its message even more compelling by providing counseling, medical attention and social services to its followers, making irrelevant corrupt governments.

The second has to do with the role that Saudi Arabia has played in creating conditions that are hospitable to the spread of radical Islam. Saudi Arabia enjoys immense prestige in the Islamic world both because Islam's holiest sites are located within its borders and because of its enormous oil wealth. It aspires to be the perfect Islamic society. In order to achieve this aspiration, it practices an austere form of Islam, Wahhabism, and sharia, the law of the Qu'ran, regulates Saudi society. Hajj pilgrims from across the Islamic world travel to Saudi Arabia and marvel at its wealth and its strict adherence to Islamic norms. More importantly, it has funded madrassas (religious schools) across the Islamic world and provides support for clerics to travel to these schools to ensure proper religious instruction. Saudi Arabia's actions serve to homogenize the practice of Islam worldwide in the direction of greater extremism and rigidity, creating a climate in which radical Islam's explanation for the present condition of Muslims and its program of action for the future make perfect sense.

In the end, however, I find myself concurring with Osama bin Laden and millions of his fellow-Muslims. Ultimately, the reason young Muslim men are willing to resort to terrorism is because of religion. It is because Islam has a particular sense of itself and its destiny. Devout Muslims believe Islam to be the most perfect expression of God's Truth. It is this absolutely sincere conviction that transforms some of them into terrorists (or religious warriors) battling non-believers for the ultimate goal of restoring God's sovereignty in the world.

Works Cited

Appleby, R. Scott 2000 *The "Ambivalence" of the Sacred: Religion, Violence and Reconciliation Lanham*, Md. : Rowman & Littlefield Publishers.

Armstrong, Karen 2000 *Islam: A Short History* New York: Modern Library.

Lewis, Bernard 2002 "The Roots of Muslim Rage" in Akbar Ahmed (ed.) *Inside Islam* New York: Marlowe and Company.

Sivan, Emmanual 1985 *Radical Islam* New Haven, CT: Yale University Press.

Zakaria, Fareed 2002 "Why They Hate Us" in Akbar Ahmed (ed.) *Inside Islam* New York: Marlowe and Company.

1 This is the reason why many governments in the Islamic world cannot reveal to their people the extent of their cooperation with the United States in the war against terrorism.

2 The proponents of this view do not see the fact that much of this terrorism occurs outside the Islamic world and is directed against non-Muslims as detracting from their argument. On the contrary, they interpret it as further evidence about the repressiveness of these governments.

M.G. Piety
Some Thoughts on Race and Intelligence

Race is in the news again. First it was the Jena Six, then Nobel laureate James D. Watson's assertion, that blacks are less intelligent than whites, and finally, a series of articles in Slate arguing that there was scientific evidence to back Watson's claim.

The reaction to these recent developments was predictable. There have been a number of heated debates on the internet concerning not only race and intelligence, but also the appropriateness of studying race and intelligence. Two crucial points have yet to be made, however. The first concerns the contentious association of intelligence with IQ score and the second is the equally contentious assumption that we have anything, or ever could have anything, like a clear scientific conception or race.

Let's take the first one first. What is intelligence anyway? We have no better grasp of this than we have of the relation of the mind to the brain. Sure, some people can solve certain sorts of puzzles faster than other people, but everyone knows people who are great at Scrabble or crossword puzzles or chess or who can fix almost any mechanical or electrical gadget, but who seem unable to wrap their minds around even the most rudimentary of social or political theories. Then there are the people with great memories who are able to retain all the elements of even the most arcane theories and who can undertake an explanation of them if pressed, but whose inability to express them in novel terms betrays that they have not really grasped them after all. Other people—I've known quite a few of this type—have keenly analytical minds. They can break individual claims, or even entire theories, down into their conceptual components, yet they appear to lack any sort of synthetic intelligence in that they are unable to see the myriad implications of these analyses. Still other people are great at grasping the big picture, so to speak, but have difficulty hanging onto the details.

Some people plod slowly and methodically toward whatever insights they achieve and others receive them almost effortlessly, through flashes of inspiration. But the insights of the former group are sometimes more profound than those of the latter group. Then there are people who are mostly mistaken in their beliefs, sometimes quite obviously so, but correct in some one belief the implications of which are so staggering that we tend to forget they are otherwise unreliable.

I'm inclined to put Watson in this last group. Perhaps that's not fair. After all, I know of only one point on which he is obviously mistaken. That mistake is so glaring, however, that it leads me to think he is probably more like an idiot savant than a genuinely intelligent human being. Watson bases his claim about the intellectual inferiority of blacks on statistical analyses of I.Q. scores, assuming, apparently that I.Q. scores are a reliable indicator of intelligence. I'll give you that I.Q. scores represent something. It just isn't all that clear what. To suggest that they represent intelligence in any significant sense is thus to betray that one has less than the ideally desirable quantity of this quality himself.

Sure the mind, and therefore intelligence, is intimately connected with the brain. Read Oliver Sacks if you want to see just how intimate that connection is. Sacks is one of my favorite authors not simply because the substance of his writings is so fascinating, but also because he is himself so clearly intelligent. Not only does he not go leaping to conclusions on issues that lie outside his area of professional expertise (though I have to say I'd be more interested to hear Sacks's social and political views than Watson's), he doesn't go leaping to conclusions about the implications of what he has observed in his own work in neurology. He'd be one of the first people, I think, to defend the claim that we do not yet have a clear enough idea of what intelligence is to be reliably able to quantify it. We don't even understand it well enough yet to be able to say confidently that it is quantifiable. At this point, all we can say is that it appears so intimately connected with the brain that it can, in some sense, be associated with, or represented by, we-know-not-yet-what neurological activities or tendencies.

OK, so far, so little. But what is a black brain and what is a white brain? Most blacks in the U.S., as opposed to blacks in Africa, have a great deal of white blood, or whatever you want to call it. If whites really were more intelligent than blacks, that would mean African-Americans would be that much more intelligent than Africans. I'm sure the chair of my department, Abioseh Porter, who hails from Sierra Leone, as well as my friend, Nigerian author, Chimamanda Ngozi Adichie, would be interested to hear that one. There may well be people who believe this. I am not aware of any empirical evidence, however, that supports such a conclusion. My own experience does not support it. I grew up in a predominantly black neighborhood and attended predominantly black schools from fourth grade to college. Since that time I have also met more than a few Africans. I couldn't detect any difference in intelligence. I'm unaware of even anecdotal evidence that would support the conclusion that there was such a difference. Do you see what I'm saying? We're not looking at a slippery slope here, but at a meteoric descent right down into a pile of deep doo-doo.

From what I've read, there is no clear scientific definition of race. "Race" is just a name we give to a collection of physical characteristics such as eye and hair color and degree of pigmentation of the skin. There is no race gene. There are just genes that encode for these individual characteristics. So how many, and what sort, of characteristics does one have to have to be either black or white? It is some kind of ineffable sum, isn't it? Blacks sometimes have very pale skin, some whites actually have darker skin than some blacks. Blacks even occasionally have blue eyes, or straight hair, just as whites often have brown eyes or kinky hair. In the past, we just arbitrarily determined what made a person black, and, by implication, white. Since, presumably, we have gotten beyond the point where we would say that even one drop of black blood makes a person black, the only reasonable definition of race (even given its circularity) would, therefore, appear to be one based on the statistical representation of the various races in one's family tree. That would mean people with predominantly white, or perhaps I should say "white-ish" ancestry, would be considered white. Have you ever seen a photo of Charles Chestnut or Anatole Broyard? Not only are these guys clearly white, according to this definition, there are a whole lot of other people walking around this country who call themselves "black" because of the social environment into which they were born, but who ought properly to consider themselves white.

Since when have scientific studies been undertaken on ineffable, or arbitrarily determined, classes of things? It's like trying to determine whether people with purportedly good taste are more intelligent than people with supposedly bad taste, or whether people who live in Chicago are more intelligent than people who live in L.A. You might undertake such a thing as a sociological study with some arbitrarily agreed upon criteria for what would constitute good and bad taste, or how far out into the suburbs you want to go before you decide you have left Chicago, as well with some equally arbitrarily agreed upon criteria for what constitutes intelligence. You cannot undertake such a thing though as a scientific study (no matter how convinced you may be in the genetic superiority of people who live in Chicago), and to think that you could betray that you have a very weak grasp of what constitutes science. Given that race, at least from the standpoint of science, is nothing more than a collection of certain physical characteristics, the view that white people are more intelligent than black people is not uncomfortably close to the view of the Nazis that blue-eyed blonds were inherently superior to everyone else—it is essentially the same thing.

As I said earlier, I spent a huge portion of my life in the almost exclusive company of black people. I've been around black people and I've been around white people and I haven't found any general differences in terms of intelligence. My experience has led me to believe that most of what often passes for intelligence is actually intellectual self confidence, confidence in one's own reasoning powers, confidence in the value of one's insights. Teachers, of which I am one, will tell you that you can just see some people's brains seize up when they are confronted with tasks they fear are beyond them, but which later prove not to have been beyond them. This fear, however, that certain tasks are beyond one, is a substantial obstacle to completing them. One stumbles again and again, fearing that his "guess" is just that, a guess, rather than understanding. One fails to pursue an insight for fear that it is not genuine, or from fear that it is so obvious that others have come to it long ago. I don't mean to suggest that there are not innate differences in intelligence among human beings. I'm sure there are, but I agree with what I believe Noam Chomsky said somewhere about how these differences, measured relative to the difference in intelligence between human beings and their closest relatives the apes, are simply vanishingly small.

I construe my job as an educator not to impart knowledge, but to nurture intellectual self confidence. Of course this could be partly a defense mechanism because I am a philosopher, which means I don't have any knowledge to impart. I try to teach critical thinking skills, of course, but even more important to me is somehow to get my students to believe in their own intellectual potential because even these skills, I believe, can, at least to a certain extent, be acquired naturally by people who are confident in their ability to acquire them. We may never know exactly what intelligence is, but I think we will make more progress in our attempts to understand it if we assume it is present in everyone and do what we can to nurture and develop it. I say, teach people to believe in themselves and then see what they are able to do with that faith. We may all be pleasantly surprised.

Donald Riggs

A Supermarket Far from California

Allen Ginsberg's poem "A Supermarket in California" was read lyrically in a reflective, aesthetically diverse yet tasteful "variety show" that I participated in during my college years—I think it occurred in the spring of 1973. The poem itself entranced me every evening I heard it, but I had no idea at the time who had written it; there were no programs, and I never thought to ask anyone. It was a celebratory melancholic verbal meditation, and somehow it never occurred to me to locate the source, any more than it would have occurred to me to look up possible Freudian interpretations of my own dream motifs.

Three years later, though, I bought a remaindered copy of Paul Carroll's The Poem in Its Skin (Chicago: Big Table, 1970) and plunged into the world of those poets he referred to as "the Generation of '62." Frank O'Hara, W.S. Merwin, John Ashbery, and Robert Creeley were among those I discovered for the first time there, and…Allen Ginsberg, whom I had known only from black-and-white posters in head shops. In those, he always wore a cardboard Uncle Sam hat and was surrounded by newsreel-footage protestors. In The Poem in Its Skin he also was pictured wearing an Uncle Sam hat, but was reading his "Wichita Vortex Sutra."

More important than the individual essays, however, was Carroll's reference to Donald M. Allen's 1960 anthology The New American Poetry: 1945-1960. I bought a copy and there discovered the beautiful text starting with "What thoughts I have of you tonight, Walt Whitman…." As monumental as "Howl" was the "Waste Land" of a generation, according to Paul Carroll—and as epically elegiac as was "Kaddish," Ginsberg's lament for his mother, it was "A Supermarket in California" that I returned to, reading it silently to myself in the library, reading it out loud to the squirrels down by the creek, and unconsciously imitating its cadences in my fledgling quasi-neo-Beat poems of that era.

When I was courting a lovely Dutch dancer-turned-graduate student named Petra who would later become my wife, I shared "Supermarket" with her, along with plenty of Bly, Ferlinghetti, Wright (James, not Charles), and others of The Generation of '62. Of "Supermarket," she remarked, "It's like Garcia Lorca's *Oda al Walt Whitman.*" I found that Ben Belitt had published his translation of Garcia Lorca's *El Poeta en Nueva York* the same year that Ginsberg wrote "Supermarket"—"and you, Garcia Lorca, what were you doing among the watermelons?" (line 3)

In comparative literature, which I was studying at the time, we had been introduced to the concept of *rapports de fait*, which are factual links that a literary scholar can use to determine whether a writer was working with a particular source in mind, or unconsciously. This promised to be a first for me—an actual rapport de fait linking Garcia Lorca to Ginsberg! Such enthusiasm can only be understood by graduate students, whose lives, during that extended pupal stage between the Problems and Methods of Comparative Literature required course and the defense of the dissertation, are characterized by a maniacal focus on discourse.

Gordon Ball, a protegé of Ginsberg's, who had transcribed and edited some of Ginsberg's talks in a volume called *Allen Verbatim* (New York: McGraw-Hill, 1974), was working on a Ph.D. in English at UNC then, and was renting a house on my way to Petra's apartment. One bright morning I passed him as he was weeding his vegetable patch, and I asked him about the possible connection. The next time he talked to Allen on the phone he asked, and he later told me that yes, Ginsberg had indeed written "Supermarket in California" after reading Garcia Lorca's "Ode to Walt Whitman" in Belitt's translation. Bingo! *Rapport de fait!*

An ode has been defined as an address, by the narrative voice of the poet, to something or someone who cannot, or will not, answer. The West Wind. A Grecian Urn. The Confederate Dead. Walt Whitman. That December, after Petra successfully completed some graduate exam, she flew to Mexico for an extended visit with relatives there. With my head filled with "A Supermarket in California" and my heart filled with longing, I wrote the following:

This afternoon, I caught myself mid-
stride: just where was I
so intent on going?
Tonight, I woke up wandering
through Frozen Foods at Fowler's:
no money on me,
nothing I wanted to buy.
Back at my apartment door, my hand dropped,
key unturned in the lock.
A streetlamp, pearl, reflected in a puddle,
imitated the moon.
Absentmindedly, it rained.
I've been able to do nothing since you left.

That spring, Gordon managed to bring Ginsberg, accompanied by his partner Peter Orlovsky and his old friend William S. Burroughs, to Chapel Hill for an Arts Festival. As one of the most junior readers on the lit mag, the *Carolina Quarterly*, it was my task to set up and take down the refreshments and their arrangement for the CQ's reception for the writers. Therefore, when Allen Ginsberg himself, looking like a wizened version of his picture on the cover of *Allen Verbatim*, stood next to me at the solid-refreshment table, he asked me a question that will live on in my memory, until death or Alzheimer's subtracts it: "What is this stuff?"

My tendency is to freeze in the presence of Living Legends. "Rabbit food" was all I could come up with. In actuality, it was a mixture of hard pretzels, salted nuts, and breakfast cereals, mixed by my own hand in a large English Departmental bowl. This was before the day of disposable plastic gloves for food handlers, as well as before my own period of eating organic foods.

I had no other contacts with Ginsberg at that party, nor for the rest of that day. The senior members of the *Carolina Quarterly* staff were busy chatting him up as I retreated from my insignificant verbal skirmish. Peter Orlovsky, whom I recognized from a photograph of Ginsberg, Kerouac, and others on the beach, was less occupied, so I confronted him.

I asked Orlovsky about his "Second Poem" from the Donald M. Allen anthology; he said it was about "life." I asked him about the line "Comes a time for everyone when they have to piss in the sink." Was it about those cheap hotel rooms in Paris where you have a sink in your own room but you share a toilet with everyone else on your floor and two others? "Yep." Then he ambled away.

I was suddenly alone. All the Writers and their followers and the undergrads in search of free snacks had folded their tents like the Arabs, and silently stolen away. I started cleaning up. Suddenly, William S. Burroughs himself, with his student guide in tow, came back for his fedora! On his way out, he looked in the little kitchen, turned towards me without breaking stride, and, pointing toward the stove, said, "Water's boiling." My day was complete. I have no idea why I had set a pan of water to boil on the stove, but there it was, described in a stark, telegraphic oral prose, pared to the essence. I turned it off.

It was three years until I would see Ginsberg again. I went to my first Modern Language Association convention, looking for a job. My first afternoon there, I looked at the cards on the job board, and found that they all said "Dissertation in Hand" on them. As I myself was just barely ABD (All But Dissertation), I figured I'd better not knock my head against that wall yet. Of course, I could always quip that I had no dissertation in hand, but two in the bush, but I doubt that would have done me any good.

I decided that as long as I was there anyway, I would have a good time. I attended a few sessions "in my field"—troubadour verse, translation theory—but for the most part I went to sessions on Modern and Contemporary Poetry. I bumped into Gordon Ball, who was there, dissertation in hand, to get a job; he invited me to hear his presentation, which was in a session on Diaries and Journals as Literature. He added, "Allen's here to support me, as I'm presenting my edition of his journals, *Early Fifties, Early Sixties*."

I had read Gordon's book, and was able to ask a "good question" on the relationship of the earlier version of "America" in it to the final, published version. After the session, I went up to Ginsberg and practically gushed about "A Supermarket in California," remarking how Garcia Lorca, like Whitman, was a Gemini. "Really, Lorca was a Gemini?" said Ginsberg, pronouncing the sign with a hard G, as in his own name. "I didn't know that."

Later, Gordon bumped into me in the hotel lobby and said that he and Allen and a few others were going to lunch, would I join them?

Wow! From a failed attempt to get a job interview, this MLA meeting had become an opportunity to rub elbows with the Literary Lion of Bop Prosody! I didn't take a chance at getting separated from Gordon, but followed him around like a nursery school boy following his teacher as we let the lunch expedition accrete to us, professor by poet by professor.

A half dozen of us were walking down the main streets of Dallas, in the period between Christmas and New Year's. The streets were wide and empty, the buildings all skyscrapers. We joked about the neutron bomb, how one had probably wiped out the population without touching the property.

Sometimes an underground stream will, without warning, burst through the surface of the earth. The subterranean stresses and tensions are comprehensible to a specialist in hydraulics, but to someone just hiking by, the geyser is a shock, and seemingly capricious. Just so with Allen Ginsberg.

Suddenly, he turned to Gordon and yelled, "Why do people keep on complimenting 'Supermarket in California?' I HATE THAT POEM! It's probably only anthologized a lot because it's short."

Gordon froze, and glanced at me once. Ginsberg turned, and walked on.

I frankly have no idea whether he knew I was the culprit. It had been over an hour since I'd said that. I walked softly and fingered a Bic in my pocket. My head retracted into my collar in an unsuccessful imitation of a turtle.

At the restaurant where we ate, I was confronted by the economic reality that divides tenured professors from graduate students. All of the others had full meals, with soup or salad and entrée; I had a cup—not even a bowl—of soup, which I stretched by taking parsimonious spoonfuls and savoring each one. From the other end of the table, Ginsberg noticed me, and passed down his plate, still half filled. "Take it," he said, "I've had enough."

When you're hungry and on a tight budget, a meal that descends from the air, like those loaves of bread that a bird would bring to one of the Desert Fathers, is miraculous. Ginsberg had asked the waiter what his personal preference was on the menu, so I was eating the waiter's favorite fish, which was tender, flaky, breaded and sprinkled with lemon juice. Then there was rice, a dish I associated more with what I had conceived of Ginsberg in India or on a commune, although that departed from Kerouac's menus in *On the Road*. Did they eat in *On the Road*? Or was it mainly drinking, the body so bopping on speed that no food cravings interrupted the constant driving? In any case, I was not driven to ask: "Who killed the pork chops? What price bananas?"

Seventeen years after that, I was finishing a second master's degree, this time in English/Creative Writing. Ginsberg's major works were on the Reading List, but I needed much more work on the canonical poets—Skelton, Sidney, the Metaphysicals, the Romantics. I had not had any subsequent live encounters with Ginsberg, though he was still alive—he would die in April of that year—but in January I was studying for my written comprehensive exams. I read Keats's "Ode on Melancholy" and marveled at the moment where the narrator rejects suicide as a way out of depression:

But shade to shade will come too drowsily
And drown the waking anguish of the soul.

I recalled "A Supermarket in California" in which Ginsberg asks Walt Whitman, "Which way does your beard point tonight? The trees add shade to shade, we'll both be lonely." Is the phrase "shade to shade"—which I take to mean, in the Keats, that the individual spirit (shade) will come to the Underworld (shade)—echoed in Ginsberg's "the trees add shade to shade," probably meaning that the shadows cast by the trees and the streetlights add to the night's darkness? The allusion seems incontestable to me, but I'd lost touch with Gordon Ball, and Ginsberg was at Naropa, at the Jack Kerouac School of Disembodied Poetics, and I couldn't countenance reminding him again of my obsession with a work he now classified among his juvenilia. I knew I could always use it in an answer on my comps, but the opportunity didn't arise.

A couple of years later, when I tried to read more Keats, I found that I couldn't, that his voice had suffered a sea change for me and, unlike Odysseus, I couldn't sacrifice a sheep for his shade to regain it momentarily. However, I take comfort in the reflection that the 1st-century rhetorician Longinus, in his treatise *On the Sublime*, notes that, of the spirits of the dead who crowd around Odysseus, hoping to drink of the blood of his slaughtered sheep and thus be able to speak to him, Ajax's noble refusal to do this, despite Odysseus' desire to ask him a question, is more sublime than any words could have been. And so my own admission that Keats no longer speaks to me, but whose silent eloquence led me to recall how Ginsberg had spoken to the shades of Whitman and Garcia Lorca, gifted me with this small poem:

I can't read Keats. I know he's great
—not merely Great, as in, The Greatest Poets
of the English Tongue—but far out; I can hear
Ginsberg raise his ironic Jersey voice
with quasi-cultivated accents queered
by self-referential irony as to myself
I read the Ode on Melancholy's choice
line where "shade to shade" appeared
before on California's supermarket shelf
—or off it, really, among the trees
and Ginsberg, Whitman, Lorca walked,
all three dead now, but over forty years
ago by neon fruit they talked
and now they cool themselves by Lethe's breeze.

Fred Siegel

Trip or Trap

On the day the drug film was to be shown in Mr. Britchkow's science class, I took my assigned seat at the rear center cluster of desks, directly across from a girl named Eileen. She was at least a head taller than me, with a few freckles and long brown hair that covered most of her face. Like all girls in my seventh grade class, she wore skirts or casual dresses over a contrasting leotard. She was not especially pretty or popular, not that I had any right to evaluate her. She never smiled, and for however many months she sat directly across from me I don't remember us ever speaking. Her face seemed to be in a permanent scowl, and like most girls, she looked at me with pure hatred.

But as scary as Eileen was, she was nothing compared to the drug film. Even the opening credits made me nervous. The screen was filled with psychedelic colors that bubbled and whirled into each other, as if a rainbow were being cooked in a lab until it suffered aneurisms. Then, the title of the film, *LSD: Trip or Trap?*, appeared luridly across the screen in bold, slanted letters. Maybe it was the colors, or the typography, or perhaps the serious-looking announcer in the doctor coat, but it was clear to me that I was not going to pass this bravery test. I didn't turn away when the young man who "thought he was God," jumped in front of the moving car, but I did wince and look away when the doctor carved up the "LSD damaged brain" as if it were a London broil.

As the carving continued, I saw I was not the only person who found the film disturbing. Eileen, too, turned away in disgust, and even though I didn't especially like her, it felt good to have a partner in cowardice. But the feelings of solidarity didn't reach their peak until the deformed babies made their appearance. As soon as I saw them, posed on a clinical-looking, white porcelain counter, I let out a feeble moan. Eileen whimpered "Oh, Jesus Christ!" and in unison we turned away from the screen. In that chaotic instant, her nastiness was replaced by a much more sympathetic vulnerability.

And then, in all the recoiling and flinching, our ankles touched.

My immediate impulse was to pull my foot back, but I maintained my original position. After all, the warmth of her ankle felt good through her leotard, and touching a girl was exciting, even though I didn't especially like her. I tried to keep the touch subtle, as if it might be unintentional. If she rolled her eyes and kicked my shins, I could act indignant and pretend I wasn't even aware of our contact. After a few seconds without an objection, however, I felt bold and rested more of my ankle upon hers. I didn't dare to look at her directly, but I could see an ever-so-slight widening of her eyes as the full gravity of what was happening became clear to her. There was a moment of tension, but soon I felt her ankle surrender to mine. While infant gargoyles flickered on the screen, the ankles of two children melted together beneath cold, metal desks.

It would be nice if I could report that our passion blossomed, that we became puppy-lovers, that we have been married now for thirty years, and that our children are now in seventh grade and making their own marvelous discoveries. The truth, however, is weirder than that. Above the desks, my relationship with Eileen did not improve. She never smiled and we never spoke. Above the desks, Eileen's hatred for me seemed as if it would bubble for eternity, like psychedelic rainbows with aneurisms.

But below the desks, it was prom night. For the remainder of seventh grade, whenever Mr. Britchkow turned out the lights to show a film about the rotation of the planets or the many uses of seaweed, two twelve year old pairs of feet escaped from their shoes to touch and dance and explore. If he had found out, Mr. Britchkow might have felt that our activities were outside of the curriculum. I would argue that we were studying anatomy. We learned that while the human foot can be surprisingly expressive, the most extraordinary organ is the human heart; a muscle capable of pumping blood and containing, simultaneously, the purest hatred and love.

Scott Stein

The Failed Playwright of Virginia Tech

After Cho Seung-Hui killed 32 people and himself at Virginia Tech on April 17, 2007, media attention quickly turned to the "warning signs." Whenever one of these mass school shootings occurs, much is made of the warning signs that were missed. How could school officials or family members not have known what these shooters were planning? How could they not have known about the bullying, the hours in the garage building pipe bombs, the rage, the isolation? How could they not have seen the violent video games and aggressive music as the clues that, in retrospect, some believed they clearly were?

This standard narrative that follows mass school shootings unraveled before it really got going in the Virginia Tech case. Cho's warning signs were everywhere, and no one seemed to miss any of them. There were stalking accusations, psychological evaluations, police reports, and freaked-out professors and students. Even Cho's creative writing—the ostensible cause of the freaked-out professors and students—was taken as a warning sign.

In fall 2005, Cho's poetry professor, Nikki Giovanni, insisted that, because his "poetry was so intimidating—and his behavior so menacing," he be removed from her course. According to cnn.com, "Giovanni went to the department's then-chairwoman, Lucinda Roy, and told her, 'I was willing to resign before I was going to continue with him.' Roy took Cho out of Giovanni's class."[i] Roy taught Cho herself, one on one, but "[h]is writings were so disturbing, she said, that she went to the police and university administrators for help."[ii] His poems, to my knowledge, have not been made available to the public. However, two of his plays have been. Shortly after the shooting, Cho's former classmate Ian MacFarlane, an AOL employee, posted an entry on AOL News Bloggers containing the full text of "Richard McBeef" and "Mr. Brownstone." Both pieces were submitted by Cho to a playwriting class that he and MacFarlane attended. The plays are described, in a warning by AOL, as containing "disturbing content."[iii] MacFarlane goes further:

> When we read Cho's plays, it was like something out of a nightmare. The plays had really twisted, macabre violence that used weapons I wouldn't have even thought of. Before Cho got to class that day, we students were talking to each other with serious worry about whether he could be a school shooter. I

was even thinking of scenarios of what I would do in case he did come in with a gun, I was that freaked out about him. When the students gave reviews of his play in class, we were very careful with our words in case he decided to snap. Even the professor didn't pressure him to give closing comments.[iv]

Early in the blog's comments section, there was broad agreement about the clear signal the plays were sending. One woman, Judi, wrote, "Why didn't his instructors see that something was very seriously wrong with this man at the time of this writing[?]"[v] Another commenter, Blackdog, wrote, "I'm very surprised that writing like this didn't get the attention of the school authorities. He was obviously a very angry young man and relayed issues that he had through his writing."[vi] A third commenter, Linda, wrote, "Guess I'm naïve, but this piece of porn should've elicited some kind of action when he turned it in. Perhaps, in our depraved society, this was not considered out of the 'norm'."[vii]

These early commenters on the blog did not know when they wrote the above that, indeed, Cho's creative writing had attracted the attention not only of school authorities but also of the police. When asked, however, "about Roy's concerns that Cho was writing troubling plays and poems in his classes," Chief Wendell Flinchum said, "These course assignments were for a creative writing course and the students were encouraged to be imaginative and artistic. The writings did not express any threatening intentions or allude to criminal activity. No criminal violation had taken place."[viii]

Giovanni said that the poems were not violent. "It's not like, 'I'll rip your heart out.' It's that, 'Your bra is torn, and I'm looking at your flesh.'" No student or professor who had read Nabokov's *Lolita* or much that has been published in recent decades would be frightened by this sexually charged content, in and of itself. If the plays—which, unlike the poems, do contain violence—are any indication of the disturbing content in Cho's creative writing, I would argue that not only hadn't a criminal violation taken place, but the writing itself wasn't much cause for concern, and wasn't enough reason to contact the police.

I've been teaching creative writing on the university level for about seven years. I've taught such courses as writing fiction, writing humor and comedy, and introductory creative writing. Before the Virginia Tech shooting, receiving a story with the kind of violence contained in Cho's plays—absent some exceptionally odd student behavior—wouldn't have elicited a second thought. Cho's classmate MacFarlane refers to the plays' "twisted, macabre violence," and a commenter refers to them as "porn." While "Richard McBeef" certainly has some violent content, it's rather tame, cartoonish violence and is not gruesome. "Mr. Brownstone" is hardly violent at all.[x]

In "Mr. Brownstone," the characters do curse a lot. They are at a casino and spend much of the play complaining about their mean teacher, Mr. Brownstone. They talk about wanting to kill him. They see him at the casino, and they taunt him. They sing a song. Then they win a slot machine jackpot, and Mr. Brownstone accuses them of stealing his jackpot. Brownstone is believed, and the kids are thrown out of the casino. The play ends with all three kids yelling, "You won't get away with this, Brownstone! You old muthafucker! Muthafucker! Muthafucker!" That's it. No one is killed or even assaulted.

In "Richard McBeef," John begins by saying to his stepfather, Richard, "What's up, Dick!" Richard attempts to have a talk with John, to try to get along with him, but John is having none of it. He chews on a cereal bar "angrily." When Richard casually rests his hand on John's knee for a second, in an apparently innocent, fatherly manner, Cho throws in a couple of lame pedophilia jokes, having John refer both to Catholic priests and to Michael Jackson's Neverland Ranch. John accuses Richard of murdering his biological father in order to get into John's mother's "pant." Richard denies it and remains calm, and John stays on the offensive, continually cutting Richard off and finally saying, "You want me to shove this remote control up your ass, buddy! You ain't even worth it man. This remote was five bucks. You are such a—"

This impertinence brings the first threat of violence from Richard, who says, "NOW THAT'S ENOUGH," and "raises his hand to strike his stepson." John's mother, Sue, walks in at this moment, confronts Richard, and mocks his "chubby face." John accuses Richard of trying to "touch my privates," and Sue then attacks Richard, slapping him in the head "multiple times" and even hitting him with her shoes, hard. The violence and over-the-top dialogue continue from here, with Sue throwing a plate at Richard and calling him a "fat piece of pork" and a "bisexual psycho rapist murderer."

John is alone in his room at this point, throwing darts at a picture of Richard's face and talking to himself about killing Richard. He then rejoins the others and once again accuses Richard of molesting him. Sue drives Richard from the home by brandishing a chainsaw. At the end of the play, alone in the car with Richard, John goes on an extended rant, insulting his stepfather for a long paragraph before sticking his "half-eaten banana cereal bar in his stepfather's mouth and [attempting] to shove it down his throat." Richard removes the cereal bar, and the play ends with stage direction: "Out of sheer desecrated hurt and anger, Richard lifts his large arms and swings a deadly blow at the thirteen year old boy."

"Richard McBeef" *does* conclude with, presumably, a murder (taken literally, John is killed by Richard's "deadly blow"), and there is the use of shoes, plates, and a cereal bar as weapons. But the violence hardly seems real, and is mostly derivative—killing with a chainsaw is a movie cliché, seen in both "The Texas Chainsaw Massacre" and "Scarface." And it should be noted that in Cho's play the chainsaw never actually harms anyone. An angry woman throwing plates at a spouse isn't original, either. We've all seen that in a movie or TV show. Richard isn't even injured by the plate that hits him in the head. The violence reads like a cartoon, without the glee, of course, though Cho makes a pathetic attempt at wit with the insults hurled at Richard by John and Sue. Only the shoving of the cereal bar down Richard's throat stands out as truly violent. It's the play's most intimate, visceral moment, coming closest to projecting real rage. Having characters chase each other with chainsaws is easily dismissed as imitation. The cereal bar, the forcing of something down another person's throat, is angrier, more personal.

Lacking the context of Cho's behavior and demeanor, even this violent use of a cereal bar would not ordinarily be viewed as a warning sign. Actually, it's the only bit in the entire play that successfully conveys what the author intends, and is just the sort of memorable detail that a writing instructor might point to as effective. It isn't genius or anything, but it beats "brandishes a chainsaw."

The violence in "Richard McBeef" is not remarkable. There's an entire genre of horror movies, and a subgenre of slasher movies. And action movie fans have delighted in high body counts for decades. Short story writers and novelists haven't shied away from scenes of torture and murder, either. The movie *Saw* and the novel *American Psycho*, just as two examples, contain far more explicit horror and violence than anything a student is likely to produce, though some students try. Whatever one thinks of such works, they have received their share of commercial success and critical attention, and it shouldn't shock anyone that writing students have been influenced by these and hundreds of other works full of violence. Every reader can name, in a minute, dozens of respected and popular works that are far more violent than anything Cho wrote.

One need not point only to contemporary examples. Cruelty and murder abound in Shakespeare's tragedies; the treachery and the body count in "Hamlet" are impressive. Just the other day I was discussing Edgar Allan Poe's short story, "The Black Cat," with my students. More than a few of them found it disturbing, particularly when the narrator tells the reader that, furious with his cat, he "took from a waistcoat-pocket a penknife, opened it, grasped the poor beast by the throat, and deliberately cut one of its eyes from the socket!"[xi] Few writers have ever commanded prose to such concisely powerful violence as when Poe's narrator tells us that, in a rage at his wife, "I withdrew my arm from her grasp and buried the axe in her brain. She fell dead upon the spot without a groan."[xii]

Whether writing students are influenced by TV shows like 24 and *The Sopranos* or by writers like Poe, some of them are going to produce violent stories and plays. I've had stories handed in to my fiction workshops about all manner of murder and mayhem. "Richard McBeef" doesn't come close. There is no shortage of mobsters and hitmen in student stories I have read, with someone always getting whacked. Students trying to write thrillers develop convoluted fight scenes, with loving descriptions of each punch and spin kick knocking some teeth loose. One student recently wrote about a suicide club that the protagonist stumbled upon; blood was on the floor and walls, and people were slashing their wrists. Another student wrote about a woman who lured men to her apartment on dates, and then, after invariably discovering that they were hiding from her the fact that they were married, killed them. An especially ugly story was about a home invasion that ended with quite graphic descriptions of people killing each other. The list goes on and continues to grow. Should I have reported the author of the suicide story to the counseling center, for the student's own protection? Pedro, responding to the comments on MacFarlane's blog post, said it well:

> You can't "turn someone in" because they create a
> piece of art that you think may say something about
> them. It's a work of imagination (or it's supposed to
> be). Perhaps he was just getting inside the mind of a
> young sociopath. Turns out he had issues obviously,
> but you know how many thousands of plays, stories
> and poems are submitted to creative writing classes
> that are way more disturbing than that? You can't just
> assume that means someone is demented.[xiii]

The violence in a creative writing piece isn't itself a warning sign. Stephen King, known for writing some violence of his own, agrees:

"Certainly in this sensitized day and age, my own college writing—including a short story called 'Cain Rose Up' and the novel *RAGE*—would have raised red flags, and I'm certain someone would have tabbed me as mentally ill because of them."[xiv] Despite the attention being paid to Cho's plays, creative writing instructors must avoid reading student stories as predictors of future real life violence. King writes, "For most creative people, the imagination serves as an excretory channel for violence: We visualize what we will never actually do."[xv] Pedro is right that these kinds of stories are handed in every semester to writing workshops across the country and that they don't tell us much about the writer. Some of the stories are even well-crafted. Cho's plays are not.

King thinks that this matters: "On the whole, I don't think you can pick these guys out based on their work, unless you look for violence unenlivened by any real talent."[xvi] CNN tells us that Cho's poetry "had no meter or structure or rhyme scheme. To Giovanni, it was simply 'a tirade.'" She said, "There was no writing. I wasn't teaching him anything, and he didn't want to learn anything."[xvii] It is true that Cho's plays are very, very bad. They aren't stories at all. But I can't agree with King that identifying violence without talent might help us "pick these guys out." There are a lot of people out there without any talent filling their screenplays with blood and guts. Most of these people will never hurt anyone. Maybe the imagination serves as an excretory channel for the untalented as well as the talented. Maybe the violent content has nothing to do with an excretory channel, and aspiring writers are just imitating what they have read and seen.

Although Giovanni was referring to Cho's poetry, I would also describe his plays as "tirades." It's just him emoting, projecting, and posing. There's no plot development, no coherence, and no attempt really to tell a story. The plays also demonstrate a lack of maturity and logical thought. As a blog commenter named Stacy asked, "This is something written by a senior in college? It reads and sounds like something a 9th grader might write."[xviii] An immature, not overly bright ninth-grader, one might add.

So it's tempting to say that, though it isn't especially violent, Cho's writing's immaturity and illogic indicate that he was dangerous. Of course, when I read the plays for the first time, I already knew that he'd killed 32 people. But had I not known that, if I am being honest with myself, I believe I would have thought, "This is a crappy play by a bad writer." Probably, even though I have read some directionless student work in my time, I would have also thought, like some blog commenters, "This is a college student?" Cho's work is markedly immature and illogical, but I just don't think I would have seen any of it as a warning sign about impending violence in the real world.

Yet his professors and fellow students did. Based on what I've seen of it, I believe that Cho's writing could not, or should not, by itself, have driven a professor to contact authorities. His behavior and demeanor were the main warning signs. He barely talked with anyone. Lucinda Roy "recalled Cho exhibiting a palpable anger and secretly taking photographs of other students while holding the camera under his desk." Giovanni described him as "menacing."[xix] The police had also received stalking complaints. It was Cho the person, not Cho the writer, who was the warning sign.

College professors become accustomed to having troubled students—students who stop showing up for weeks at a time; students who grumble under their breath; students dealing with depression or drug problems or family crises; students with odd personalities; students who are socially awkward or say inappropriate things; students who cry because of a recent breakup with a boyfriend or girlfriend; students who are angry at the whole world. Long before Cho's rampage at Virginia Tech, many professors have found themselves becoming wary of a student or two and have had to decide whether to seek outside assistance, and not necessarily because they were expecting a violent outburst. In creative writing classes especially, where the order of every day is critiquing a student's work—work in which a student may have a great deal invested emotionally—tactfully managing the personality of the occasional troubled student is required.

Even given all the troubled students whom a career in teaching exposes professors to, Cho's demeanor and behavior must have stood out. The raw, pointless anger in his writing might have completed the picture for his professors, but that alone doesn't explain their concern. It's worth keeping all of this in mind as the fear caused by the massacre at Virginia Tech brings an inevitable overreaction when dealing with students' writing and other forms of self-expression. Already, little more than a week after the shootings, a high school senior was arrested for the violence in his creative writing assignment.[xx] Eighteen-year-old Allen Lee's essay seemed to contain an outright threat, and he faces two disorderly conduct charges. Given recent events, the least that can be said is that Lee's work was monumentally stupid:

> According to the complaint, Lee's essay reads in part, "Blood, sex and booze. Drugs, drugs, drugs are fun. Stab, stab, stab, stab, stab, s...t...a...b...puke. So I had this dream last night where I went into a building, pulled out two P90s and started shooting everyone, then had sex with the dead bodies. Well, not really, but it would be funny if I did."[xxi]

It seems clear that this student is messing around, but he also wrote, "[D]on't be surprised on inspiring the first CG [Cary-Grove High School] shooting."[xxii] Does a high school teacher ignore this? Should he? Note that the assignment told students to "write whatever comes to your mind. Do not judge or censor what you are writing."[xxii] Whether you think Lee is guilty only of poor judgment or of making a serious threat, whether you think the school and police overreacted or were vigilant, this one case is just the beginning, if we fool ourselves into thinking that we can prevent future horrors by looking for warning signs in student writing.

Notes

[i] "Killer's manifesto: 'You forced me into a corner'" CNN.com (April 18, 2007);
< http://www.cnn.com/2007/US/04/18/vtech.shooting/index.html>
[ii] Ibid.
[iii] "Cho Seung-Hui's Plays" posted by Ian McFarlane, AOL News Bloggers (April 17. 2007); < http://newsbloggers.aol.com/2007/04/17/cho-seung-huis-plays/>
[iv] Ibid.
[v] Ibid comment by Judi at 2:59PM Apr 17, 2007
[vi] Ibid comment by Blackdog at 3:02PM Apr 17, 2007
[vii] Ibid comment by Linda at 2:56PM Apr 17, 2007
[viii] "Killer's manifesto: 'You forced me into a corner'"
[x] Allen G. Breed, "Giovanni confronted Cho in poetry class" The Enquirer (April 19, 2007);
< http://news.enquirer.com/apps/pbcs.dll/article?AID=/AB/20070419/NEWS01/704190350/>
[xi] All references to and quotations from "Richard McBeef" and "Mr. Brownstone" are based on the version accessible through AOL News Bloggers. "Cho Seung-Hui's Plays"; < http://newsbloggers.aol.com/2007/04/17/cho-seung-huis-plays/>
[xii] Edgar Allan Poe, "The Complete Tales and Poems" (New York: Dorset 1989).478.
Poe 481.
[xiii] "Cho Seung-Hui's Plays" comment by Pedro at 2:55PM Apr 17, 2007
[xiv] Stephen King, "On Predicting Violence," Entertainment Weekly (EW.com; April 20, 2007); < http://www.ew.com/ew/article/0,,20036014,00.html>
[xv] Ibid.
[xvi] Ibid.
[xvii] "Giovanni confronted Cho in poetry class."
[xviii] "Cho Seung-Hui's Plays" comment by Stacy at 2:28PM; April 17, 2007;
< http://newsbloggers.aol.com/2007/04/17/cho-seung-huis-plays/>
[xix] "Killer's manifesto: 'You forced me into a corner.'"

[xx] "Student arrested for essay's imaginary violence," CNN.com. (April 27, 2007); <http://www.cnn.com/2007/US/04/27/student.essay.arrest.ap/index.html>

[xxi] Ibid.

[xxii] Ibid.

[xxiii] Ibid.

Michael Sullivan

American Adventurism Abroad: Invasions, Interventions, and Regime Changes since World War II

As of mid-2008, the United States was mired in a military mess in Iraq that had been dragging on longer than it had taken to win World War II. US combat forces had also been in Afghanistan for a year and a half beyond this, meaning President George W. Bush had spent more time fighting wars than either Lyndon Johnson or Richard Nixon in Vietnam.

It was not supposed to be this way after America ascended to the heights of hegemony over the global capitalist system after winning the Cold War in the early 1990s. But by declaring a "war on terror" after the attack of 9-11-01, the United States returned to its historic pattern of robust military interventionism abroad. Like the Cold War before it, the "war on terror" has provided a paradigm for a new generation of invasions and other types of regime change. Such activity has not been limited to the arguably terror-related sites in the Middle East where the most dramatic interventions have occurred; there have also been two cases of forceful intervention in the Western Hemisphere (Venezuela, 2002, and Haiti, 2004), and two in Africa (Liberia, 2003, and Somalia, 2005). In short, the announced rationales for such foreign adventures ("fighting communism" in the earlier era, "war on terror" since 9/11) are insufficient to explain totally US actions abroad; a more historic perspective is needed.

American foreign policy since 1945 has mainly been motivated by the goal of being hegemon of the global capitalist economic system. As chief protector of transnational capitalism, the United States has replaced the United Kingdom, which played this role for more than a century before World War II. Although the 1947-91 Cold War presented an easy-to-understand threat to this objective, US diplomacy in these years was not primarily about keeping the USSR out of Western Europe (the original explanation for containment), but rather about projecting its own power, globally. It was not about making the world safe for democracy (the usual ideological justification), but rather about being the leader of the capitalist world, the upholder of the global economic system.

The primary strategic goal of the United States since 1945 has been to supplant the major imperial powers of the pre-World War II era—United Kingdom, France, Germany, and Japan—as the sole economic hegemon of the global capitalist system. This generally meant America's competing against the Soviet Union (its main bilateral strategic rival in Europe) over which of the two post-World War II Super Powers would succeed Western Europe and Japan as leader of the "Third World" of developing nations in the Middle East, Africa, Asia and the Western Hemisphere.

A corollary to this thesis (which relates primarily to politics) is another pertaining more specifically to *economics*. The US objective, in most of its 30-plus interventions since 1945, has primarily been to make the world safe not for democracy (as is often claimed), but rather to make the world *safe* for capital. This is especially true in the periphery of the global capitalist system where there is opportunity for the greatest economic growth and profit, and for demonstrations of the superiority of the system. To this end, US interventions are not limited to the protection of specific business investments of *American* corporations, but rather to upholding the economic system, the idea of capitalism itself.

In defense of this policy, it is often argued that safeguarding capitalism in a developing nation sometimes leads to an improved quality of life for a small number of local capitalists and some upper-middle-class managers, and *in the long run* to democracy (or at least to "electoral" or "procedural" democracy). In the short run, however, economic hegemony by nations of the core over those in the periphery—a continuing goal in this current era of globalization and "war on terror"—leads to control not only of the weaker states' economic systems, but of their politics as well. For many of the states encroached upon, the "political systems" that have been promoted to preserve capitalism range from one-party rule and military dictatorship, to monarchies, colonies, and recurring civil wars.

It might also be noted that there has been a reluctance by the United States to accept any "third way" in these developing nations between left-wing "socialist nationalists" and right-wing "unreconstructed fascists." Transnational corporations, not governments, must organize these Third World economies; alternate models of development are rejected as not congenial to global capital. Not acceptable under this formula are social-democratic reformers with mixed economies where some private property is respected, and moderate capitalist governments sympathetic to labor unions or the poor (in the form of food subsidies or significant spending for health and education). Welfare must have a lower priority than repayment of international debt, or spending on infrastructure to entice investment from countries of the core.

These themes and patterns (of preferring right over center, embracing dubious allies, and employing nefarious means) may have resulted in some short-term US foreign policy successes, but nearly always have proved tragic for the countries affected. Terrible disasters have been visited upon the local societies targeted in many US interventions. These range from the "mere" loss of democracy to the consolidation of authoritarianism where it was already the rule. Finally, in almost all instances, the overwhelming military technology accompanying American interventions into wars has led to disproportionate destruction of life in these developing nations. In fact, with respect to war-related *deaths*, there are many instances where US intervention either caused, or prolonged and exacerbated, some 200 years of war involving several million deaths. Despite these appalling levels of death, destruction, and disruption related to American diplomacy, many of these interventions did not even result in any gains for US foreign policy. In many cases it can be argued that American action actually produced long-term diplomatic losses.

In short, US foreign policy in the periphery of the global capitalist system in the years before 9/11/01 may have succeeded in securing the United States as hegemonic successor to earlier imperialist powers. However, it was at a tremendous cost, especially for the societies besieged by American belligerence, and in lesser measure for the United States itself.

Since 9/11/01, it has become conventional wisdom that the world has changed and international politics will never again be the same. Indeed, the George W. Bush administration has done its utmost to create a new paradigm for American foreign policy, including a novel strategic doctrine of pre-emptive war, and a re-structuring of government comparable to that at the start of the Cold War. The latter even includes a Department of Homeland Security, exposing the pretense that the Department of "Defense" was for something other than the projection of global power.

Thus, the basic thesis concerning American intervention in the Third World remains valid. The United States still aspires to be the global hegemon. Only the name of the enemy has been changed. Instead of "fighting communism," the US is engaged in a "war against terrorism." Both of these rubrics are essentially cover stories for a policy of global power projection in pursuit of world hegemony.

It remains to be seen whether the initial overwhelming support within the United States for the "war on terror" lasts as long as the bipartisan consensus for fighting communism did (about 20 years without discernible elite dissent until it broke over Vietnam). To date, the US has not been as successful in getting state support for the "war on terror" in numbers comparable to the more than 50 partners in NATO and other alliances that formally embraced the "war on communism."

The "war against terrorism"—in whose name the massive military deployments into Afghanistan and, especially, Iraq have been made—has resulted in US troops being spread from Kenya and Somalia in east Africa to Kyrgyzstan and Tajikistan among the central Asian republics of the former Soviet Union. It is no coincidence that this swath of territory roughly embraces the "arc of crisis" described by President Jimmy Carter at the time of the Soviet invasion of Afghanistan. But within this realm there is little talk today of human rights or democracy, the justifications for American adventures in the Third World during the Cold War and the Carter and Reagan years. Rather, the United States is striving for mere stability and governments that can sustain and defend themselves in the two cauldrons of chaos that have been created in the wake the American invasions of 2001 and 2003.

This area from the horn of Africa to central Asia, represents one of the last places on the periphery of the capitalist world to which the America can hope to fill the role of hegemon. To the extent that east Asia is now a zone of competition vis-a-vis a resurgent neo-capitalist nuclear China, and that eastern Europe is once again a focus for Russia and Germany (via the European Union), the "arc of crisis" represents the last fruitful area for American aspirations unlikely to be of immediate interest to any other Great Power. (Sub-Saharan Africa is at a more primitive stage of development and therefore not yet a factor in such calculations.)

It would be too easy to say the American wars in Afghanistan and Iraq are only about oil and bases. What is at stake is the future development of one of the final outposts of the global capitalist system. As hegemon, the United States desires to make this latest frontier stable, and hopes to set the general parameters, for the next expansion of global capitalism.

From a longer historical perspective, the model is American neo-colonialism in the Western Hemisphere. In the latest phase of its role as global hegemon, the intent is for the United States to eschew genuine "nation-building" and political micro-management in the conquered areas, contenting itself with mere "regime change." As soon as the government "harborers of terrorists" or "makers of weapons of mass destruction" are overthrown, America would prefer to withdraw most of its forces and to allow the newly-installed local satrap to resume normal activities in service to global capital.

But the interventions in Afghanistan and Iraq did not work out as planned. By getting bogged down in two wars now in their seventh and fifth years, respectively, the United States has overextended its military capacity and put in jeopardy its role as hegemon of the global capitalist system. The era of American adventurism abroad may be coming to an end.

Exerpted from American Adventurism Abroad: Invasions, Interventions, and Regime Changes since World War II, revised and expanded paperback edition (Wiley-Blackwell, 2008).

Eva Thury

The Old Refugee and Me

Bozeman. Billings. Miles City. I'm a timid middle-class creature, the kind who makes reservations ahead on a long car trip, sometimes two or three at various points on the road, allowing for every eventuality. Travelodge. Comfort Inn. Motel 6. I don't usually go as upscale as the Holiday Inn, but if that's all I find on the back of my AAA Trip-Tik, I could succumb. I once went to Venice with some friends and produced a large table with an hour-by-hour and day-by-day schedule for each person, taking into account the interests of each traveler. It was worked out like a lesson plan. Early in the visit we were all programmed to move together, building the basic skills of Kati, the first-time traveler among us, so midway through she could pluck up her courage and head off *senza italiano* to the Doge's Palace while the rest of us could proceed to more advanced venues.

So why was I driving through Montana at three in the morning, the neon "Full" signs slapping me in the face, one after the other? It's the company I was keeping. My father didn't do reservations. He smiled and got a faraway look in his eyes at the first suggestion. When I persisted, he shook his head, a dog, jaws clamped, thrashing the life out of a rabbit. I had just finished the summer at the University of Washington, studying Aristotle, toasting the sunset with martinis by the shore of Lake Union, helping my marriage unravel by sneaking off whenever I could to screw one of my classmates. It was going to be a long drive back to Toledo, Ohio by myself. The old man and I didn't talk very well, ever really, so I still didn't know what to make of his Sunday-night-phone-call announcement that he was flying out to Seattle to drive back with me.

Did he want to help? Was it an adventure for him? Was my overprotective mother fueling the trip? Did he see himself as exploring the country, old newspaperman that he was? In Hungary, he had been a journalist and writer. His most famous piece, the one that made him a fugitive from the Soviet government, was investigative journalism about Hungarians whose lives were metastasized when their homes were reallocated to Slovakia, while the government did nothing. "Poof! You're a Slovak now! What do you mean you don't speak your national language? You'd better learn it or you can kiss your job good-bye." That week, he was visited by thugs from the secret police telling him not to write a story like that *ever again* I don't know what made a hotel room in Billings such a hot ticket tonight, but we drove on, ending up in Miles City, saved by a kindly

Holiday Inn clerk who located a room unrented because it was left uncleaned by mistake. She prepared the room herself as my father and I waited in the furniture-less, just-being-renovated lobby, nearly passed out on the rug, barely speaking to each other.

From then on, despite my father's protests, I made reservations ahead along the road, no matter how bourgeois he thought I was. It was an amusing taunt for him to be able to make, and we both knew it. Usually, I was the left-leaning daughter who got to sling that epithet at him. But in this instance, he was the old refugee who has been through a thing or two that I had not. We forged an uneasy truce born not out of understanding but from the determination to get along. It was only later that I understood the old man, when I remembered the account he wrote in 1956:

I arrived in Austria on March 13, 1948 at three in the morning. In the first village, a peasant took care of me; he spoke Hungarian as well as German. Washing up. Toweling dry. After breakfast, he offered me a cigarette,and suddenly, the rising smoke made me forget the stinging soles of my feet. I quietly repacked my belongings into the pocket of my winter coat while my host, stabbing the air with broad gestures, explained where I should get on the Vienna bus to avoid Soviet guards. There was this then too. I watched his movements, but I no longer heard his voice. I was sleepy and watchful at the same time. Twenty-four hours earlier I was in Budapest, saying my good-byes. I hardly said anything different from what is customary at such a time. I asked them to wait. Four-five years and I'll be back.

"Four-five years?" repeated the person I was hugging.

"Yes," I answered then, while worrying about something else.

"I don't think I'll live that long," was the answer.

This sentence and its emphasis suddenly came back to me now. Only three and a half miles separated me from the border. Rough terrain, a two-hour walk.

"I'll come this way, when I go home," I thought, "and I'll stop in this village."

I tried to imagine how they would look when I saw them again: this room, the gesticulating peasant, his silent wife. No wonder I got on the

Vienna bus in the wrong place, and almost got in trouble. New pictures were swarming in my head. I was embellishing my homecoming. This is what ties us to all the other drifters in the world.

What is it like alone in a foreign land? Back then, I first settled in Linz, inside the American sector of Austria. The first night I slept on a ship on the Danube. This little respite took all the money I had left.

There was a Red Cross booth in front of the bombed-out railroad station. I started there the next day: could I sleep for free somewhere? I got an entry slip for the Red Cross shelter from a tall brown-haired girl. As I was leaving, the girl called me back and gave me a two-pound loaf of bread. I could have thought about what I must have looked like if handing over a loaf of bread went without saying. But this peripheral matter did not hold my attention. The bread was still fresh and warm. The next day I strolled around the area of the Linz train station until the brown-haired girl took up her post. I went to her regularly for shelter entry slips and loaves of bread.

The Red Cross shelter was a wooden building with bunk beds and many different kinds of people. The custodian was a one-armed Austrian war casualty; he distributed his two or three blankets to us every night. In the morning he bought milk with his own money for those with children. There was no real rest at night. The weak-bladdered went in and out constantly. Others told stories, or argued, or bantered with each other half the night. The police raided the shelter just about every night. They snapped on the lights, and pulled the ragged covers from people's faces, inspecting each person in the place. They shook awake six or seven of those who were sleeping, or pretending to sleep. They studied their papers. They took away those who didn't have identity cards validated by the Americans. In principle at least, refugees were liable for crossing a forbidden border. Some were actually jailed; others had better luck. Those collected night after night in the shelters were not among the fortunate. The penalty was being locked up for eight, ten or even thirty or sixty days.

I always awoke when the lights were turned on. I waited to see if they shook my leg and took me away. The third or fourth night, I was surprised to discover that I wasn't afraid, just curious. There was also worry mixed in with the curiosity. The thought of being locked up for eight, or thirty days didn't thrill me, but the rhythm of my heart remained regular and calm when the Austrian police came and turned on the light. I studied them on the sly. They were always a little ashamed and did their job in a hurry. I sang the same refrain of curses as the others when the police closed the door behind them, but my anger was more for show. I swiftly went back to sleep in the barracks made warm by our stench.

There were times in my upbringing when I found my father remote. He would stare off into space, and I sensed that the scenes playing on his pupils were more vivid than the world around him. That night in Montana, you could almost say we slept in different barracks.[xxiv]

The excerpt in this essay comes from Zoltán Thury's *Menekültek Kalauza (The Refugee's Handbook)* Munich: Greif, 1957, translated from the Hungarian by his daughter Eva Thury. The Refugee's Handbook tells the story of the author's emigration from Hungary in 1948, following government threats for his anti-Soviet activities; his exile lasted for 40 years. The work is autobiographical, but its focus is somewhat ironic: it explains how to live if you have lost your homeland. This essay is part of a larger project to translate and comment upon the whole work.

Kathleen Volk Miller

Feeding People

I had to have my roof redone a few months ago. The man doing the roof was a man I had just begun dating, and he had his friends helping, doing my 100-year-old, 20-pitch, two-and-a-half story house for about half of what my neighbors had paid.

So I cooked. I made hot lunches the six days they were there barbecued beef on crusty rolls, chicken soup with spinach and tortellini, carved ham and cheese, buffalo wings and pepperoni bread. These meals were accompanied by side dishes like homemade cole slaw, carrot and raisin salad, tortilla chips with cheese. I timed desserts to come out of the oven just as the men were finishing their lunches—chocolate chip cookies, cherry dump cake, brownies, plum cobbler. Each morning I had donuts or coffeecake, muffins or Danish waiting on the kitchen table. All day, I made sure there was a fresh pot of coffee available.

I was so happy to do this for them. So happy to have one say I should market the cole slaw to local delis; to have another ask me to marry him; to have them tease the man I was seeing mercilessly, telling him he didn't deserve me. I was a happy *hausfrau*. My mother had died less than a year before, and I "called her up" for ideas and to thank her—to thank her for my cooking skills and for the simple fact that I was happy to please these people through food, as she has given me that character attribute, too.

We've always noticed the connection between sex and death, but food might be more complicated. Cooking for someone, and even eating, might be the antithesis of death—it's an act of optimism. We expect the guests to show up. We expect to be around long enough to burn the calories. It's overtly primal, of course, a base instinct, and "I'm hungry" is more acceptable to say aloud than "I'm horny." Food satisfies. Eating is a sensual experience. Going out for a lovely dinner or cooking a meal for someone, then having sex with them, is a perfect date, a perfect way of sharing time, of sharing ourselves. When someone dies, food memories stay connected to them; smells and tastes can bring them back.

When my mother was still alive, and her back was too bad for her to stand in the kitchen peeling potatoes, I had taken over the responsibility of "Mom's Potato Salad." That's what we always called it and what we still do, and though I'm a mother, too, even my own children know whose it is. When my brother came in the kitchen the first time I had attempted to replicate her potato salad, he kissed me on the cheek and said, "You nailed it." There was no greater reward, no greater compliment, except for when my mother said, "You did it. It's yours now."

One time, she tried to read me the homemade bread recipe, and I was eager, writing it all down, anxious to master this long-time Christmas-and-Easter-only bread. Halfway through the long and complicated instructions, I stopped writing. She knew it, and said, "You're not going to try this, are you?" I just started laughing, surprised yet pleased that she knew. "Mom," I said, "I just don't think I can do it." And she said, "You could. But it's okay. Maybe next holiday." Optimistic.

And last week, my Dad and I were alone in his storage basement, culling through boxes whose contents were a mystery to him. We found lots of things that made us laugh, lots of things that hurt our hearts, often concurrently.

Then he found the recipe card box. He said, "I don't think there's anything in here she made often; we haven't opened this box in twenty years." I said, still, "I'll take anything in her handwriting." And we found out he was wrong. These were the recipes for things she made so often she no longer needed the cards.

We gasped when we read "Banana Bread." We laughed when we found the one for barbecued beef, as I no longer need the recipe either. We both got misty-eyed over how many called for crushed pineapple, Dad saying simply, "She loved crushed pineapple." I kept them all, and made her "Harvey House Cole Slaw" for the first time this past weekend. I nailed it.

I sent a dear friend home with an extra loaf of pepperoni bread, his favorite, the food item he's thanked me for for twenty years. He texted me the next day—"hmm." And then, "pepperoni bread massages my heart." I texted back, "I'm glad." I am.

After ten years of living next door to the same family, the women of the household only recently let me know that her family stands in their driveway, sniffing in our direction, then comes in the house and tells her how good it smells next door. I had no idea this had been going on, and even though I wasn't feeding them, somehow, there's even gratification knowing that our dinner wafting into their driveway will be part of their memories.

Of course we know that food is love, that our relationship with it is ingrained early, and frequently, it is instilled by our mothers. I am a professor, a writer, and an editor. My mother graduated high school, got married, and had five children. I love that I still love to cook, that she gave me this, this urge to feed, to please this way. I can't see it as sexist or demeaning. When my husband was still alive, he mowed the lawn, maintained the cars, painted, and hammered when things needed painting or hammering. I cooked.

Another faculty member and I once had a conversation on this topic, on the division of labor in the home. When I told her that my husband and I had what might be seen as very sexist, traditional roles, she went into a flurry of protestations: "Why should the cooking be your responsibility? Why should you cook dinner every night when he is perfectly capable of cooking his own dinner?" My response: "Look. I have no desire, ever, to push a lawnmower. We are each doing what we want to do for the household." She could not be assuaged. She accused me of adapting to my socialization, not doing what I truly wanted.

I remember sitting there, watching her face redden, and thinking, "I want to have my husband call me on his way home from work and ask me what's for dinner, and when I answer, I want him to say, 'Sounds great, honey.' It's a good language for us to speak." And that's what he and continued to say to each other.

About five months after he died, I was making spaghetti and meatballs, and it was raining. The kids weren't home yet from their after-school activities. It was winter. It was only about 5 p.m. but it was pitch black outside. I thought I heard a car pull up in the driveway and then I thought, "Don will be so happy when he sees what's for dinner." And then I realized that it couldn't be him, that he would never pull up in the driveway again. I slid to the kitchen floor, sobbing. I couldn't stop crying and didn't sleep that night. I had to cancel classes the next day. I stayed in bed. He had died five months prior, but the realization, the true ownership of the knowledge that I would never cook for him again, put me into a state of grief I had not yet been in.

When he was alive, he'd walk in the back door and his eyes would go to the stove, rather than me, and I loved it, took no offense at all. Happy, happy that my cooking could please him. When I first met him, his vegetable repertoire consisted of corn and peas. I took great pride in turning him on to ratatouille, cauliflower sautéed in garlic and Italian breadcrumbs, broccoli steamed and buttered, snow peas with lemon. He frustrated me by his gag reflex to mayonnaise, though I managed to hide it from him in dishes all the time; his love of Stovetop made me question his character, but I got over his addition of ketchup to a steak.

It's been three years and there are certain dishes he loved that I still can't make.

I have interns at the university where I teach, and one of the first things I show them is where I keep the cereal bars and the Hershey kisses.

When my brother and his family come to visit from Pittsburgh I make "Welcome to Our House Soup." When I have buffet parties, after fifteen people have eaten, the buffet looks as full as if no one has come through. But, see, that's what my mother did. Just tonight, my daughter thought she was invited to a friend's house for hot dogs (Hot dogs! Hot dogs for dinner!) and then got called back and was told there was not enough. My daughter said, "Mom. If I invite someone to dinner and you're afraid there's not enough, even though there always is, you add another side dish, you go to the freezer and you just... make more." I want her to see it that way, that if we turn someone away from our table, we are turning them away.

My children and I skew the national statistics by having dinner together at least four nights a week. We will sit around the table for half an hour after we're done eating, enjoying the talk, not wanting to break off just yet, into our separateness.

Eventually, regretfully, we will, and I'll go back into the kitchen, prep tomorrow's coffee for myself, pack their lunches—three different kinds of sandwiches for three different kinds of kids. I will pack their lunches while the smell of dinner is still in the air, and I will find this satisfying, a celebration of our life, optimistic.

Of course there have been failures. I forgot to put the lid on the chuck roast, and so it wouldn't pull apart, no matter how long I kept cooking it. The time I made a baked ham for a Jewish couple, not thinking they followed Judaic Law. (But it was okay anyway, as I had also roasted a turkey breast, and made three types of salads as side dishes.) I've set chicken on fire on the grill, and I once locked us out of the house with pork chops in the oven.

My husband died at forty-five and won't ask me what's for dinner anymore. But the kids will. And they'll ask if their friends can stay, and they can. I will cook for other men, but not whole chicken legs stuffed with spinach and cheese, because that was one of my husband's favorites. I cannot call my mother and ask her how she made the green peppercorn sauce for the strip steak, but I can remember watching her make it, I can remember what it tasted like, and I can try to make it my own. I can make Mom's potato salad.

I like food. I like to cook. I like sex. I've survived the deaths of my mother and my husband. But I get to feed people. I can hope that people will remember my hummus, my pumpkin chocolate chip bread. I get to keep coming out from the kitchen with dish after dish or plate after plate and the people say, "Thank you." And the people are pleased. And so am I.

Contributors

Zahra Ahmed, a native of New Delhi, India, is a rising sophomore pursuing her bachelor's degree in Biomedical Engineering. She is currently the Public Relations Chair for the Society of Women Engineers and plans to pursue a Ph.D. and a career in research after graduating from Drexel University.

Stacey Ake has received Ph.D.s in Biology and Philosophy from Pennsylvania State University. She was the editor of *Metanexus: from Religion and Science*. Ake is currently an Assistant Professor of Philosophy at Drexel University in Philadelphia.

Tom Bennett is a computer scientist originally from Philadelphia, PA. He enjoys exploring new approaches to art, and is a strong proponent for exploring different methods of utilizing video game mechanics as a means of storytelling and artistic expression.

Ronald C. Bishop, a Professor in the Department of Culture and Communications, teaches courses in journalism and mass media, including a course on the cultural significance of fame. Bishop received his Ph.D. from Temple University.

Robert Brulle is an Associate Professor of Sociology and Environmental Science in the Department of Culture and Communications at Drexel University. He received his Ph.D. in Sociology at George Washington University.

Paula Marantz Cohen, is Distinguished Professor of English at Drexel University, where she teaches courses in literature, film, and creative writing. She is the author of four nonfiction books: *The Daughter's Dilemma: Family Process and the Nineteenth-Century Domestic Novel; The Daughter as Reader: Encounters Between Literature and Life; Alfred Hitchcock: The Legacy of Victorianism; and Silent Film and the Triumph of the American Myth*. Her novels include *Jane Austen in Boca, Much Ado About Jessie Kaplan,* and *Jane Austen in Scarsdale or Love, Death, and the SATs*. Cohen's essays and stories have appeared in *The Yale Review, Raritan, The American Scholar, Boulevard, The Hudson Review, the Times Literary Supplement,* and other publications. She is the host of the *Drexel Interview*, a cable TV show based in Philadelphia, and a co-editor of *jml: The Journal of Modern Literature*.

Ali Cahill is a junior majoring in English with a concentration in creative writing. While she considers herself primarily a poet, she enjoys all dimensions of writing. She is the Managing Editor of *ASK*, the online journal of the College of Arts & Sciences at Drexel, and the Editor-in-Chief of *Maya*, the student literary magazine at Drexel. Her non-literary hobbies include solving the Rubik's cube and drinking chai, and her dream job is to be Poet Laureate.

Kelly Collett is a first-year mechanical engineering major from Pasadena, Maryland. She enjoys Batman comics, coffee, giraffes, taking naps, and spending time with her family and friends. In the future, Kelly hopes to obtain her masters degree in aerospace engineering, and design spaceships.

Lisa Collins hails from Phoenixville, Pennsylvania. Double majoring in English and International Area Studies with a concentration in International Business and Economics, she hopes to obtain an overseas representative position in an international firm after graduation.

Ryan Cooper received a B.S. in Mechanical Engineering and Mechanics at Drexel University. He has received the Augustus H. Hess Scholarship for his research as an undergraduate, as well as the Dolphin Scholarship for Academic Excellence, and is a member of the Pi Tau Sigma Honors fraternity of Mechanical Engineers, and the National Society of Collegiate Scholars. Currently continuing his graduate studies at Columbia University, Cooper's research has focused on the characterization of carbon nanotubes at Drexel University.

Ingrid G. Daemmrich teaches writing and literature in the Department of English and Philosophy at Drexel. Her textbook, *The Changing Seasons of Humor in Literature*, now in its sixth edition, aligns humorous literature with the seasons in moving from springtime fun to winter absurdity.

Albert DiBartolomeo is the Editor-in-Chief of *ASK*, the Journal of the College of Arts and Sciences at Drexel University where he teaches writing and Literature in the Department of English and Philosophy. He is also the founding editor of the *Drexel Online Journal*. He is the author of two novels, *The Vespers Tapes (Blood Confessions* in paperback) and Fool's Gold.

Rebecca Dorne came to Drexel from Los Angeles to study nursing, and is also a member of Drexel's women's rugby team. After college she plans to attend graduate school on the west coast and pursue a career as a nurse anesthetist.

Leonard Finegold teaches in the Department of Physics at Drexel University.

Andrew Fiorentino is majoring in journalism at Drexel University. He plans to write the next great American novel.

Valerie Fox is the author of *The Rorschach Factory* (Straw Gate Books) and *Bundles of Letters Including A, V and Epsilon* (Texture Press). She co-edits the online magazine Press 1.

Emily Greenberg is a Business Administration major with concentrations in Marketing and Entrepreneurship, and a member of the LeBow College of Business and the Pennoni Honors College. Emily was elected treasurer of the Drexel University chapter of Phi Beta Lambda, a national business organization, for the 2008-2009 school year.

Michael B. Harris-Peyton is an English Major at Drexel University. Originally from Drexel Hill, Pennsylvania, he currently lives in Philadelphia. An avid writer, he intends to get a doctoral degree in English and teach. His interests include writing, philosophy, languages, biology, politics and stand-up comedy.

Shanowya Jackson is a history major from Brooklyn, New York. She plans to obtain her undergraduate degree in history, and her graduate degree in education.

Samantha Kats is a sophomore at the Lebow College of Business with concentrations in Economics and Legal Studies. She plans to extensively study analytical writing and psychology. After graduating Drexel University, she plans to attend law school to study criminal justice or business law.

Scott Gabriel Knowles is Assistant Professor of History and Director of the Great Works Symposium at Drexel University. He is currently working on a book about the history of disaster management titled *Experts in Disaster: A History of Risk and Authority in the Modern United States*. Additionally, he is editor of a forthcoming book titled *Philadelphia in the Year 2009: Looking Backward at Edmund Bacon's Vision for the City*.

Miriam N. Kotzin is the co-founding editor of Per Contra: The international Journal of the Arts, Literature and Ideas. She is the author of *A History of Drexel University*, Drexel University: 1983. Her poetry and fiction have been published in more than one hundred magazines. A book of her poems, *Reclaiming the Dead,* will be published by New American Press (November 2008). She teaches literature and creative writing in the Department of English and Philosophy and directs the Certificate Program in Writing and Publishing

Ashley Landicho is a freshman from Seattle, Washington majoring in Biological Sciences at Drexel University. She is a member of the seven year accelerated medical program, and aspires to become a neurosurgeon after graduating medical school. Ashley loves singing Disney songs in the shower, playing Scrabble, and having taco eating contests with her friends.

Krista Lewis grew up in Lino Lakes, Minnesota, and graduated from Drexel University in 2008 with a major in history and minors in art history and architecture.

Matthew Lucas received a Bachelor's degree in English Literature and Creative Writing from the University of Scranton, and is currently enrolled in Drexel University's ACE Nursing Program. In his free time he enjoys backpacking, photography, and fresh New Jersey produce. His career plans seem to change annually, so he hopes that a few years of Travel-Nursing will serve as sinecure. He is working on a chapbook entitled, *The Old Codger: and other Poems for Daily Living*, soon to be published

Pearl Mathew is a dual degree student pursuing a Bachelor's degree in Business Administration (Finance) and Economics at the Lebow School of Business.

Amanda McArthur is a fifth-year English major at Drexel. After graduation she hopes to get a scholarship to teach English abroad and later study linguistics. She will miss studying literature though, and may ultimately return to it, preferably as an insane, octogenarian professor.

Usha Menon is Associate Professor of Anthropology in the Department of Culture and Communication at Drexel University. She received her Ph.D. from the University of Chicago in 1995. She has done fieldwork in the temple town of Bhudaneswar in Orissa, eastern India, as well as in the northern Indian city of Meerut. She has written extensively on different aspects of Hindu society and civilization.

Ian Micir is the editorial assistant for the Drexel Publishing Group and also works on the editorial staff of *Maya* and *Painted Bride Quarterly*. Over the past year, Ian has discovered his love for performance of both written pieces and original songs. In a few semesters, he will receive his B.A. in English from Drexel. Ian is a cheese steak and fine scotch connoisseur, and on most nights can be found enjoying both while writing pieces for his comedy blog, *Time to Feed the Goldfish*, which is not recommended for children under 2, the blind, or anyone who can't read.

Sarah Munroe, originally from Maine, grew up in Lancaster County and came to Philadelphia to be a part of the Circle of Hope church community. Munroe has tried various majors at various colleges, but has stayed at Drexel the longest and will graduate in 2009, possibly with a degree in Political Science. While Sarah enjoys writing in most styles, her particular interests are children's books and poetry. She currently lives in Kensington and loves dinosaurs, kites, and whiskey.

Trevor Nederlof, from Westport, Connecticut, is a Business Administration major in the Lebow School of Business at Drexel University, concentrating in Economics. He is a collegiate, as well as an international sailboat racer, competing in world championship events. He plans on working in the financial industry upon graduation from Drexel University.

Madeline Olsen grew up in South Jersey in Mullica Township and is pursuing a degree in Biomedical Engineering at Drexel University. She is the vice president of the Drexel Club Track Team and enjoys running, soccer, and the beach.

Monica Pace received her master's degree in Communication from Drexel University in June 2008. Her myriad of interests include languages and cultures, painting, writing, guitar, singing, travel, cooking, and education. She aspires to a career in international journalism or travel writing.

Michelle Pagnani is from a small-town outside of Atlantic City, NJ. She majored in English at Drexel and graduated in June 2008. She intends to eventually get her Ph.D. in Rhetoric and Composition. In the near future she plans to teach at a prep school somewhere in the Northeast and spend her summers being a beach bum.

Barkha Patel is an undergraduate student in the College of Arts and Sciences majoring in Political Science with a minor in Philosophy. She is in the six-year Accelerated Law Program at Drexel. She hopes to continue participating in the many organizations in which she is involved while balancing her academic endeavors.

Ram Pathak is from Jacksonville, Florida and has recently graduated as a BS/MD student from Drexel University. He plans to continue his medical studies at Drexel University College of Medicine. His aspirations for becoming a doctor and passion for the sciences have been cultivating since a very young age. He loves to read and write, play basketball, and most of all enjoy the company of his friends.

M.G. Piety is an associate professor of philosophy at Drexel University. She has published scholarly articles on the philosophy of Soren Kierkegaard and on business ethics. She has also published several pieces of creative nonfiction in literary journals and a number of popular articles on Kierkegaard on a variety of social and political topics in publications such as the *Times Literary Supplement, Counterpunch, Per Contra, The Smart Set, Commonsense2* and *ASK*.

Furrah Qureshi is a Drexel undergraduate currently enrolled in the English program. Her future goals meet somewhere in between the blunt honesty of the journalism world, and the manipulation and power of the legal world. When asked what she would want people to say about her after she's gone, she replied, "The same thing I said after I read *Catch-22*, What else is there to say?"

Regina Ram graduated from Drexel with a degree in Biology. She writes poetry when inspired, and enjoys music and museums. Her favorite poet is Charles Bukowski.

Don Riggs earned his Ph.D. in Comparative Literature at UNC-Chapel Hill, and has been writing ever since.

Elizabeth Rosenthal has just completed her freshman year in the LeBow College of Business at Drexel University where she is doing a triple major in finance, marketing, and legal studies. She is working towards receiving a combined B.S./M.B.A degree through Drexel's accelerated five-year program, and plans to attend law school. Elizabeth is a native of Huntingdon Valley, Pennsylvania, a suburb of Philadelphia.

Sondra Schreibman's love of small things first became evident at five years old, when she became an avid collector of insects, much to the chagrin of her devoted but macrocentric mother. Schreibman obtained a Bachelor's degree in environmental science from California State University at Monterey Bay in 2005 and is currently working toward a Ph.D. in molecular biology at Drexel University.

Anjali Sethi, is from Montgomery, NJ. She is a senior and biology major in the BS/MD program at Drexel University. Along with writing, she enjoys playing foosball, the piano, painting, and reading.

Fred Siegel teaches several courses for the Department of English and Philosophy, including Horror in American Culture, Readings in Drama, Creative Nonfiction and Freshman Writing. Dr. Siegel has articles in *The Drama Review* and had an autobiographical column, "Fred's Dreams," in the *Drexel Online Journal.*

Scott Stein is the author of the novels *Lost* and *Mean Martin Manning* and the editor of *When Falls the Coliseum: a journal of American culture (or lack thereof)* < whenfallsthecoliseum.com>. His short fiction, reviews, and essays have appeared in such places as the *Philadelphia Inquirer, Liberty, New York* magazine, *The G.W. Review,* and *Art Times*. He teaches writing fiction, writing humor and comedy, creative writing, and freshman writing in the Department of English and Philosophy.

Michael J. Sullivan III is Professor of History and Politics at Drexel University. He has authored numerous articles on arms control and nuclear non-proliferation and has been awarded fellowships from the National Endowment for the Humanities (NEH), the North Atlantic Treaty Organization (NATO), and the Pew Foundation. He is the author of *Measuring Global Values: The Ranking of 162 Countries* (1991) and *Comparing Nation-State Polities: a Framework for Analyzing 100 Governments.*

Karna Sura is a third year BS/MD Biological Science major from Ellicott City, MD. In his free time he enjoys playing videos games and watching movies. He plans on continuing researching stem cells and their potential therapies.

Eva Thury is an Associate Professor in the Department of English and Philosophy at Drexel. She wrote a column for the *Drexel Online Journal* called "with a small c." Her work has also appeared in ASK, the journal of the College of Arts and Sciences at Drexel. She is the co-author of *Introduction to Mythology: Contemporary Approaches to Classical and*

World Myths (Oxford: second edition forthcoming in 2009) with Margaret K. Devinney. Dr. Thury teaches such courses as Mythology, the Mystery Story, Classical Literature in Translation, and Freshman Writing. She received her Ph.D. from the University of Pennsylvania.

Amber Turner is a Global Journalism major, but does not intend to use her degree. She suffers from "Peter Pan Syndrome" and will become a professional student to avoid adult responsibility. While furthering her education, she plans on acting and singing, occasionally writing when inspiration strikes, and generally trying not to be a hack.

Sonia Voleti is a Biology Major at Drexel University, currently enrolled in the Seven Year Accelerated Medical Program. She was born and raised in New Jersey, near Princeton. In her free time she loves to read and also enjoys playing the violin.

Kathleen Volk Miller is the Managing Editor of the *Painted Bride Quarterly*. She teaches writing and literature for the English and Philosophy Department at Drexel University. She has fiction, personal essays, and articles in numerous publications, including *Red Booth Review*, *The Smart Set* and the *Philadelphia Inquirer*.

Alyssa Woodman was born in Kaltenkirchen, Germany and moved to California at age four. She is a Design and Merchandising major and plans to work in advertising. She loves traveling, snowboarding, and going to the beach with friends.

The 33rd

Drexel
UNIVERSITY